Dictionary of
GERONTOLOGY

Dictionary of
GERONTOLOGY

Diana K. Harris

GREENWOOD PRESS

NEW YORK • WESTPORT, CONNECTICUT • LONDON

Library of Congress Cataloging-in-Publication Data

Harris, Diana K.
  Dictionary of gerontology.

  Includes index.
  1. Gerontology—Dictionaries.   2. Gerontology—
Bibliography.   I. Title.
HQ1061.H338   1988   016.3052'6'03   87-25142
ISBN 0-313-25287-4 (lib. bdg. : alk. paper)

British Library Cataloguing in Publication Data is available.

Library of Congress Catalog Card Number: 87-25142
ISBN: 0-313-25287-4

First published in 1988

Greenwood Press, Inc.
88 Post Road West, Westport, Connecticut 06881

Printed in the United States of America

The paper used in this book complies with the
Permanent Paper Standard issued by the National
Information Standards Organization (Z39.48-1984).

10 9 8 7 6 5 4 3 2 1

Contents

Figures

Preface

Gerontology is one of the newest and most rapidly growing fields of inquiry. Accompanying the growth of any new field is the development of its own special language. Gerontology is no exception. Precise concepts and terms are not only needed to carry on a scientific discussion, but their formulation leads to increased ideas and knowledge.

This dictionary has a twofold purpose: (1) to further the development of a specialized gerontological terminology; and (2), because of the multidisciplinary nature of gerontology, to assist students, scholars, researchers, and practitioners in the field in understanding the terminology that is used in the various disciplines that gerontology encompasses.

A number of features have been incorporated in this dictionary to increase its effectiveness as a reference tool and to make it more "user friendly." The most unique and distinctive feature of this work is that it does double duty by serving both as a dictionary and a detailed bibliography. At least one complete reference, often three or four, immediately following each entry, is given for every term contained in this work. This placement eliminates the chore of repeatedly turning to the back of the book to look up references. In those cases where terms are not limited to the field of aging, first general references are given in chronological order, followed by specific references to aging also in chronological order.

A dual cross-referencing system also has been provided. First, terms within an entry that are themselves the subjects of definitions in their proper alphabetical place are followed by an asterisk. Second, related and relevant terms are listed at the end of most entries. Another feature of this work is that whenever possible the name of the person who originated the term is given along with the date when it was first used. As an additional aid to the user, this dictionary contains some of the most important and most commonly used statistical and research terms in gerontology.

All terms are defined as clearly and concisely as possible with the minimum amount of jargon. In most cases, examples or short sentences are given to further clarify the definition or to show the relationship to aging. Commonly used synonyms are also included in many of the entries. Since all the entries have been written by one author, there is a consistency of style and a continuity of coverage throughout this volume.

The entries all appear in alphabetical order. Compound terms and phrases are not inverted (e.g., primary group is listed under primary group and not group, primary). Some entries are more lengthy than others because of the listing of the various usages of the term or because additional information is given.

I am grateful to Erdman Palmore, who reviewed the manuscript. I have benefited greatly from his suggestions. In addition, in the two years that I have spent working on this volume, my respect and admiration for such men as Samuel Johnson and Noah Webster have increased enormously.

Timetable of Important Developments

1935 Passage of the Social Security Act

1943 First senior center established (New York City)

1945 Gerontological Society of America

1946 Friendly Visitors Program

1947 National Retired Teachers Association (NRTA)

1950 National Council on the Aging (NCOA)

1956 Reduced social security benefits for women at age 62

1958 American Association of Retired Persons (AARP)

1961 First White House Conference on Aging (WHCOA)
      Special Committee on Aging, U.S. Senate
      National Council of Senior Citizens (NCSC)
      Reduced social security benefits for men at age 62

1964 National Association of State Units on Aging (NASUA)

1965 Older Americans Act (OAA)
      Administration on Aging (AoA)
      Medicare and Medicaid
      Foster Grandparent Program (FGP)
      Service Corps of Retired Executives (SCORE)
      Green Thumb

1967 Age Discrimination in Employment Act (ADEA) covering workers between
      the ages of 40 and 65

1970 Gray Panthers

1971 Second White House Conference on Aging (WHCOA)
      ACTION agency
      Retired Senior Volunteer Program (RSVP)

1972 National Nutrition Program for the Elderly
      Day Care Centers

1973 Area Agencies on Aging (AAA)
      Federal Council on Aging

1974 Employee Retirement Income Security Act (ERISA)
      Supplemental Security Income (SSI)
      Association for Gerontology in Higher Education (AGHE)
      National Institute on Aging (NIA)
      Senior Companions Program (SCP)

1975   Age Discrimination Act (ADA)
        Ombudsman program for long-term care institutions
1976   First hospice in the United States
1978   Amendments to Age Discrimination in Employment
        Act of 1967 (ADEA) raising upper age limit to 70
1981   Third White House Conference on Aging (WHCOA)
1986   Amendments to Age Discrimination in Employment
        Act of 1967 (ADEA) removing upper age limit

All of the above legislation, organizations, and programs on aging are defined alphabetically in this book.

Dictionary of
GERONTOLOGY

A

academic gerontology. An area of study that focuses on an empirical description of the aging processes and the situation of the elderly population. (David A. Peterson and Christopher R. Bolton. *Gerontology Instruction in Higher Education*. New York: Springer, 1980; Clark Tibbitts et al. *Academic Gerontology: Dilemmas of the 1980s*. Ann Arbor: Institute of Gerontology, University of Michigan, 1980.)

accessory apartments. The conversion of surplus space in an existing single-family home into a separate living unit with its own kitchen, bathroom, and often its own entrance. Also referred to as "mother-in-law apartments." (Norma Blackie, Jack Edelstein, Pamela S. Matthews et al. *Alternative Housing and Living Arrangements for Independent Living*. National Policy Center on Housing and Living Arrangements for Older Americans. Ann Arbor: University of Michigan Institute of Gerontology, 1982; P. H. Hare, S. Connor, and D. Merriam. *Accessory Apartments: Using Surplus Space in Single Family Houses*. Chicago: American Planning Association, 1982.)

accidental hypothermia. An unexpected drop in body temperature below 95°F. or 35°C., which may occur after prolonged exposure to cold or even mildly cool temperatures. Older persons may become hypothermic with indoor temperatures lower than 60°F. and sometimes even lower than 65°F. Hypothermia is characterized by impaired speech, lethargy, and disorientation.* Coma and even death may result if the environment is not changed. (R. W. Besdine. "Accidental Hypothermia: The Body's Energy Crisis." *Geriatrics*, 1979, 34, pp. 51-59; Nicholas Rango. "The Social Epidemiology of Accidental Hypothermia among the Aged." *The Gerontologist*, 1985, 25, pp. 424-30.)

acculturation. (1) The process by which individuals or groups modify their culture* through direct and continuous contact with another culture. (2) The term is also used to describe the outcome of such a contact. The meeting of two cultures usually produces a clash of values and creates conflict between the minority group elderly of the first generation* and their families, which may last through several generations; for example, see Christie W. Kiefer's account of aging Japanese immigrants in San Francisco. (3) Occasionally used to designate the process of transmitting culture from one generation to the next. ("Memorandum for the Study of Accul-turation," *American Anthropologist*, 1936, 38, pp. 149-52; Christie W. Kiefer. "Lessons from the Issei." In Jaber F. Gubrium, ed., *Late Life: Communities and Environmental Policy*. Springfield, Ill.: Charles C. Thomas, 1974, pp. 167-97; Donald E. Gelfand. *Aging: The Ethnic Factor*. Boston: Little, Brown, 1982; Lowell D. Holmes. *Other Cultures, Elder Years: An Introduction to Cultural Gerontology*. Minneapolis, Minn.: Burgess, 1983.) *See also* assimilation, socialization.

accumulative waste theory. According to this nongenetic cellular theory of aging, waste products and harmful substances that cannot be eliminated build up in the cells and in time interfere with their normal metabolism and eventually lead to cell death. (Nathan W. Shock. "Biological Theories of Aging." In James E. Birren and K. Warner Schaie, eds., *Handbook of the Psychology of Aging*. New York: Van Nostrand Reinhold, 1977, pp. 103-15.)

achieved status. A status* that is filled through competition and individual effort, as opposed to ascribed status,* which is assigned to persons on the basis of age, sex, and other factors and over which they have no control. Examples of achieved statuses are a spouse, a college graduate, or a retiree. (Ralph Linton. *The Study of Man*. New York: Appleton-Century-Crofts, 1936.)

ACTION. This federal volunteer agency was established in 1971 under a reorganization plan that consolidated seven existing volunteer programs into a single agency. ACTION programs allow for part-time and full-time service with some volunteers serving on stipends and others on a nonpaid basis. The Office of Older American Volunteer Programs (OAVP), a part of the ACTION agency, manages the Foster Grandparent Program (FGP),* the Retired Senior Volunteer Program (RSVP),* and the Senior Companion Program (SCP).* (Catherine B. Healy. "Volunteer Services Rendered by the Aging." In Lorin Baumhover and Joan D. Jones, eds., *Handbook of American Aging Programs*. Westport, Conn.: Greenwood, 1977; U.S. Senate. *Developments in Aging: 1984*. Vol. 1. A Report of the Special Committee on Aging. Washington, D.C.: U.S. Government Printing Office, 1985; ACTION, 806 Connecticut, N.W., Washington, D.C. 20525.)

Action for Independent Maturity (AIM). A division of the American Association of Retired Persons (AARP),* which was created in 1972 for the purpose of providing preretirement planning information and assistance to persons between the ages of 50 and 64. AIM has developed a complete series of preretirement planning programs* which are available to organizations and employers. (Steve Mehlman and Duncan Scott. "The Advocacy Role of

NRTA-AARP." In Lorin Baumhover and Joan D. Jones, eds., *Handbook of American Aging Programs*. Westport, Conn.: Greenwood Press, 1977, pp. 161-71.)

Active Corps of Executives (ACE). This program uses executives and professionals who are still active in the business world as consultants to small businesses that are just getting started or are having operational problems. (Frances Tenenbaum. *Over 55 Is Not Illegal: A Resource Book for Active Older People*. Boston: Houghton Mifflin, 1979.) *See also* Service Corps of Retired Executives.

active euthanasia. The deliberate termination of the life of a patient who is hopelessly ill or nonfunctional. The most common method is for the physician to increase the dosage of pain-killing drugs to the extent that the medication becomes toxic. Also referred to as "mercy killing." (Wayne Sage. "Choosing the Good Death." *Human Behavior*, June 1974, pp. 16-23; John A. Behnke and Sisela Bok, eds. *The Dilemmas of Euthanasia*, Garden City, N.Y.: Anchor Books, 1975.) *See also* passive euthanasia.

Activities of Daily Living, Index of (ADL). Developed by S. Katz and his associates to assess personal self-maintenance in the elderly, this scale focuses on the unaided performance of six basic personal care activities: eating, toileting, dressing, bathing, transferring (e.g., getting in and out of bed), and continence. Ratings are done both by the observer and the patient and are limited to the present and a two-week period preceding the assessment. Also called physical ADL (PADL). (S. Katz et al. "Studies of Illness in the Aged: The Index of ADL—A Standardized Measure of Biological and Psychosocial Function." *Journal of the American Medical Association*, 1963, 185, pp. 914-19; S. Katz et al. "Progress in the Development of the Index of ADL." *The Gerontologist*, 1970, 10, pt. 1, pp. 20-30.) *See also* Instrumental Activities of Daily Living Scale, Older Americans Resources and Services Multidimensional Functional Assessment Questionnaire.

activity theory. Often referred to as the "common-sense theory" of aging, the activity theory stresses a continuation of role performances and asserts that the more active older persons are, the higher their life satisfaction and morale. According to this theory, older persons who age optimally are those who find substitutes for the activities and roles that they are forced to relinquish. In this way, they stay active and resist the narrowing of their social world. (Robert J. Havighurst. "Successful Aging." *The Gerontologist*, 1961, 1, pp. 8-13; Robert J. Havighurst, Bernice L. Neugarten, and Sheldon S. Tobin. "Disengagement and Patterns of Aging." In B. Neugarten, ed., *Middle Age and Aging*. Chicago: University of Chicago Press, 1968, pp. 161-72; Bruce W. Lemon, Vern L. Bengtson, and James A. Peterson. "An

Exploration of the Activity Theory of Aging: Activity Types and Life Satisfaction among In-movers to a Retirement Community." *Journal of Gerontology*, 1972, 27, pp. 511-23.) *See also* disengagement theory; Kansas City
Studies of Adult Life.

acute care. Care that is provided within a hospital or similar setting. About
60 percent of all hospital beds are occupied by older persons. (Theodore H.
Koff. *Long-Term Care: An Approach to Serving the Frail Elderly*. Boston:
Little, Brown, 1982; Terry Fulmer, June Ashley, and Catherine Reilly.
"Geriatric Nursing in Acute Settings." In Carl Eisdorfer, ed., *Annual
Review of Gerontology and Geriatrics*. Vol. 6. New York: Springer, 1986,
pp. 27-80.)

acute disease. A pathological condition of a definite and rapid onset, short-
term in duration, and pronounced symptoms that usually respond well to
the use of drugs or therapy. Examples are a cold or influenza. In general,
older persons have fewer afflictions with acute disorders than younger
persons. (C. S. Kart, E. S. Metress, and J. F. Metress. *Aging and Health:
Biologic and Social Perspectives*. Menlo Park, Calif.: Addison-Wesley,
1978.) *See also* chronic disease; disease.

adaptation. (1) In biology, where the term originated, it refers to any
change in an organism that makes it better suited to its environment. (2) The
way in which an individual or group fits into its social or physical environment. Sometimes used interchangeably with "coping," which is a form of
adaptive behavior. The relationship between aging and successful adaptation is one of the most persistent and widely studied issues in the field of
aging. (3) A temporary change in the responsiveness of a sense organ.
(R. W. White. "Strategies of Adaptation: An Attempt at Systematic Description." In G. V. Coelho, D. A. Hamburg, and J. E. Adams, eds., *Coping and Adaptation*. New York: Basic Books, 1974; Ewald W. Busse and
Eric Pfeiffer. *Behavior and Adaptation in Late Life*. Boston: Little, Brown,
1977; Eric Pfeiffer, "Psychopathology and Social Pathology." In James E.
Birren and K. Warner Schaie, eds., *Handbook of the Psychology of Aging*.
New York: Van Nostrand Reinhold, 1977, pp. 650-71.) *See also* adjustment.

adaptive paranoia (in old age). A term first used by Morton A. Lieberman
to describe a pattern of combativeness and grouchiness used by some elderly
persons as a survival technique. (M. A. Lieberman. "Some Issues in Studying Psychological Predictors of Survival." In Erdman B. Palmore and F. C.
Jeffers, eds., *Prediction of Life-span*. Lexington, Mass.: D. C. Heath,
1971, pp. 167-79.)

addiction. A physiological dependence on a chemical substance to the point
where withdrawal symptoms occur if it is removed. (S. Zimberg. "The

Elderly Alcoholic.'' *The Gerontologist*, 1974, 14, pp. 222-24; D. M. Peterson, F. J. Whittington, and E. T. Beer. ''Drug Use and Misuse among the Elderly.'' *Journal of Social Issues*, 1979, 9, pp. 5-26; Alexander Simon. ''The Neuroses, Personality Disorders, Alcoholism, Drug Use and Misuse, and Crime in the Aged.'' In James E. Birren and R. Bruce Sloane, eds., *Handbook of Mental Health and Aging*. Englewood Cliffs, N.J.: Prentice-Hall, 1980, pp. 653-70; Brian L. Mishara and Robert Kastenbaum. *Alcohol and Old Age*. New York: Grune & Stratton, 1980.)

adjustment. (1) The relationship an organism has with its environment. (2) A process in which an individual has a harmonious relationship with his or her social or physical environment; the end result of adaptation. Influences on good adjustment of older persons include health and personal security, independent action, group membership and social experience, and worthwhile activity (W. Donahue and E. E. Ashley). (Ruth S. Cavan. ''Self and Role in Adjustment during Old Age.'' In Arnold M. Rose, ed., *Human Behavior and Social Processes*. Boston: Houghton Mifflin, 1962, pp. 526-36; Irving Rosow. ''Adjustment of the Normal Aged.'' In Richard H. Williams, Clark Tibbitts, and Wilma Donahue, eds., *Processes of Aging: Social and Psychological Perspectives*. Vol. 2. New York: Atherton Press, 1963, pp. 195-223; W. Donahue and E. E. Ashley. ''Housing and the Social Health of Older People in the United States.'' In A. A. Katz and J. S. Felton, eds., *Health and the Community*. New York: The Free Press, 1965, pp. 149-63; Hans Thomae. ''Personality and Adjustment to Aging.'' In James E. Birren and R. Bruce Sloane, eds., *Handbook of Mental Health and Aging*. Englewood Cliffs, N.J.: Prentice-Hall, 1980, pp. 285-309.) *See also* personal adjustment.

ADL. *See* Activities of Daily Living, Index of.

Administration on Aging (AoA). Located within the Department of Health and Human Services, the AoA is the principal agency for carrying out the Older Americans Act* of 1965. Its functions and duties include developing and conducting research in the field of aging, coordinating and assisting federal, state, and local agencies in planning and developing programs for older persons, and the dissemination of information relating to the problems of the elderly. (Lorin A. Baumhover and Joan D. Jones, eds. *Handbook of American Aging Programs*. Westport, Conn.: Greenwood, 1977.)

adult day care. *See* day-care center/geriatric day hospital.

adult education. Education for and of the older adult had its beginnings in the latter half of the 1940s when the National Education Association established a Committee on Education and Aging. Adult education became

firmly established when it was officially recognized by the 1961 White
House Conference on Aging.* Since 1974 the education of the older adult
has been one of the most rapidly growing areas in the field of lifelong
learning.* Educational services available to older persons include programs
at senior citizens centers, libraries, and museums as well as regular courses
at colleges and universities for credit and noncredit. Many universities and
colleges, especially community colleges, offer programs designed for older
persons. (Howard Y. McClusky. "Education for Aging: The Scope of the
Field and Perspectives for the Future." In D. Mason and S. Brabowski,
eds., *Learning for Aging*. Washington, D.C.: Adult Education Association
of the USA, 1974; Howard Y. McClusky. "Education for Older Adults."
In Carl Eisdorfer, ed., *Annual Review of Gerontology and Geriatrics*. Vol.
3. 1982, pp. 403-28.) *See also* educational gerontology, Elderhostel, Institute for Retired Professionals, Institutes of Lifetime Learning, lifelong
learning.

adult progeria. *See* progeria.

adult protective services. *See* protective services.

adult socialization. "The process of inculcating new values and behavior
appropriate to adult positions and group memberships" (Irving Rosow).
Examples of adult socialization include becoming a husband, an employee,
or a retiree. (Orville G. Brim, Jr., and Stanton Wheeler. *Socialization after
Childhood: Two Essays*. New York: John Wiley, 1966; Matilda W. Riley et
al. "Socialization for the Middle and Later Years." In David A. Goslin,
ed., *Handbook of Socialization Theory and Research*. Chicago: Rand
McNally, 1969, pp. 951-82; Irving Rosow. *Socialization to Old Age*. Berkeley: University of California Press, 1974.) *See also* socialization.

Adults Only Movement in Arizona. Started in 1973, this movement, composed of older persons, was successful in influencing the passage of legislation to legalize adult communities in the state. Its success was linked to the
emerging aging subculture* within adult and retirement communities.
(William A. Anderson and Norma D. Anderson. "The Politics of Age Ex-
clusion: The Adults Only Movement in Arizona." *The Gerontologist*, 1978,
18, pp. 6-12.)

adult stability model. This model asserts that once an individual has reached
maximum levels of performance or learning, behavior tends to remain
stable for the remainder of one's life. (K. Warner Schaie. "Methodological
Problems in Descriptive Developmental Research in Adulthood and
Aging." In J. R. Nesselroade and H. W. Reese, eds., *Life-Span Developmental Psychology: Methodological Issues*. New York: Academic Press,
1973.)

age. (1) The number of years a person has lived. When used unmodified, this term refers to chronological age.* (2) For census purposes, the United Nations defines age "as the interval of time between the date of birth and the date of the census, expressed in completed solar years." (United Nations. *Principles and Recommendations for Population and Housing Censuses*. Statistical Papers, Series M, No. 67. New York: Department of Economic and Social Affairs, 1980.) *See also* age in completed years, exact age.

age-category. *See* age grade.

age changes. Changes in an individual as a result of development and maturation; for example, vision, motor skills, and reaction time change with age. Not to be confused with age differences.* (K. Warner Schaie and Sherry L. Willis. *Adult Development and Aging*. Boston: Little, Brown, 1986.)

age composition. The structure of the population according to the number or proportion of different age categories in a population.* Used synonymously with "age structure." (David M. Heer. *Society and Population*. Englewood Cliffs, N.J.: Prentice-Hall, 1975; Henry Shryock, Jacob Siegel, and Associates. *The Methods and Materials of Demography*. New York: Academic Press, 1976.) *See also* age-sex structure, population pyramid.

age concentration. (1) An unplanned and unintentional pattern of neighborhood age segregation* within metropolitan areas; (2) A pattern of density of population settlement by age, such as a retirement community.* (Mark Messer. "The Possibility of an Age-Concentrated Environment Becoming a Normative System." *The Gerontologist*, 1967, 7, pp. 247-51; Stephen M. Golant. "Residential Concentrations of the Future Elderly." *The Gerontologist*, 1975, 15, pt. 2, pp. 16-23; Susan R. Sherman, Russell A. Ward, and Mark LaGory. "Socialization and Aging Group Consciousness: The Effect of Neighborhood Age Concentration." *Journal of Gerontology*, 1985, 40, pp. 102-9.)

age consciousness. The awareness of one's own aging and the aging of others. (Gordon F. Streib. "Social Stratification and Aging." In Robert H. Binstock and Ethel Shanas, eds., *Handbook of Aging and the Social Sciences*. New York: Van Nostrand Reinhold, 1985, pp. 339-68.)

age-cycle effect. Events that characterize the life course* as cohort members grow older. (Matilda W. Riley. "Social Gerontology and the Age Stratification of Society." *The Gerontologist*, 1971, 2, pp. 79-87.)

aged. *See* older person.

age dependency ratio. The ratio of the number of persons under 15 and over 65 years of age to the number of persons in the age group 15 to 64 years. A component of the age dependency ratio is the old-age dependency ratio which is defined as the ratio of persons 65 and over to persons 15 to 64 years. (R. L. Clark and J. J. Spengler. "Changing Demography and Dependency Cost: The Implications of New Dependency Ratios and Their Composition." In B. Herzog, ed., *Aging and Income*. New York: Human Sciences Press, 1978; William H. Crown. "Some Thoughts on Reformulating the Dependency Ratio." *The Gerontologist*, 1985, 25, pp. 166-71.) *See also* working age population.

age deviance. Behavior that violates the age norms* of a group* or society.* (Bernice L. Neugarten, Joan W. Moore, and John C. Lowe. "Age Norms, Age Constraints, and Adult Socialization." *American Journal of Sociology*, 1965, 70, pp. 710-17.)

age differences. The variation that occurs among individuals of different ages. The differences may be due to the cohort* to which they belong, and/or the aging process. Not to be confused with age changes.* (K. Warner Schaie and Sherry L. Willis. *Adult Development and Aging*. Boston: Little, Brown, 1986.)

age differentiation. The process by which different roles and statuses for people of various ages are developed and maintained within a society. (P. H. Gulliver. "Age Differentiation." In David L. Sills, ed., *International Encyclopedia of the Social Sciences*. New York: Macmillan, 1968, pp. 157-61; G. H. Elder. "Age Differentiation and the Life Course." In Alex Inkeles, ed., *Annual Review of Sociology*. Vol. 1. Palo Alto, Calif.: Annual Reviews Inc., 1975, pp. 165-90; Matilda W. Riley, Marilyn Johnson, and Anne Foner. *Aging and Society: A Sociology of Age Stratification*. Vol. 3. New York: Russell Sage, 1972.)

age discrimination. The unfavorable treatment of individuals or groups on the basis of age; the denying of opportunity to persons based solely on age. (Jacob Tuckman and Irving Lorge. "Attitudes toward Older People." *Journal of Social Psychology*, 1953, 7, pp. 249-60; Alex Comfort. "Age Prejudice in America." *Social Policy*, 1976, 7, pp. 3-8.) *See also* ageism.

Age Discrimination Act (ADA). Passed in 1975 and amended in 1978, this federal law prohibits any discrimination (except in employment) based on the age of any recipient of federal financial assistance. In addition, it states that no person on the basis of age shall be barred from participation in or be subjected to discrimination under any program receiving federal funds. (Lawrence M. Friedman. *Your Time Will Come: The Law of Age Discrimination and Mandatory Retirement*. New York: Russell Sage, 1984; Howard Eglit. "Age and the Law." In Robert H. Binstock and Ethel Shanas, eds., *Handbook of Aging and the Social Sciences*. New York: Van Nostrand Reinhold, 1985, pp. 528-52.)

Age Discrimination in Employment Act (ADEA). Enacted in 1967 to promote equal employment opportunities for older persons, this legislation protects workers between the ages of 40 and 65 against age discrimination in hiring, promoting, demoting, firing, withholding benefits, and discriminatory advertising. Amendments in 1978 raised the upper age limit to 70 years for employees in the private sector as well as in state and local governments and removed the upper age limit for most federal employees. In 1986 this act was amended to remove the upper age limit of 70 for all workers. As a result, age alone cannot be used as a basis for dismissal of a worker at any age. (M. Malin. "Employment Discrimination: The Age Discrimination in Employment Act: Protections, Prohibitions, and Exceptions." In Howard Eglit, *Age Discrimination*. Vol. 1. Colorado Springs, Colo.: Shepard's/McGraw-Hill, 1981; Lawrence M. Friedman. *Your Time Will Come: The Law of Age Discrimination and Mandatory Retirement*. New York: Russell Sage, 1984; U.S. Senate. *Developments in Aging: 1984*. Vol. 1. A Report of the Special Committee on Aging. Washington, D.C.: U.S. Government Printing Office, 1985, pp. 111-12.)

age distribution. *See* age composition, age-sex structure.

aged nations. Those nations with 7 percent of their population age 65 and over. Sometimes over 10 percent is used. (E. Rosset. *The Aging Process of Population*. New York: Macmillan, 1964; Philip M. Hauser. "Aging and World-Wide Population Change." In Robert H. Binstock and Ethel Shanas, eds., *Handbook of Aging and the Social Sciences*. New York: Van Nostrand Reinhold, 1976, pp. 59-86.)

age effect. (1) The impact of maturation on one's performance or behavior. (2) A change between two measured points in time, which is thought to be due to the aging process. Also referred to as the "maturational" or "developmental" effect. (J. Hobcraft, J. Menken, and S. Preston. "Age, Period, and Cohort Effects in Demography: A Review." *Population Index*, 48, 1982, pp. 4-43.) *See also* cohort effect, period effect.

age grade. Culturally defined stages or divisions of the life course* (e.g., childhood, adulthood, and old age). All societies have at least three or four age grades and some have many more. The age grade forms the structure through which age sets pass. Age grade is often used interchangeably with age category. (Arthur R. Radcliffe-Brown. "Age Organization Terminology." *Man*, 1929, 29; Shmuel N. Eisenstadt. *From Generation to Generation: Age Groups and Social Structure*. New York: Free Press, 1956; P. H. Gulliver. "Age Differentiation." In David L. Sills, ed., *International Encyclopedia of the Social Sciences*. Vol. 1. New York: Macmillan, 1968, pp. 157-61; Gordon V. Bultena. "Age Grading in the Social Interaction of an Elderly Male Population." *Journal of Gerontology*, 1968, 23, pp. 539-43.) *See also* age set, rites of passage.

age-grade system. The successive movement of persons from one age grade* to the next and the prescribed relationships between persons in different age grades. (P. H. Gulliver. "Age Differentiation." In David L. Sills, ed., *International Encyclopedia of the Social Sciences*. Vol. 1. New York: Macmillan, 1968, pp. 157-61; Shmuel N. Eisenstadt. *From Generation to Generation: Age Groups and Social Structure*. New York: Free Press, 1956; Bernice L. Neugarten and W. A. Peterson. "A Study of the American Age-Grade System." In *Proceedings 4th Congress International Association of Gerontology*. 1957, 3, pp. 497-502.)

age groups. (1) A collection of people of roughly the same age who have a degree of unity, who engage together in particular activities, and function as a group* in relations with outsiders. Examples include a Boy Scout troop, a neighborhood gang, or a Golden Agers club. According to Pitirim Sorokin, who introduced the concept of age groups, individuals close in age share similar biological, psychological, and social characteristics that bring them together with their own set of values, attitudes, and norms. (2) Used in demography* to refer to the grouping of persons into age intervals, often a period of five years; for example, 55-59 and 60-64. Also used in demography to refer to broad classifications of the population, such as dependent children, working population, and retirees. (P. Sorokin. *Society, Culture and Personality: Their Structure and Dynamics*. New York: Harper and Brothers, 1947; Shmuel N. Eisenstadt. *From Generation to Generation: Age Groups and Social Structure*. New York: Free Press, 1956; P. H. Gulliver. "Age Differentiation." In David L. Sills, ed., *International Encyclopedia of the Social Sciences*. Vol. 1. New York: Macmillan, 1968, pp. 157-61; Roland Pressat. *Demographic Analysis: Methods, Results, Applications*. Chicago: Aldine-Atherton, 1972.)

age heaping. A pattern of systematic distortion in age statistics that results from persons reporting some ages at the expense of others; for example, by rounding one's age off to a number ending in 0 or 5. Also referred to as digit preference or age preference. (Henry S. Shryock, Jacob S. Siegel, and

Associates. *The Methods and Materials of Demography*. New York: Academic Press, 1976; David H. Fischer. *Growing Old in America*. New York: Oxford University Press, 1978.)

age heterogamy. Marriage between persons of widely varying ages. (William J. Goode. *The Family*. Englewood Cliffs, N.J.: Prentice-Hall, 1982.)

age heterogeneity. Persons dissimilar in age; for example, the population of a city, state, or nation. (Irving Rosow. *Social Integration of the Aged*. New York: Free Press, 1967.)

age homogamy. The marriage between persons of similar age. (William J. Goode. *The Family*. Englewood Cliffs, N.J.: Prentice-Hall, 1982.)

age homogeneity. Persons similar in age; for example, persons in a retirement community or at a senior citizens center. (Irving Rosow. *Social Integration of the Aged*. New York: Free Press, 1967.)

age homophily. The tendency for friendships to form between persons close in age. (Paul F. Lazarfeld and Robert K. Merton. "Friendship as Social Process: A Substantive and Methodological Analysis." In M. Berger et al., eds., *Freedom and Control in Modern Society*. New York: Octagon, 1964; Beth B. Hess. "Friendship." In Matilda W. Riley, Marilyn Johnson, and Anne Foner, eds., *Aging and Society: A Sociology of Age Stratification*. Vol. 3. New York: Russell Sage, 1972, pp. 357-93.)

age identification. An individual's self-definition of his or her stage in the life course;* for example, whether a person thinks of himself or herself as middle-aged or old. (Carleton S. Guptill. "A Measure of Age Identification." *The Gerontologist*, 1969, 9, pt. 1, pp. 96-102; Robert C. Atchley and Judith A. Seltzer. "Prediction of Age Identification." In Robert C. Atchley, ed., *Research Studies in Social Gerontology*. Oxford, Ohio: Scripps Foundation, 1975; Russell A. Ward. "The Impact of Subjective Age and Stigma on Older Persons." *Journal of Gerontology*, 1977, 32, pp. 227-32; Gordon L. Bultena and Edward A. Powers. "Denial of Aging: Age Identification and Reference Group Orientation." *Journal of Gerontology*, 1978, 33, pp. 748-54.) *See also* self-concept.

age in completed years. The number of complete years a person has lived. Also called "age at last birthday." (Roland Pressat. *Demographic Analysis: Methods, Results, Applications*. Chicago: Aldine-Atherton, 1972.) *See also* exact age.

age incongruity. The violation of age-related expectations or of age criteria for individuals occupying a certain role.* (Matilda W. Riley, Marilyn Johnson, and Anne Foner. *Aging and Society: A Sociology of Age Stratification.* Vol. 3. New York: Russell Sage Foundation, 1972, pp. 413-14.)

age-integrated community. A community* which contains people of all age groups. Also referred to as a "heterogeneous community." (Gordon L. Bultena. "Structural Effects on the Morale of the Aged: A Comparison of Age-Segregated and Age-Integrated Communities." In Jaber F. Gubrium, ed., *Late Life Communities and Environmental Policy.* Springfield, Ill.: Charles C. Thomas, 1974, pp. 18-31.) *See also* age-segregated community.

age integration. Residential areas, services, and other facilities that promote the interaction* of individuals of all ages. (Irving Rosow. *Social Integration of the Aged.* New York: Free Press, 1967; Gordon L. Bultena. "Age-Grading in the Social Interaction of an Elderly Male Population." *Journal of Gerontology*, 1968, 23, pp. 539-43; Susan R. Sherman. "Patterns of Contacts for Residents of Aged-Segregated and Age-Integrated Housing." *Journal of Gerontology*, 1975, 30, pp. 103-7; Joseph D. Teaff et al. "Impact of Age Integration on the Well-Being of the Elderly Tenants in Public Housing." *Journal of Gerontology*, 1978, 33, pp. 126-33.) *See also* age segregation, social integration.

age-irrelevant society. A society in which there is no single appropriate age for taking on given roles. (Bernice L. Neugarten. "Time, Age and Life Cycle." *American Journal of Psychiatry*, 1979, 136, pp. 887-94.) *See also* role.

ageism. (1) The prejudices and stereotypes* that are applied to older persons based solely on their age. According to Robert Butler, who coined the term in 1968: "Ageism, can be seen as a process of systematic stereotyping of and discrimination against people because they are old, just as racism* and sexism* accomplish this with skin color and gender." (2) When one or more age groups* discriminate* against other age groups. Sometimes the term is spelled "agism" or is hyphenated, "age-ism." (Robert N. Butler, "Age-ism: Another Form of Bigotry." *The Gerontologist*, 1969, 9, pp. 243-46; Robert N. Butler. *Why Survive? Being Old in America.* New York: Harper and Row, 1975; Jack Levin and William C. Levin. *Ageism: Prejudice and Discrimination against the Elderly.* Belmont, Calif.: Wadsworth, 1980.) *See also* prejudice.

age mobility. The movement from one age status* to another; unlike social mobility, "age mobility is universal, unidirectional, and irreversible"

(Matilda W. Riley). (M. W. Riley. "Social Gerontology and the Age Stratification of Society." *The Gerontologist*, 1971, 11, pp. 79-87.)

age norms. Social expectations of what is considered appropriate behavior
at different ages. (Bernice L. Neugarten, Joan W. Moore, and John C.
Lowe. "Age Norms, Age Constraints, and Adult Socialization." *American
Journal of Sociology*, 1965, 70, pp. 710-17; Vivian Wood. "Age-Appro-
priate Behavior for Older People." *The Gerontologist*, 1971, 11, pt. 2, pp.
74-78.) *See also* social clock.

age overstatement. To exaggerate one's age. There is a tendency for persons
of extreme old age, their relatives, or other persons who live in the same
household with them to overstate their ages. (Jacob S. Siegel and Jeffrey S.
Passel. "New Estimates of the Number of Centenarians in the United
States." *Journal of the American Statistical Association*, 1976, 71, pp.
559-66.) *See also* age heaping.

age prejudice. *See* ageism.

age pyramid. *See* population pyramid.

age role. The expected behavior of one who holds a certain age status.*
(Ralph Linton. "Age and Sex Categories." *American Sociological Review*,
1942, 7, pp. 589-603; Irving Rosow. "Status and Role Change throughout
the Life Cycle." In Robert H. Binstock and Ethel Shanas, eds., *Handbook
of Aging and the Social Sciences*. New York: Van Nostrand Reinhold, 1985,
pp. 62-93.) *See also* age status.

age-segregated community. An intentionally planned community* designed
and designated for one age group. Also referred to as an "age-
homogeneous community." (Sheila K. Johnson. *Idle Haven: Community
Building among the Working-Class Retired*. Berkeley: University of California Press, 1971; Gordon L. Bultena. "Structural Effects on the Morale
of the Aged: A Comparison of Age-Segregated and Age-Integrated Communities." In Jaber F. Gubrium, ed., *Late Life: Communities and Environmental Policy*. Springfield, Ill.: Charles C. Thomas, 1974, pp. 18-31;
Frances M. Carp, "Housing and Living Environments of Older People." In
Robert H. Binstock and Ethel Shanas, eds., *Handbook of Aging and the
Social Sciences*. New York: Van Nostrand Reinhold, 1976, pp. 244-71.) *See
also* age-integrated community.

age segregation. Residential areas, communities, services, and other facilities that limit interaction* mainly to those individuals in the same age

group. Segregation may be voluntary or involuntary. Some writers prefer to use the term "age concentration"* instead of age segregation when referring to residences or communities. (Arnold M. Rose. "The Subculture of Aging: A Framework for Research in Social Gerontology." In A. M. Rose and W. A. Peterson, eds., *Older People and Their Social World*. Philadelphia: F. A. Davis, 1965; Frances M. Carp. *A Future for the Aged*. Austin: University of Texas Press, 1966; Irving Rosow. *Social Integration of the Aged*. New York: Free Press, 1967; Ruth H. Jacobs. "The Friendship Club: A Case Study of the Segregated Aged." *The Gerontologist*, 1969, 9, pt. 1, pp. 276-80; Arlie R. Hochschild. *The Unexpected Community*. Berkeley: University of California Press, 1973.) *See also* age integration, retirement communities.

age set. (1) A specific group of individuals who are roughly the same age, perform the same roles, engage in similar activities, and advance together from one age grade* to the next (e.g., childhood, adolescence, etc.). Members of an age set maintain a distinctive group identity over a period of time or even throughout life. (2) A group of people who belong to the same age grade. (Arthur R. Radcliffe-Brown. "Age Organization Terminology." *Man*, 29, 1929; P. H. Gulliver, "Age Differentiation." In David L. Sills, ed., *International Encyclopedia of the Social Sciences*. Vol. 1. New York: Macmillan, 1968; Pierre van den Berghe. *Age and Sex in Human Societies*. Belmont, Calif.: Wadsworth, 1973.) *See also* rites of passage.

age-sex pyramid. *See* population pyramid.

age-sex structure. The number or proportion of males and females in each age group in a population. The age-sex structure is graphically shown by use of a population pyramid.* (Roland Pressat. *Demographic Analysis: Methods, Results, Applications*. Chicago: Aldine-Atherton, 1972; David M. Heer. *Society and Population*. Englewood Cliffs, N.J.: Prentice-Hall, 1975.)

age-specific rate. The incidence of a demographic process at a given age or within a certain age group. For example, the age-specific birthrate is the number of births per 1,000 women in a specific age group and the age-specific death rate is the number of deaths per 1,000 persons in a given age group. (Roland Pressat. *Demographic Analysis: Methods, Results, Applications*. Chicago: Aldine-Atherton, 1972; Henry Shryock, Jacob Siegel, and Associates. *The Methods and Materials of Demography*. New York: Academic Press, 1976.)

age status. A social position based on one's age, which carries certain rights and obligations. (Ralph Linton. "Age and Sex Categories." *American*

Sociological Review, 1942, 7, pp. 589-603; Leonard D. Cain, Jr. "Age Status and Generational Phenomena: The New Old People in Contemporary America." *The Gerontologist*. 1967, 7, pp. 83-92; Irving Rosow. "Status and Role Change throughout the Life Cycle." In Robert H. Binstock and Ethel Shanas, eds., *Handbook of Aging and the Social Sciences*. New York: Van Nostrand Reinhold, 1985, pp. 62-93.) *See also* age role, life course.

age-status asynchronization. A situation in which social definitions of the various age statuses that one holds vary from one institution* to the next. For example, a young person may be eligible to vote but not to buy liquor. While this asynchronization is present at most stages of the life course,* it is most evident in the transition from youth to adulthood. The term is used interchangeably with age-status inconsistency. (Leonard D. Cain, Jr. "Life Course and the Social Structure." In Robert E. L. Faris, ed., *Handbook of Modern Sociology*. Chicago: Rand McNally, 1964.) *See also* age status.

age-status inconsistency. *See* age-status asynchronization.

age stereotypes. Oversimplified, exaggerated beliefs about people in a certain age category. Age stereotypes most often pertain to the elderly. (Bill D. Bell and Gary G. Stanfield. "The Aging Stereotype in Experimental Perspective." *The Gerontologist*, 1973, 13, pt. 1, pp. 341-44; Timothy H. Brubaker and Edward A. Powers. "The Stereotype of 'Old': A Review and Alternative Approach." *Journal of Gerontology*, 1976, 31, pp. 441-47.)

age strata. The categorizing of persons in a society on the basis of age (e.g., young, middle-aged, and old). The singular form is age stratum. (Matilda W. Riley, Marilyn Johnson, and Anne Foner. *Aging and Society: A Sociology of Age Stratification*. Vol. 3. New York: Russell Sage, 1972; Matilda W. Riley. "Age Strata in Social Systems." In Robert H. Binstock and Ethel Shanas, eds., *Handbook of Aging and the Social Sciences*. New York: Van Nostrand Reinhold, 1985, pp. 369-411.) *See also* age stratification, age stratification model.

age stratification. Strata or categories of persons who have differential access to social rewards (wealth, power,* and prestige*) as a result of their age; structured social inequality on the basis of age. (Matilda W. Riley. "Social Gerontology and the Age Stratification of Society." *The Gerontologist*, 1971, 11, pt. 1, pp. 78-87; Matilda W. Riley, Marilyn Johnson, and Anne Foner. *Aging and Society: A Sociology of Age Stratification*. Vol. 3. New York: Russell Sage, 1972.) *See also* age strata, social strata, social stratification.

age stratification model. According to this model put forth by Matilda W. Riley and her associates, people and roles are stratified by age. Age, like class,* divides the population* into strata or categories on the basis of the amount of wealth, power,* and prestige* (social rewards) that they possess. Age functions as a means of control over society's rewards because it is built into the social structure as a criterion for when one takes on or gives up certain roles. In this way, age leads to inequality between the various age strata* because people in some age strata have less access than others to valued roles and their rewards. The term "age stratification" was first used by Karl Mannheim in 1928 in comparing and contrasting age and class. (Matilda W. Riley, Marilyn Johnson, and Anne Foner. *Aging and Society: A Sociology of Age Stratification.* Vol. 3. New York: Russell Sage, 1972; Matilda W. Riley, "Age Strata in Social Systems." In Robert H. Binstock and Ethel Shanas, eds., *Handbook of Aging and the Social Sciences.* New York: Van Nostrand Reinhold, 1985, pp. 369-411.) *See also* age strata, social strata, social stratification.

Figure 1.
Elements and Processes in the Age Stratification Model

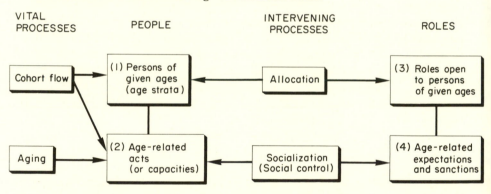

Source: Matilda W. Riley, Marilyn Johnson, and Anne Foner, eds. *Aging and Society: Sociology of Age Stratification*, Vol. 3. New York: Russell Sage Foundation, 1972, p. 9. © 1972 by the Russell Sage Foundation. Used by permission of the Russell Sage Foundation.

age structure. *See* age composition, age-sex structure, population pyramid.

aging. "The regular changes that occur in mature genetically representative organisms living under representative environmental conditions as they advance in chronological age" (James E. Birren and V. Jayne Renner). Also spelled "ageing" (British variation). (J. E. Birren and V. J. Renner. "Research on the Psychology of Aging: Principles and Experimentation."

In James E. Birren and K. Warner Schaie, eds., *Handbook of the Psychology of Aging*. New York: Van Nostrand Reinhold, 1977, pp. 3-38.) *See also* biological aging, psychological aging, senescence, social aging.

aging-based interest group. A group that is organized to obtain certain goals that the members consider beneficial to themselves. Three prominent interest groups related to aging are the American Association of Retired Persons,* the National Council of Senior Citizens,* and the National Association of Retired Federal Employees.* Also referred to as pressure groups. (Michael K. Carlie. "The Politics of Age: Interest Group or Social Movement?" *The Gerontologist*, 1969, 8, pp. 259-63; Robert H. Binstock. "Interest-Group Liberalism and the Politics of Aging." *The Gerontologist*, 1972, 12, pp. 265-80; Henry J. Pratt. *The Gray Lobby*. Chicago: University of Chicago Press, 1976; M. Olson. *The Political Economy of Aging*. New York: Columbia University Press, 1982.) *See also* aging-based organization.

aging-based organization. A highly organized group that depends to a great extent upon the existence of older persons for its activities. Older persons may be members, consumers, clients, or subjects for research. Some aging-based organizations are also interest or pressure groups. Examples include the American Association of Retired Persons,* American Nursing Home Association, and the Gerontological Society of America.* (Henry J. Pratt. "Old Age Associations in National Politics." *Annals of the American Academy of Political and Social Science*. 1974. Vol. 415, pp. 106-19; Robert B. Hudson and Robert H. Binstock. "Political Systems and Aging." In Robert H. Binstock and Ethel Shanas, eds., *Handbook of Aging and the Social Sciences*. New York: Van Nostrand Reinhold, 1976, pp. 381-90.) *See also* aging-based interest group.

aging clock theory. A neural and endocrine theory of aging that proposes that aging is timed by a mechanism located in the hypothalamus. As a result, aging consists of an orderly succession of changes programmed from conception until death. Also referred to as a hypothalmic aging clock. (Arthur V. Everitt and J. A. Burgess, eds. *Hypothalamus, Pituitary and Aging*. Springfield, Ill.: Charles C. Thomas, 1976.) *See also* pacemakers.

aging effect. *See* age effect.

aging enterprise. A term coined by Carroll L. Estes to describe the vast array of programs, bureaucracies, industries, and so on that serve the elderly. According to Estes, this aging enterprise treats older persons as a commodity as well as isolating and stigmatizing them. (C. L. Estes. *The Aging Enterprise*. San Francisco, Calif.: Jossey-Bass, 1979.)

aging-group consciousness. A situation in which older persons think of themselves as members of an aging group and begin to identify and associate with fellow-agers. Also referred to as "aging-group identification." (Arnold Rose. "The Subculture of Aging: A Framework for Research in Social Gerontology." In Arnold Rose and Warren Peterson, eds., *Older People and Their Social World*. Philadelphia: F. A. Davis, 1965, pp. 3-16; Pauline K. Ragan and James J. Dowd. "The Emerging Consciousness of the Aged: A Generational Interpretation." *Journal of Social Issues*, 1974, 30, pp. 137-58; Russell A. Ward. "Aging Group Consciousness: Implications in an Older Sample." *Sociology and Social Research*, 1977, 61, pp. 496-519.)

aging-in-place. The effect of time on a nonmobile population; remaining in the same residence where one has spent his or her earlier years. (Michael Gutowski and Tracey Field. *The Graying of Suburbia*. Washington, D.C.: The Urban Institute, 1979; Phyllis Myers. *Aging in Place: Strategies to Help the Elderly Stay in Revitalizing Neighborhoods*. Washington, D.C.: The Conservation Foundation, 1982.)

aging network. The agencies and organizations created and funded under the Older Americans Act* at the federal, state, and local levels. The network includes the federal Administration on Aging,* State Units on Aging,* and Area Agencies on Aging,* nutrition programs, and senior citizens centers. Arthur Flemming, former Commissioner of the Administration on Aging, introduced the term. (Donald E. Gelfand and Jody K. Olsen. *The Aging Network*. New York: Springer, 1983.)

aging of the population. An increase in the proportion of the population aged 65 and over. This situation is influenced by changes in mortality, fertility, and migration. The proportion of older persons in the population increases as birth rates and death rates decrease. (Philip M. Hauser. "Aging and World-Wide Population Change." In Robert H. Binstock and Ethel Shanas, eds., *The Handbook of Aging and the Social Sciences*. New York: Van Nostrand Reinhold, 1976, pp. 59-86; G. Myers. "The Aging of Populations." In Robert H. Binstock, W. Sun Chow, and James Schulz, eds., *International Perspectives on Aging: Population and Policy Challenges*. New York: United Nations Fund for Population Activity, 1982; Jacob S. Siegel and Cynthia M. Taeuber. "Demographic Dimensions of an Aging Population." In Alan Pifer and Lydia Bronte, eds., *Our Aging Society: Paradox and Promise*. New York: W. W. Norton, 1986, pp. 79-110.) *See also* graying of America, graying of suburbia.

aging subculture. This concept is an extension of interactionist theory and was first proposed by Arnold M. Rose. He states that "the elderly tend to interact more with one another as they grow older and less with younger persons because of the common interests and concerns that the elderly share and also because in some ways they are excluded from interacting with other age groups.* This segregation results in the development of an aging subculture." (Arnold M. Rose. "The Subculture of the Aging: A Topic for Sociological Research." *The Gerontologist*, 1962, 2, pp. 123-27.) *See also* subculture.

alienation. A feeling of estrangement or separation from society. Alienation may arise from feelings of powerlessness, meaninglessness, and isolation. Georg Hegel was the first to use the term in the modern sense. According to D. K. Kent, alienation is a major problem facing the elderly. He notes that the older person "becomes a stranger in a society that is both his and of his making. Yet he no longer belongs nor can he participate." (F. Johnson, ed. *Alienation: Concept, Term and Meanings.* New York: Seminar Press, 1973; J. Israel. *Alienation from Marx to Modern Sociology.* Boston: Allyn and Bacon, 1971; D. K. Kent. "Social and Cultural Factors Influencing the Mental Health of the Aged." *American Journal of Orthopsychiatry*, 1966, 36, pp. 680-85; William C. Martin, Vern L. Bengtson, and Alan C. Adcock. "Alienation and Age: A Context-Specific Approach." *Social Forces*, 1974, 53, pp. 266-74.) *See also* anomie.

almshouses. In existence from colonial times up to the mid-thirties, almshouses housed poor, aged, and infirm persons who could not provide for themselves and had no family that could help them. Also called "poor houses" and "poor farms." ("Almshouse Care and the Old Age Assistance Program." *Social Security Bulletin*, March 1938; W. Andrew Achenbaum, *Old Age in the New Land.* Baltimore: Johns Hopkins University, 1978.)

altruistic suicide. One of the types of suicide* identified by Emile Durkheim in 1897 in which persons are so well integrated into the group that their own self interests become subordinate to that of the group. They completely accept the groups' norms and are willing to sacrifice themselves for the welfare of the group. For example, in some preindustrial societies when conditions become intolerable and an elderly person becomes a burden and can no longer make a contribution to the group, he or she may choose to commit suicide. (Emile Durkheim. *Suicide.* Translated by J. A. Spaulding and G. Simpson. Glencoe, Ill.: Free Press, 1951; Leo W. Simmons. *The Role of the Aged in Primitive Society.* New Haven, Conn.: Yale University Press, 1945; Anthony P. Glascock and Susan L. Feinman. "Social Asset or Social Burden: Treatment of the Aged in Non-Industrial Societies." In C. L. Fry, ed., *Dimensions: Aging, Culture, and Health.* Brooklyn, N.Y.: Praeger, 1981, pp. 13-31.) *See also* anomic suicide, egoistic suicide.

Alzheimer's disease (AD). An irreversible, organic mental disorder characterized by a progressive deterioration of mental functioning that includes loss of memory, especially for recent events, impairment of judgment and abstract thinking, and a deterioration of personality. Presently, Alzheimer's disease and senile dementia* of the Alzheimer's type (SDAT) are neuropathologically indistinguishable and are frequently treated as a single entity. The former usually appears between the ages of 45 and 70. Alois Alzheimer, a German neurologist, first recognized this disease in 1907. (Lissy F. Jarvik. "Diagnosis of Dementia in the Elderly: A 1980 Perspective." In Carl Eisdorfer, ed., *Annual Review of Gerontology and Geriatrics*. New York: Springer, 1980; N. E. Miller and G. D. Cohen, eds. *Clinical Aspects of Alzheimer's Disease and Senile Dementia*. New York: Raven Press, 1981; Ethel Shanas and George Maddox. "Health, Health Resources, and the Utilization of Care." In Robert H. Binstock and Ethel Shanas, eds., *Handbook of Aging and the Social Sciences*. New York: Van Nostrand Reinhold, 1985, p. 713.) *See also* Alzheimer's Disease and Related Disorders Association, dementia, presenile dementia.

Alzheimer's Disease and Related Disorders Association (ADRDA). A national voluntary organization composed of families and professionals working together to assist with caregiving to Alzheimer's patients through support groups, counseling, and educational forums. (ADRDA National Headquarters, 70 E. Lake St. Chicago, Illinois 60601.)

American Association of Retired Persons (AARP). The largest voluntary association of older persons (retired or not) with a membership of over 20 million persons. Its goal is to improve every aspect of living for persons aged 50 years or over. Some of the many benefits and services it provides for its members are group health insurance, pharmacy service, temporary employment service, adult education,* and travel service. The association works closely with members of Congress and state legislatures to represent the interests of older persons. The AARP was founded in 1958 by Ethel Percy Andrus, a retired high school principal. Eleven years earlier (1947), she founded the National Retired Teachers Association (NRTA), which has remained as a smaller but autonomous group within the NRTA-AARP structure. ("The Story of AARP." *Modern Maturity*. August-September 1976, pp. 57-64; Steve Mehlman and Duncan Scott, "The Advocacy Role of NRTA-AARP." In Lorin A. Baumhover and Joan D. Jones, eds., *Handbook of American Aging Programs*, Westport, Conn.: Greenwood, 1977, pp. 161-77.)

American Geriatrics Society (AGS). Established in 1942 by biomedical researchers and clinicians, this society encourages and directs research in the field of aging, publishes *The Journal of the American Geriatrics Society*, and assists in the creation and expansion of geriatric training centers. (American Geriatric Society, 10 Columbus Circle, New York, New York 10019.)

Analysis of Variance (ANOVA). A statistical technique to test whether there are significant differences between two or more means. (Ann E. MacEachron. *Basic Statistics in the Human Services*. Baltimore: University Park Press, 1982.) *See also* mean.

angina pectoris. An intense pain in the chest due to narrowing of the coronary arteries, which results in the interference of the oxygen supply to the heart. Not to be confused with a heart attack (myocardial infarction).* (Edward G. Lakatta. "Heart and Circulation." In Caleb E. Finch and Edward L. Schneider, eds., *Handbook of the Biology of Aging*. New York: Van Nostrand Reinhold, 1985, pp. 377-413.) *See also* cardiovascular disease, coronary artery disease.

anomic suicide. One of the types of suicide* identified by Emile Durkheim in 1897 in which the normal equilibrium of society becomes disturbed and, as a result, individuals lack clear-cut rules and guidelines to regulate their behavior. They feel a sense of despair and hopelessness and thus are more likely to commit suicide. Some writers suggest that because the aged role has few meaningful norms and guidelines, the elderly are left to structure their own role without any clear prescriptions as to the appropriate behavior. For some this leads to a state of disequilibrium which may result in suicide. (Emile Durkheim. *Suicide*. Translated by J. A. Spaulding and G. Simpson. Glencoe, Ill.: Free Press, 1951; Asser Stenback. "Depression and Suicidal Behavior in Old Age." In James E. Birren and R. Bruce Sloane, eds., *Handbook of Mental Health and Aging*. Englewood Cliffs, N.J.: Prentice-Hall, 1980, pp. 616-52; Nancy J. Osgood. "Suicides." In Erdman B. Palmore, ed., *Handbook on the Aged in the United States*. Westport, Conn.: Greenwood Press, 1984, pp. 371-90.) *See also* altruistic suicide, egoistic suicide.

anomie. (1) A state of society that is characterized by a weakening of the rules of conduct, insecurity, and/or confusion. Emile Durkheim introduced the term in 1897 to describe an inadequate regulation in a society where traditional values and norms have become weak or absent. Some writers point out that there is a normlessness in old age because there are few clear-cut norms and guidelines for the elderly to follow and they are left to structure the aged role themselves. (2) Robert K. Merton in 1938 redefined anomie to refer to a widespread frustration that occurs when there is an acute disparity between culturally prescribed goals and socially approved ways to achieve them. One response to this situation is retreatism.* (Emile Durkheim. *Suicide*. Translated by J. A. Spaulding and G. Simpson. Glencoe, Ill.: Free Press, 1951; Robert K. Merton. *Social Theory and Social Structure*. New York: Free Press, 1968.)

antediluvian theme. This notion asserts that people in ancient times lived much longer than they do today. Examples of antediluvian beliefs are found in Genesis where Methuselah was reputed to have lived 969 years, Noah 950 years, and Adam 930 years. (Gerald J. Gruman. "History of Ideas about the Prolongation of Life: The Evaluation of Prolongevity Hypotheses to 1800." *Transactions of the American Philosophical Society*, 1966, vol. 56, pt. 9, pp. 1-102.) *See also* fountain theme, hyperborean theme.

anthropology. The systematic study of human beings and their works. The term is a composite of two Greek words: *anthropos* (man) and *logia* (study). Anthropology is primarily divided into cultural anthropology and physical anthropology. Cultural anthropology focuses on the study of culture,* whereas physical anthropology is concerned with similarities and differences between human beings and other animals. (Sol Tax et al., eds. *An Appraisal of Anthropology Today*. Chicago: University of Chicago Press, 1953; John J. Honigmann. *Handbook of Social and Cultural Anthropology*. Chicago: Rand McNally, 1973; Leo W. Simmons. *The Role of the Aged in Primitive Society*. New Haven, Conn.: Yale University Press, 1945; Jennie Keith. "The Best Is Yet to Be: Toward an Anthropology of Age." In B. J. Siegel, ed., *Annual Review of Anthropology*. Palo Alto, Calif.: Annual Reviews, 1980.) *See also* social sciences.

anticipatory grief. The grief that is experienced prior to the impending death of a loved one. (Bernice L. Neugarten. *Middle Age and Aging*. Chicago: University of Chicago Press, 1968; Bernard Schoenberg et al. *Anticipatory Grief*. New York: Columbia University Press, 1974; I. Gerber et al. "Anticipatory Grief and Aged Widows and Widowers." *Journal of Gerontology*, 1975, 30, pp. 225-29.) *See also* rehearsal for widowhood.

anticipatory socialization. Advance preparation for a new role;* role rehearsal. Examples include preretirement planning programs* and rehearsal for retirement.* The term was introduced by Robert K. Merton and Alice S. Kitt. (R. K. Merton and A. S. Kitt. "Contributions to the Theory of Reference Group Behavior." In R. K. Merton and P. F. Lazarsfeld, eds., *Continuities in Social Research*. Glencoe, Ill.: Free Press, 1950, pp. 40-105.)

anxiety. A vague, generalized feeling of uneasiness and worry that comes from an unrecognized or unknown source. This feeling is often intensified in older persons because of increased stress from illness, fears of loneliness and abandonment, and becoming a burden on others. (Adrian Verwoerdt. "Anxiety, Dissociative and Personality Disorders in the Elderly." In Ewald W. Busse and Dan G. Blazer, eds., *Handbook of Geriatric Psychiatry*. New York: Van Nostrand Reinhold, 1980, pp. 368-80.)

aphasia. Partial or total loss of the ability to speak or to understand speech due to a disorder in the cerebrum of the brain. Cerebrovascular accidents account for the greatest incidence of aphasia in older persons. (M. L. Albert. "Language in Normal and Dementing Elderly." In L. Obler and M. Albert, eds., *Language and Communication in the Elderly: Clinical, Therapeutic, and Experimental Issues*. Lexington, Mass.: D. C. Heath, 1980.) *See also* cerebrovascular accident.

applied gerontology. (1) The use of the findings from research on aging to improve the quality of life for the elderly. (2) The planning, development, and delivery of services to the elderly. (Jan D. Sinnot et al. *Applied Research in Aging: A Guide to Methods and Resources*. Boston: Little, Brown, 1983; Albert J. E. Wilson. *Social Services for Older Persons*. Boston: Little, Brown, 1984.)

applied research. Research that is designed to provide answers to solve immediate practical problems. (Jan D. Sinnot et al. *Applied Research in Aging: A Guide to Methods and Resources*. Boston: Little, Brown, 1983; David J. Mangen, and Warren A. Peterson. *Research Instruments in Social Gerontology: Social Roles and Social Participation*. Vol. 2. Minneapolis: University of Minnesota Press, 1982.) *See also* basic research.

Area Agencies on Aging (AAA). Created by the 1973 Comprehensive Services Amendments to the Older Americans Act,* these agencies range in size from a municipality to several counties and are the chief advocates of the elderly at the community level. They are charged with planning services for the elderly, coordinating and evaluating the delivery of services, and identifying needs and new resources within their areas. Each area agency is responsible for developing an area plan that is submitted to the state unit and becomes a part of the state plan. (Robert B. Hudson. "Rational Planning and Organizational Imperatives: Prospects for Area Planning in Aging." *Annals of the American Academy of Political and Social Science*, 1974, Vol. 415, pp. 41-54; Carroll Estes. *The Aging Enterprise*. San Francisco: Jossey-Bass, 1979.)

area-wide model projects. This concept was introduced through the 1971 amendments to the Older Americans Act* to encourage local communities to develop new and innovative approaches for providing needed services to the elderly to delay institutionalization* and help older persons to remain in their homes as long as possible. (Theodore H. Koff. *Long-Term Care: An Approach to Serving the Frail Elderly*. Boston: Little, Brown, 1982.)

armored personality. This personality type, which was first identified by Suzanne Reichard and others in 1962, consisted of men who had highly developed defenses against aging. They warded off the fear of growing old by keeping active and rated high on adjustment to aging. A similar personality type, "the defended," was later delineated by Bernice Neugarten and associates. This type is composed of persons who are ambitious, striving, and maintain strong defenses against anxieties associated with aging. (Suzanne Reichard, Florine Livson, and Paul G. Petersen. *Aging and Personality*. New York: John Wiley, 1962; Bernice L. Neugarten, Robert Havighurst, and Sheldon S. Tobin. "Personality and Patterns of Aging." In B. Neugarten, ed., *Middle Age and Aging*. Chicago: University of Chicago Press, 1968, pp. 173-77.)

arteriosclerosis. A generic term for degenerative changes in which the arterial walls thicken and lose their elasticity resulting in an impairment of blood circulation. (*Arteriosclerosis 1981*. Report of the Working Group on Arteriosclerosis of the National Heart, Lung and Blood Institute (NHLBI). Washington, D.C.: U.S. Dept. of Health and Human Services, National Institutes of Health (NIH) Publication No. 81-2034, 1981; Edwin L. Bierman. "Arteriosclerosis and Aging." In Caleb E. Finch and Edward L. Schneider, eds., *Handbook of the Biology of Aging*. New York: Van Nostrand Reinhold, 1985, pp. 842-58.) *See also* atherosclerosis.

artery. Any of a large number of tubular vessels that carry blood away from the heart to all parts of the body. (Edwin L. Bierman. "Arteriosclerosis and Aging." In Caleb E. Finch and Edward L. Schneider, eds., *Handbook of the Biology of Aging*. New York: Van Nostrand Reinhold, 1985, pp. 842-58.) *See also* arteriosclerosis.

arthritis. A general term used to describe any inflammation of the joints. The most common forms of arthritis seen in the elderly are rheumatoid arthritis and osteoarthritis. It is the leading cause of physical disability in the United States. (D. Grob. "Prevalent Joint Diseases in Older Persons." In W. Reichel, ed., *Clinical Aspects of Aging*. Baltimore: Williams and Wilkins, 1978; Roland W. Moskowitz and Marie R. Haug. *Arthritis and the Elderly*. New York: Springer, 1985.)

ascribed status. A status* that is assigned to individuals, usually at birth, by society without regard to innate abilities or differences. The most universally ascribed statuses are age and sex. (Ralph Linton. *The Study of Man*. New York: Appleton-Century-Crofts, 1936). *See also* achieved status.

Asian-American and Pacific-Islander elderly. The 1980 United States census included the following nine ethnic groups in this category: Asian Indian, Chinese Filipino, Cambodian, Guamanian, Hawaiian, Japanese,

Korean, Samoan, and Vietnamese. About 6 percent of the Asian and Pacific Islanders are age 65 and over and of these 6.7 percent are age 85 and over. Of all the minority elderly, they have the greatest proportion of high school graduates and the largest number remaining in the labor force. Over 55 percent of the Asian-American and Pacific-Islander elderly are concentrated in California, Washington, and Hawaii. (Ron C. Manuel, ed. *Minority Aging: Sociological and Social Psychological Issues*. Westport, Conn.: Greenwood, 1982; Toshi Kii. "Asians." In Erdman B. Palmore, ed., *Handbook on the Aged in the United States*. Westport, Conn.: Greenwood, 1984, pp. 201-17.) *See also* ethnic group, minority group.

assimilation. (1) The process in which two or more groups come to share the same cultural patterns, and there is a mutual blending of the two (a two-way process). (2) Sometimes used to refer to the process in which the subordinate group becomes absorbed into the dominant group (a one-way process). This usage was popular after World War I with the large wave of immigrants coming to the United States and became synonymous with the term "Americanization." Sometimes used interchangeably with acculturation.* Assimilation affects older people in that often their formerly respected and honored roles in the family and community are lost when complete assimilation takes place with another group. (Robert E. Park. *The Collected Papers of Robert Ezra Park*. New York: Free Press, 1950; Milton M. Gordon. *Assimilation in American Life*. New York: Oxford University Press, 1964; Donald E. Gelfand. *Aging and the Ethnic Factor*. Boston: Little, Brown, 1982.)

associational solidarity. The degree to which family* members interact in shared behavior and common activities. (Vern L. Bengtson, Edward B. Olander, and Anees A. Haddad. "The 'Generation Gap' and Aging Family Members." In J. Gubrium, ed., *Times, Roles, and Self in Old Age*. New York: Behavioral Publications, 1976, pp. 237-63; Vern L. Bengtson and Sandi Schrader. "Parent-Child Relations." In David J. Mangen and Warren A. Peterson, eds., *Research Instruments in Social Gerontology: Social Roles and Social Participation*. Vol. 2. Minneapolis: University of Minnesota Press, 1982, pp. 115-85.)

Association for Gerontology in Higher Education (AGHE). Founded in 1972 for the purpose of increasing the commitment and development of higher education in the field of aging through education, research, and public service. Membership is open to colleges and universities with programs in aging. (Tom Hickey. "Association for Gerontology in Higher Education: A Brief History." In Mildred M. Seltzer, Harvey Sterns, and Tom Hickey, eds., *Gerontology in Higher Education: Perspectives and*

Issues. Belmont, Calif.: Wadsworth, 1978; David A. Peterson and Christopher Bolton. *Gerontology Instruction in Higher Education*. New York: Springer, 1980.)

associations. *See* voluntary association.

asynchronization. *See* age-status asynchronization.

atherosclerosis. The most prevalent type of arteriosclerosis* in which in addition to the thickening and reduced elasticity of the arteries, deposits of plaques, a fatty substance, cause the inner walls of the larger arteries to narrow. Over 80 percent of atherosclerotic cardiovascular disease in the United States occurs in persons over age 65. (Edwin L. Bierman and R. Ross. "Aging and Atherosclerosis." In R. Paoletti and A. M. Grotto, eds., *Atherosclerosis Reviews*. Vol. 2. New York: Raven Press, 1977, pp. 79-111; Edwin L. Bierman. "Arteriosclerosis and Aging." In Caleb E. Finch and Edward L. Schneider, eds., *Handbook of the Biology of Aging*. New York: Van Nostrand Reinhold, 1985, pp. 842-58.) *See also* cardiovascular disease.

atrophy. Wasting away of organ or tissue cells from disease or lack of use. (Morris Rockstein and Marvin Sussman. *Biology of Aging*. Belmont, Calif.: Wadsworth, 1979.)

attitude. A learned predisposition to act in a consistent way toward persons, objects, or situations. In addition to conceiving of attitudes in behavioral terms, some writers view them as including cognitive components (beliefs), conative components (intentions regarding actions), and affective components (emotions or feelings) toward persons, objects, or situations. The study of attitudes toward the elderly and old age has long been a significant area of research in gerontology. (Gordon W. Allport. "Attitudes." In C. Murchison, ed., *Handbook of Social Psychology*. Worcester, Mass.: Clark University Press, 1935, pp. 798-894; W. J. McGuire. "Attitudes and Attitude Change." In Gardner Lindzey and Elliot Aronson, eds., *Handbook of Social Psychology*, Vol. 2, New York: Random House, 1985, pp. 233-346; Jacob Tuckman and Irving Lorge. "Attitudes towards Old People." *Journal of Social Psychology*, 1953, 37, pp. 249-60; Donald G. McTavish. "Perceptions of Old People: A Review of Research, Methodologies, and Findings." *The Gerontologist*, 1971, 11, pt. 2, pp. 90-101; N. Kogan. "Beliefs, Attitudes and Stereotypes about Old People: A New Look at Some Old Issues." *Research on Aging*, 1979, 1, pp. 11-36; Neil S. Lutsky. "Attitudes toward Old Age and Elderly Persons." In Carl Eisdorfer, ed., *Annual Review of Gerontology and Geriatrics*. Vol. 1. New York: Springer, 1980, pp. 287-336.) *See also* ageism, conservatism.

autoimmune theory. A physiological theory of aging, originally proposed by Roy L. Walford, that postulates that aging results from the development of antibodies that attack and destroy the normal cells in the body that they are supposed to protect. With age, according to this theory, defects occur in the body's autoimmune system so that it cannot distinguish itself from foreign structures. (R. L. Walford. *The Immunologic Theory of Aging.* Baltimore: Williams and Wilkins, 1969; H. T. Blumenthal and Aline W. Berns. "Auto-Immunity and Aging." In Bernard L. Strehler, ed., *Advances in Gerontological Research*. Vol. 1. New York: Academic Press, 1964, pp. 289-342; W. H. Adler. "An 'Autoimmune' Theory of Aging." In M. Rockstein, ed., *Theoretical Aspects of Aging*. New York: Academic Press, 1974, pp. 33-42.)

B

baby boom. A dramatic increase in births lasting for a number of years. Most often it refers to the significant increase in births in the United States that extended from 1946 to 1964, peaking in 1957. (R. Easterlin. *Birth and Fortune*. New York: Basic Books, 1980.)

bag ladies. Impoverished, homeless elderly women in urban areas who carry all of their possessions in shopping bags. The term was introduced by Sharon Curtin. Also referred to as shopping-bag women. (S. Curtin. *Nobody Ever Died of Old Age*. Boston: Little, Brown, 1972, chap. 6; Ann M. Rousseau. *Shopping Bag Ladies: Homeless Women Speak about Their Lives*. New York: The Pilgrim Press, 1981; Jennifer Hand. "Shopping-Bag Women: Aging Deviants in the City." In Elizabeth W. Markson, ed., *Older Women: Issue and Prospects*. Lexington, Mass.: Lexington Books, 1983, pp. 155-77.)

baldness. Male pattern baldness, which is related to heredity, androgen hormones, and aging, begins with the hairline receding at the temples, followed by thinning on the top of the head. Most men are partially bald or completely bald by age 60. A tendency to baldness may be inherited from either side of the family. Previously, the transmission was believed to be only from the mother's side. (L. Giacometti. "Hair Growth and Aging." In W. Montagna, ed., *Advances in Biology of the Skin*. Oxford: Pergamon, 1965, pp. 97-118.)

Baltimore Longitudinal Study of Aging. This study was initiated n 1958 for the purpose of examining aging in healthy, upper-middle-class persons with regard to certain physiological and psychological variables. The subjects were recruited from the Baltimore-Washington, D.C., area. (Nathan W. Shock et al. *Normal Human Aging: The Baltimore Longitudinal Study of Aging*. Washington, D.C.: U.S. Government Printing Office, National Institutes of Health Publication No. 84-2450, 1984.)

bank examiner scheme. A confidence game that victimizes primarily older persons, usually women. The swindle takes place in the following manner. A man calls an older woman on the phone and poses as a bank examiner. He explains that he is trying to trap a dishonest teller at the bank and asks her help in apprehending the culprit. If she agrees, the "bank examiner" then asks her to go to the bank and withdraw all her money. Later he phones saying that the plan worked and the teller has been caught. He offers to send a bank messenger to pick up her money and redeposit it in her account. The messenger arrives, takes the money, and gives the woman a receipt. She never sees the messenger or her money again. (Amram Ducovny. *The Billion Dollar Swindle: Frauds against the Elderly*. New York: Fleet Press, 1969.)

basic research. Research that deals with knowledge for its own sake without regard for its application and use. (George L. Maddox and Richard T. Campbell. "Scope, Concepts, and Methods in the Study of Aging." In Robert H. Binstock and Ethel Shanas, eds., *Handbook of Aging and the Social Sciences*. New York: Van Nostrand Reinhold, 1985, pp. 3-31.) *See also* applied research.

battered old person syndrome. The physical abuse of older persons in the home by family members or acquaintances. (Robert N. Butler. *Why Survive? Being Old in America*. New York: Harper and Row, 1975; Suzanne K. Steinmetz. "Battered Parents." *Society*, 1978, 15, pp. 54-55; Marilyn R. Block and Jan D. Sinnott, eds. *The Battered Elder Syndrome: An Exploratory Study*. Center on Aging. College Park: University of Maryland, 1979.) *See also* elder abuse.

bed-disability day. When a person is kept in bed either all or most of the day because of an illness or injury. This would include hospital days even if the patient is not actually in bed at the hospital. (Mortimer Spiegelman. *Introduction to Demography*. Cambridge, Mass.: Harvard University Press, 1968.)

bedsores. *See* decubitus ulcers.

bereavement. (1) A feeling of loss of or separation from a person or object to which one was attached. (2) In a narrower sense it refers to the loss of a loved person by death. Edmund H. Volkart and Stanley T. Michael define bereavement as "the emotional state, behavior, and conduct of the survivors immediately following the experience of separation by death from a person who fulfilled dependency needs, especially needs related to emotional interaction." (Erich Lindemann. "The Symptomatology and Management of Acute Grief." *American Journal of Psychiatry*, 101, 1944, pp. 141-48; E. H. Volkart and S. T. Michael. *Explorations in Social Psychiatry*. New York: Basic Books, 1957; Colin M. Parkes. *Bereavement: Studies of Grief in Adult Life*. New York: International Universities Press, 1972.) *See also* grief, mourning.

bilateral descent. A family* in which descent or inheritance is traced equally through both the father and male line and the mother and female line. (Meyer F. Nimkoff. *Comparative Family Systems*. Boston: Houghton Mifflin, 1965; William J. Goode. *The Family*. Englewood Cliffs, N.J.: Prentice-Hall, 1982.)

biogerontology or biological gerontology. The study of the three primary aspects of life: aging,* longevity,* and death.* (George A. Sacher. "Theory in Gerontology, Pt. 1." In Carl Eisdorfer, ed., *Annual Review of Gerontology and Geriatrics*. Vol. 1. New York: Springer, 1980, pp. 3-25; Leonard Hayflick. "When Does Aging Begin?" *Research on Aging*, 1984, 6, pp. 99-103.)

biological age. One's present position in regard to the probability of survival. A determination of biological age would include assessing and measuring the functional capacities of the life-limiting organ systems (e.g., the cardiovascular system). (James E. Birren and Walter R. Cunningham. "Research on the Psychology of Aging: Principles, Concepts and Theory." In James E. Birren and K. Warner Schaie, eds., *Handbook of the Psychology of Aging*. New York: Van Nostrand Reinhold, 1985, pp. 3-34; Juliene L. Stafford and James E. Birren. "Changes in the Organization of Behavior with Age." In James E. Birren, Pauline K. Robinson, and Judy E. Livingston, eds., *Age, Health, and Employment*. Englewood Cliffs, N.J.: Prentice-Hall, 1986, pp. 1-26.) *See also* aging, functional age, psychological age, social age.

biological aging. (1) "The time-related changes in the anatomy and physiology of the individual" (Morris Rockstein and Marvin Sussman); all the changes that normally occur in an organism with the passage of time ending with death. Also referred to as the process of "senescing" by J. J. F. Schroots and James E. Birren. (2) The progressive loss of functional capacity after an individual has reached maturity. (Morris Rockstein and Marvin Sussman. *Biology of Aging*. Belmont, Calif.: Wadsworth, 1979; J. J. F. Schroots and J. E. Birren. "A Psychological Point of View toward Human Aging and Adaptability "In *Adaptability and Aging*. Proceedings of 9th International Conference of Social Gerontology, Quebec, Canada, 1980, pp. 43-54.) *See also* aging, primary aging, psychological aging, secondary aging, social aging.

birth cohort. An aggregate of individuals born within the same year (e.g., 1900) or time interval (e.g., 1910-1914). (Norman B. Ryder. "The Cohort as a Concept in the Study of Social Change." *American Sociological Review*, 1965, 30, pp. 843-61.) *See also* cohort, generation.

birthrate. *See* crude birthrate.

black/white crossover. *See* crossover phenomenon.

blood pressure. This term refers to the force of the blood against the artery*
walls. Two measures are usually taken, the systolic and the diastolic. The
top number or systolic pressure represents the force with which the blood
flows through the arteries when the heart is contracting. The bottom
number or diastolic pressure represents the force of blood through the heart
when it is relaxing between contractions. Blood pressure usually rises with
age but it is not clear whether the rise is caused by aging per se. (William B.
Kannel. "Hypertension and Aging." In Caleb E. Finch and Edward L.
Schneider, eds., *Handbook of the Biology of Aging*. New York: Van Nostrand Reinhold, 1985, pp. 859-93.) *See also* hypertension.

body monitoring. Techniques used by middle-aged persons to maintain
their bodies at certain levels of performance and appearance. Wives tend to
be more concerned about their husbands than themselves in regard to body
monitoring. The term was originated by Bernice L. Neugarten and her
associates. (B. L. Neugarten. "The Awareness of Middle Age." In B. L.
Neugarten, ed., *Middle Age and Aging*. Chicago: University of Chicago
Press, 1968, pp. 93-98.)

brain clock. *See* aging clock theory.

brain death. The cessation of brain function for a 24-hour period, which is
determined by data from an electroencephalogram (EEG). Other criteria
include unresponsivity, no movements or breathing, and no reflexes. (Ad
Hoc Committee of the Harvard Medical School to Examine the Definition
of Brain Death. "Definition of Irreversible Coma." *Journal of the
American Medical Association*, 1968, 205, pp. 337-40; R. M. Veatch.
Death, Dying and the Biological Revolution. New Haven, Conn.: Yale
University Press, 1976; J. Korein. "Brain Death: Interrelated Medical and
Social Issues." *Annals of the New York Academy of Sciences*, 1978, 315,
pp. 1-10.) *See also* death, dying.

bureaucracy. (1) A formal, large-scale organization in which there is a
highly formalized division of labor, and activities are explicitly defined by
rules and procedures and coordinated by a hierarchal system of authority.
(2) The administrative aspect of an organization. Max Weber was the first
to systematically study bureaucracy. Social security and the medical care
system are two examples of bureaucracies that directly affect the elderly.
Often times older persons will have family members act as mediators in

their dealing with these complex bureaucratic organizations. (H. H. Gerth and C. Wright Mills. *From Max Weber: Essays in Sociology*. London: Routledge and Kegan Paul, 1948, pp. 196-98; Ethel Shanas and Marvin B. Sussman. *Family, Bureaucracy and the Elderly*. Durham, N.C.: Duke University Press, 1977.)

C

cancer. *See* neoplasia.

cardiovascular disease. A disorder of the heart and blood vessels that can take many forms including coronary artery disease,* congestive heart failure,* and myocardial infarction.* It is the leading cause of death in the 65-plus age group worldwide. (S. E. Gould, ed. *Pathology of the Heart and Blood Vessels*. Springfield, Ill.: Charles C. Thomas, 1968; Edward G. Lakatta. "Heart and Circulation." In Caleb E. Finch and Edward L. Schneider, eds., *Handbook of the Biology of Aging*. New York: Van Nostrand Reinhold, 1985, pp. 377-413.) *See also* atherosclerosis, Framingham Study.

career. (1) The succession of occupational status changes that occur over the individual's working life. (2) A series of successive stages or events in a given area of activity that individuals go through on the way to some recognizable goal or series of goals (Julius Roth). Some events in an aging career may be: retirement, loss of a spouse, and an incapacitating illness. Others careers include a dying career, or the career of the nursing home patient. (S. Spilerman. "Careers, Labor Market Structure, and Socio-Economic Achievement." *American Journal of Sociology*, 1977, 83, 551-93; J. Roth. *Timetables: Structuring the Passage of Time in Hospital Treatment and Other Careers*. Cleveland: Bobbs-Merrill, 1963; Elizabeth Gustafson. "Dying: The Career of the Nursing Home Patient." *Journal of Health and Social Behavior*, 1972, 13, pp. 226-35; B. Myerhoff and A. Simic, eds. *Life's Career-Aging: Cultural Variations on Growing Old*. Beverly Hills, Calif.: Sage, 1978.

career timetable. The timing and sequence of events in a given area of activity. According to Julius Roth, socially shared expectations about when these events should occur are called "timetable norms." (Julius Roth. *Timetables: Structuring the Passage of Time in Hospital Treatment and Other Careers*. Cleveland: Bobbs-Merrill, 1963.) *See also* career, social clock.

caregiver. Anyone who is involved in the treatment, rehabilitation, or care of the patient. In the family of later life the primary caregiver (the family member who is the main provider of assistance) is the spouse. If the spouse is absent or incapacitated, then it is an adult child. (Marjorie H. Cantor. "Strain among Caregivers: A Study of Experience in the United States." *The Gerontologist*, 1983, 23, pp. 597-604; Dolores E. Gallagher. "Intervention Strategies to Assist Caregivers of Frail Elders: Current Research Status and Future Research Directions." In Carl Eisdorfer, ed., *Annual Review of Gerontology and Geriatrics*. Vol. 5. New York: Springer, 1985, pp. 249-82.)

case management. An approach to obtaining all the needed services for a client by using a case manager to link the client to direct service providers. The case manager's responsibilities include a comprehensive needs assessment, the development of an overall case plan for the client, coordinating the delivery of services, continuously monitoring the services provided to the client, and frequent reassessment. Case management is a particularly valuable approach to meeting the service needs of the homebound elderly as well as other persons with mental or physical disabilities. Sometimes referred to as service management. (Raymond M. Steinberg and Genevieve W. Carter. *Case Management and the Elderly*. Lexington, Mass.: Lexington Books, 1983.)

case study design. A detailed, in-depth analysis of a single unit; for example, a person, a group,* an event, or a place. (W. J. Goode and P. K. Hatt. *Methods in Social Research*. New York: McGraw-Hill, 1952; Susan G. Philliber, Mary R. Schwab, and G. Sam Sloss. *Social Research*. Itasca, Ill.: F. E. Peacock, 1980; Jaber F. Gubrium. *Living and Dying at Murray Manor*. New York: St. Martin's, 1975; Jerry Jacobs. *Older Persons and Retirement Communities: Case Studies in Social Gerontology*. Springfield, Ill.: Charles C. Thomas, 1975.) *See also* community study.

Cassandra complex. The overinvolvement and worry of middle-aged women about the well-being of their husbands, elderly parents, and adult children and their families. Lillian E. Troll and Barbara F. Turner named the term for Cassandra, the Trojan princess who was always predicting doom. (Lillian E. Troll, Sheila J. Miller, and Robert C. Atchley. *Families in Later Life*. Belmont, Calif.: Wadsworth, 1979.)

cataract. The gradual clouding or opacity of the normally transparent lens inside the eye. This leads to impaired passage of light, and vision becomes blurred and hazy. Cataracts are one of the most common eye problems of the elderly. (A. Spector. "Aging of the Lens and Cataract Formation." In Robert Sekuler, Donald W. Kline, and Key Dismukes, eds., *Aging and Human Visual Function*. New York: Alan R. Liss, 1982.)

Cavan Activity Inventory. This inventory was originally designed to measure adjustment* but measures activity levels instead. Topics addressed include family,* friends, leisure,* and economic activity. (Ruth S. Cavan et al. *Personal Adjustment in Old Age*. Chicago: Science Research Associates, 1949.)

Cavan Adjustment Rating Scales. These two, ten-step scales are used as social participation instruments. One scale measures primary relationships and the other secondary relationships. (Robert J. Havighurst and Ruth Albrecht. *Older People*. New York: Longmans, Green, 1953.)

cellular clock theory. *See* Hayflick limit.

census of population. According to the United Nations, a census of population is "the total process of collecting, compiling, evaluating, analyzing, and publishing or otherwise disseminating demographic, economic and social data pertaining, at a specified time, to all persons in a country, or in a well-delimited part of a country." The United States census of population has been taken regularly every ten years since 1790. (United Nations. *Principles and Recommendations for Population and Housing Censuses*. Statistical Papers, Series M, No. 67. New York: Department of International Social and Economic Affairs, 1980.)

centenarians. Persons 100 years of age or older. Septuagenarians are persons 70 to 80 years old, and octogenarians are persons 80 to 90 years old. (Belle Boone Beard. *Social Competence of Centenarians*. Social Science Institute. Athens: University of Georgia, 1967; Robert E. Pieroni. "Centenarians" in Erdman B. Palmore, ed., *Handbook on the Aged in the United States*. Westport, Conn.: Greenwood Press, 1984, pp. 3-16.)

cerebral arteriosclerosis. *See* multi-infarct dementia.

cerebrovascular accident (CVA). Commonly known as stroke, this condition occurs when the blood supply to a particular part of the brain is interrupted or when there is a hemorrhage into the substance of the brain. It may result in partial paralysis (usually on one side of the body), complete paralysis, loss of some bodily function, coma, or even death. (W. B. Kannel et al. "Systolic Blood Pressure, Arterial Rigidity, and Risk of Stroke: The Framingham Study." *Journal of the American Medical Association*, 1981, 245, pp. 1225-29; S. Locke. "Neurological Disorders of the Elderly." In William Reichel, ed., *Clinical Aspects of Aging*. Baltimore: Williams and Wilkins, 1983.)

chi square (x^2). A statistical test indicating the probability that the observed distribution of two variables or attributes has resulted from chance. (H. M. Blalock. *Social Statistics*. New York: McGraw-Hill, 1979; Ann E.

MacEachron. *Basic Statistics in the Human Services: An Applied Approach*. Baltimore: University Park Press, 1982.)

cholesterol. An organic compound that is found in almost all animal tissue. The liver manufactures cholesterol, and additional amounts are obtained through food. Elevated levels of dietary and blood cholesterol have been associated with atherosclerosis* (Molly S. Wantz and John E. Gay. *The Aging Process: A Health Perspective*. Cambridge, Mass.: Winthrop, 1981.)

chronic disease. A pathological condition of gradual onset that usually persists over a long period of time and for which there is no medical cure. Chronic conditions most common among the elderly include arthritis,* diabetes,* hypertension,* and cardiovascular disease.* Since chronic disorders constitute the bulk of health-care problems of the elderly, they have been called the "companions of the aged." More than four out of five persons age 65 and over have at least one chronic condition, and multiple conditions are common among the elderly. (Mortimer Spiegelman. *Introduction to Demography*. Cambridge, Mass.: Harvard University Press, 1968; Molly S. Wantz and John E. Gay. *The Aging Process: A Health Perspective*. Cambridge, Mass.: Winthrop, 1981; Lon R. White. "Geriatric Epidemiology." In Carl Eisdorfer, ed., *Annual Review of Gerontology and Geriatrics*. Vol. 6. New York: Springer, 1986, pp. 215-311.) *See also* acute disease, disease.

chronological age. The calculation of age in terms of the number of years a person has lived, the time elapsed from birth, calendar age. (Glen H. Elder. "Age Differentiation and the Life Course." In Alex Inkeles, ed., *Annual Review of Sociology*. Vol. 1. Palo Alto, Calif.: Annual Reviews Inc., 1975, pp. 165-90; Vern L. Bengtson, Patricia L. Kasschau, and Pauline K. Ragan. "Impact of Social Structure on Aging Individuals." In James E. Birren and K. Warner Schaie, eds., *Handbook of the Psychology of Aging*. New York: Van Nostrand Reinhold, 1977, pp. 327-53.) *See also* biological age, functional age, psychological age, social age.

circuit breakers. A type of property tax relief for low-income elderly homeowners that provides complete or partial relief for property tax payments that exceed a certain fraction of one's income. (Henry J. Aaron. "What Do Circuit Breaker Laws Accomplish?" In George E. Peterson, ed., *Property Tax Reform*. Washington, D.C.: The Urban Institute, 1973.) *See also* homestead exemptions.

class. (1) A group of people who are relatively similar in status* or rank. (2) "An aggregation or group* of people who are alike with respect to something that affects their access to power,* privilege, and prestige"* (Gerhard Lenski). (3) In Marxist usage, a group of people that share the same relationship to the means of production: those who own and control the means of production (bourgeoisie) and those who do not (proletariat). Social stratum is sometimes used interchangeably with social class. The experience of growing old varies by social class affecting one's lifestyle* and world view. (Max Weber. *From Max Weber: Essays in Sociology*. New York: Oxford University Press, 1946; Gerhard Lenski. *Power and Privilege: A Theory of Social Stratification*. New York: McGraw-Hill, 1966; Karl Marx. *Das Kapital*. New York: International Publishers, 1967; Ethel Shanas. "Family Help Patterns and Social Class in Three Countries." *Journal of Marriage and the Family*, 1967, 29, pp. 257-86; Thomas Tissue. "Social Class of the Senior Citizen Center." *The Gerontologist*, 1971, 2, pt. 1, pp. 196-200; James J. Dowd. *Stratification among the Aged*. Monterey, Calif.: Brooks/Cole, 1980.) *See also* social strata, social stratification.

class consciousness. The shared awareness of members of a social class* regarding their situation (e.g., political role, equalities, etc.); one's conception of his or her place in the stratification system. Marxists first used this term to describe a process in which the proletariat becomes aware of its class position in relation to the bourgeoisie. This consciousness tends to vary in its importance throughout the life course. (Robert W. Hodge and Donald J. Treiman. "Class Identification in the United States." *American Journal of Sociology*, 1968, 73, pp. 535-47; George S. Rosenberg. *The Worker Grows Old*. San Francisco: Jossey-Bass, 1970; James J. Dowd. *Stratification among the Aged*. Monterey, Calif.: Brooks/Cole, 1980; Gordon F. Streib. "Social Stratification and Aging." In Robert H. Binstock and Ethel Shanas, eds., *Handbook of Aging and the Social Sciences*. New York: Van Nostrand Reinhold, 1985, pp. 339-68.)

climacteric. (1) A period that may extend over many years as females make the transition from the reproductive to the nonreproductive stage of life. It is characterized by certain physiological and morphological changes and may be viewed as the counterpart of puberty. (2) Sometimes used to refer to the corresponding period in males. Also called "change of life" or menopause.* However, in the strictest sense menopause may be be considered as an event that occurs during the climacteric. (Abraham E. Rakoff and Khosrow Nowroozi. "The Female Climacteric." In Robert B. Greenblatt, ed., *Geriatric Endocrinology*. Vol. 5. New York: Raven Press, 1978, pp. 165-90; Nan Corby and Robert L. Solnick. "Psychosocial and Physiological Influences on Sexuality in the Older Adult." In James E. Birren and R. Bruce Sloane, eds., *Handbook of Mental Health and Aging*. Englewood Cliffs, N.J.: Prentice-Hall, 1980, pp. 893-921.)

closed-ended question. A question which the respondent* must answer on the basis of certain alternatives or categories; for example, multiple choice or the simple dichotomy of yes or no. (Charles F. Cannell and Robert L. Kahn. "Interviewing." In Gardner Lindzey and Elliot Aronson, eds., *Handbook of Social Psychology*. Vol. 2. Reading, Mass.: Addison-Wesley, 1968, pp. 526-95; H. W. Smith. *Strategies of Social Research*. Englewood Cliffs, N.J.: Prentice-Hall, 1981.)

cluster sample. A sample* selected by grouping the population into units or clusters that are in close physical proximity to one another; for example, using counties or blocks. (Leslie Kish. *Survey Sampling*. New York: Wiley, 1965; S. Sudman. *Applied Sampling*. New York: Academic Press, 1976.) *See also* simple random sample, stratified sample.

cohort. (1) A number of persons who have experienced the same significant life event* within a specified time period. If the event is birth, those persons born in 1920 would form a birth cohort* for that year; if the event is marriage, those persons who married in 1986 would form a marriage cohort for that year. There are a number of other types of demographic cohorts such as retirement cohorts, divorce cohorts, educational cohorts, and so on. When used unmodified, cohort usually means birth cohort. Generation* is frequently used as a synonym for birth cohort. (2) A companion, peer, or associate, or collectively a group or band. Originally, cohort referred to a Roman military unit. (Norman B. Ryder. "The Cohort as a Concept in the Study of Social Change." *American Sociological Review*, 1965, 30, 843-61.) *See also* birth cohort.

cohort analysis. The comparison of the characteristics of one or more cohorts* at two or more points in time. The simplest cohort analysis would involve studying one cohort* at two different times. For example, individuals born in 1900-1904 might be studied in 1950 when they are 50-54 years old and again in 1970 when they are 70-74 years old. Although the same cohorts are studied each time, the individuals studied in each cohort may be different. (Norman B. Ryder. "Cohort Analysis." In David L. Sills, ed., *International Encyclopedia of the Social Sciences*. Vol. 2. New York: Macmillan, 1968, pp. 546-50; Norval D. Glenn and Richard E. Zody. "Cohort Analysis with National Survey Data. *The Gerontologist*, 1970, 10, pp. 233-40; Norval D. Glenn. *Cohort Analysis*. Beverly Hills, Calif.: Sage, 1977; Donald W. Hastings and Linda G. Berry, eds., *Cohort Analysis*. Oxford, Ohio: Scripps Foundation for Research in Population Problems, 1979.) *See also* longitudinal design, panel study.

cohort-centrism. The tendency to view the world from the perspective of the cohort* to which one belongs. This term was coined by Matilda W. Riley.

(M. W. Riley. "Social Gerontology and Age Stratification of Society." *The Gerontologist*, 1971, 11, pt. 1, pp. 81-86). *See also* cohort effect.

cohort effect. (1) Socialization* experiences that are largely shared with other members of the same cohort* that result in persons perceiving and interpreting the same situation differently from others who grew up in another time period. In other words, people in different cohorts age in different ways. The Vietnam War would be an example of the cohort effect because of its primary impact on persons who were of the age to be drafted into military service. Also referred to as a generational effect. (2) A difference between individuals or groups of different ages that is thought to be due to their belonging to different cohorts. (H. Hobcraft, J. Menken, and S. Preston. "Age, Period and Cohort Effects in Demography: A Review." *Population Index*, 48, 1982, pp. 4-43; K. Warner Schaie. "Historical Time and Cohort Effects." In K. A. McCluskey and H. W. Reese, eds., *Life-Span Developmental Psychology: Historical and Generational Effects*. New York: Academic Press, 1984.) *See also* age effect, period effect.

cohort succession or flow. The process of existing cohorts aging* and dying* and new cohorts being born into the system. (Matilda W. Riley, Marilyn Johnson, and Anne Foner. *Aging and Society: A Sociology of Age Stratification*. Vol. 3. New York: Russell Sage, 1972; Matilda W. Riley. "Aging and Cohort Succession: Interpretations and Misinterpretations." *Public Opinion Quarterly*, 1973, 37, pp. 35-49.) *See also* cohort.

collagen. A natural protein found throughout the body, especially in the bones, tendons, and skin, which forms a network of fibers that acts as a framework into which blood vessels and cells can grow. With age the collagen network weakens and it cannot support the skin properly. As a result, the skin begins to wrinkle and lose its shape and resilency. (D. A. Hall. *The Aging of Connective Tissue*. New York: Academic Press, 1976.) *See also* wrinkles.

community. (1) People living in a limited territorial area where they have a sense of belonging and fulfill most of their daily needs and activities; for example, a retirement community. (2) A number of individuals who share common interests, functions, and traditions; for example, the academic community or members of an ethnic group* though widely scattered would be considered a community in this sense. (G. A. Hillery. "Definitions of a Community: Areas of Agreement." *Rural Sociology*, 1955, 20, pp. 111-123; Donald L. Warren. *The Community in America*. Chicago: Rand McNally, 1972; Arlie R. Hochschild. *The Unexpected Community*. Berkeley: University of California Press, 1973; Jerry Jacobs. *Older Persons* *and Retirement Communities*. Springfield, Ill.: Charles C. Thomas, 1975.) *See also* retirement community.

community study. A case study in which the unit of analysis is a community.* (Bernard S. Phillips. *Social Research: Strategy and Tactics*. New York: Macmillan, 1976; Sheila K. Johnson. *Idle Haven: Community Building among the Working-Class Retired*. Berkeley: University of California Press, 1971; Arlie R. Hochschild. *The Unexpected Community*. Englewood Cliffs, N.J.: Prentice-Hall, 1973.) *See also* case study design.

comparative design. The comparison of one or more large-scale social units or the same social unit at different points in time to show similarities or differences between them. These units include organizations, institutions, societies, or regions of the world. This term includes both historical design* and cross-cultural design.* (I. Vallier, ed. *Comparative Methods in Sociology*. Berkeley: University of California Press, 1971; Donald P. Warwick and S. Osherson. *Comparative Research Methods*. Englewood Cliffs, N.J.: Prentice-Hall, 1973; Ethel Shanas et al. *Old People in Three Industrial Societies*. New York: Atherton Press, 1968.)

compensation. (1) A defense mechanism by which a person attempts to make up for real or imagined deficiencies in one area by overemphasizing competency in another area. (2) A strategy to offset a loss or losses; for example, an older person may compensate for poor vision by reading books in large type. (Anna Freud. *The Ego and Mechanisms of Defense*. New York: International Universities Press, 1946; Laurance F. Shaffer and Edward J. Shoben. *Psychology of Human Adjustment*. Boston: Houghton Mifflin, 1956; B. F. Skinner and M. E. Vaughan. *Enjoy Old Age: A Program of Self-Management*. New York: W. W. Norton, 1983.) *See also* decrement-with-compensation model, defense mechanisms.

competence. *See* personal competence.

compulsory retirement. *See* mandatory retirement.

Concern for Dying. Organized in 1967, this educational council is composed of professionals and private citizens who provide information about the problems of terminal care. Concern's major project has been the development and the distribution of the living will.* Its goals are twofold: (1) to assure patient autonomy in regard to treatment during terminal illness, and (2) to prevent needless suffering and the futile prolongation of life through advanced medical technology. Formerly it was called the Euthanasia Educational Council. (Concern for Dying, 250 West 57th Street, New York, N.Y. 10107.) *See also* death with dignity, heroic measures.

confusion. *See* disorientation.

congestive heart failure. A condition in which the heart muscles become weakened and are unable to pump enough blood to maintain normal circulation. When this occurs, blood backs up into the lungs and veins leading to the heart. Usually there is also an accumulation of fluid into various parts of the body, especially in the legs and ankles. (Edward G. Lakatta. "Heart and Circulation." In Caleb E. Finch and Edward L. Schneider, eds., *Handbook of the Biology of Aging*. New York: Van Nostrand Reinhold, 1985, pp. 377-413.) *See also* cardiovascular disease.

congregate housing. A type of housing that provides individual living units combined with a central dining room, housekeeping, transportation, and social services* for older persons who range from being independent to those at the institutional level of dependence. (M. Powell Lawton. *Environment and Aging*. Monterey, Calif.: Brooks/Cole, 1980; Robert D. Chellis, James F. Seagle, and Barbara M. Seagle, eds., *Congregate Housing for Older People: A Solution for the 1980s*. Lexington, Mass.: Lexington Books, 1982.)

congregate meals program. A federal program, created in 1972, that provides nutritional meals to groups of elderly persons at midday in central locations, such as senior citizen centers, schools, and churches. Each meal site offers a variety of services and programs. (U.S. Senate. *Developments in Aging: 1977*. A Report of the Special Committee on Aging. Washington, D.C.: U.S. Government Printing Office, 1978; Annette B. Natow and Jo-Ann Heslin. *Nutritional Care of the Older Adult*. New York: Macmillan, 1986). *See also* home-delivered meals program.

conjugal family. *See* nuclear family.

conservatism. (1) In politics, the view that resists change and defends the status quo. (2) The unwillingness to take risks. Contrary to popular opinion, as people age they tend to be less conservative. However, compared to others in the population the elderly are more conservative. But compared with their younger attitudes, they have become more liberal in conformity with general societal trends. (Norval Glenn. "Aging and Conservatism." *Annals of the American Academy of Political and Social Science*, 1974. Vol. 415. pp. 176-86.)

content analysis. A social research technique for systematically and quantitatively studying oral, written, or pictorial communication in which the material is coded on the basis of some conceptual framework. Communication may refer to books, movies, television, art, and other media. (Bernard

Berelson. "Content Analysis." In Gardner Lindzey, ed., *Handbook of Social Psychology*. Cambridge, Mass.: Addison-Wesley, 1954, pp. 488-522; Ole R. Holsti. *Content Analysis for Social Sciences and Humanities*. Reading, Mass.: Addison-Wesley, 1969; Mildred M. Seltzer and Robert C. Atchley. "The Concept of Old: Changing Attitudes and Stereotypes." *The Gerontologist*, 1971, 2, pt. 1, pp. 226-30.)

continuing care community. *See* life care communities.

continuity theory. An outgrowth of the disengagement and activity theories of aging, the continuity theory asserts that as people grow older they are predisposed toward maintaining for as long as possible the habits, preferences, lifestyles, and many other patterns that they developed earlier in life. (George L. Maddox. "Persistence of Life Style among the Elderly." In Erdman B. Palmore, ed., *Normal Aging*. Durham, N.C.: Duke University Press, 1970; Bill D. Bell. "Role Set Orientations and Life Satisfaction: A New Look at an Old Theory." In Jaber F. Gubrium, ed., *Time, Roles and Self in Old Age*. Human Sciences Press, 1976, pp. 148-64.)

continuum of care. The full range of preventive, supportive, rehabilitative, and social services available in a community* to older persons at various levels of need and impairments. These services, which include nutrition, housing, employment, health, and support services may be offered in the home, at aging centers, or at institutional facilities. (George L. Maddox. "The Continuum of Care: Movement toward the Community." In E. W. Busse and D. G. Blazer, eds., *Handbook of Geriatric Psychiatry*. New York: Van Nostrand Reinhold, 1980; Albert J. E. Wilson. *Social Services for Older Persons*. Boston: Little, Brown, 1984.)

control group. A group of subjects that is not exposed to the experimental variable* or treatment and is used for making comparisons with an experimental or test group. The control group should match the experimental group in all other important aspects. (H. W. Smith. *Strategies of Social Research*. Englewood Cliffs, N.J.: Prentice-Hall, 1981.) *See also* experimental group.

control variable. The variable in a particular study or experiment that is "held constant" in order to clarify the relationship between two other variables. (Earl R. Babbie. *The Practice of Social Research*. Belmont, Calif.: Wadsworth, 1983.) *See also* variable.

coronary artery disease. A condition in which one or more of the coronary arteries become blocked. As a result, blood flow is inadequate and the heart muscle cannot get enough oxygen. This may lead to chest pain (angina pectoris*) or a heart attack (myocardial infarction*). (Edward G. Lakatta.

"Heart and Circulation." In Caleb E. Finch and Edward L. Schneider, eds., *Handbook of the Biology of Aging*. New York: Van Nostrand Reinhold, 1985, pp. 377-413.) *See also* cardiovascular disease.

correlation. The relationship between two variables. A correlation is positive (or direct) when increases in one variable are associated with increases in the other; whereas a correlation is negative (or inverse) when increases in one variable are associated with decreases in the other. (Hubert M. Blalock. *Causal Inferences in Nonexperimental Research*. New York: W. W. Norton, 1972; Bernard S. Phillips. *Social Research Strategy and Tactics*. New York: Macmillan, 1976.) *See also* variable, correlation coefficient.

correlation coefficient. A number that expresses the direction and degree of a relationship between two variables. A correlation coefficient may range from $+1.0$ (a perfect positive correlation) to -1.0 (a perfect negative correlation). A coefficient of zero indicates no correlation between variables. (Ann E. MacEachron. *Basic Statistics in the Human Services: An Applied Approach*. Baltimore: University Park Press, 1982.) *See also* correlation, variable.

countermigration. A new trend in which persons 60 and over who migrated to the sunbelt* states in their early retirement years return to their home state or to a state in which family members live. (U.S. Senate. *Developments in Aging: 1985*. A Report of the Special Committee on Aging. Washington, D.C.: U.S. Government Printing Office, 1986.)

counterphobia. A defense mechanism* in which one overcompensates for feared situations. Counterphobia is related to denial.* For example, an elderly man with a severe heart condition attempts to paint his house. (Robert N. Butler and Myrna I. Lewis. *Aging and Mental Health*. St. Louis: C. V. Mosby, 1982.)

covariance. Variables that occur in some regular relationship to each other. Changes in one variable are accompanied by changes in the other variable; for example, height and weight. (Susan G. Philliber, Mary R. Schwab, and G. Sam Sloss. *Social Research*. Itasca, Ill.: Peacock, 1980.) *See also* variable.

crib job. A slang expression for the ease in committing crimes against older persons. (Jack Goldsmith and Sharon S. Goldsmith. *Crime and the Elderly*. Lexington, Mass.: Lexington Books, 1976.)

cross-cultural design. A widely used method in the social sciences that involves the systematic gathering and comparison of data from two or more cultures. The focus is usually on the comparison of various traits and practices in different cultural settings. The terms "holocultural" and "cross-cultural" have been used interchangeably. However in recent years anthropologists have begun to distinguish between the two. Holocultural refers to studies that utilize a world sample of human societies, mainly the Human Relations Area Files. An example of a holocultural study would be Leo W. Simmons' work on the aged in primitive societies. (L. W. Simmons. *The Role of the Aged in Primitive Society*. New Haven, Conn.: Yale University Press, 1945; Ethel Shanas. "Family Kin Networks and Aging in Cross-Cultural Perspective." *Journal of Marriage and the Family*, 1973, 35, pp. 505-11; Jay Sokolovsky. *Growing Old in Different Societies*. Belmont, Calif.: Wadsworth, 1983.) *See also* comparative design.

cross-disciplinary research. *See* interdisciplinary research.

cross-linking theory. A theory that proposes that the accumulation of cross-link molecules is a major cause of aging. Cross-linking refers to the attachment of any two large molecules to one another inside or outside the cell. When this occurs, these large molecules become immobilized. The result, according to this theory, is that an accumulation of a "frozen metabolic pool" clogs the tissues and cells and impairs their function. This theory was first proposed by John Bjorksten in 1968. (J. Bjorksten. "The Crosslinkage Theory of Aging." *Journal of American Geriatrics Society*, 1968, 16, pp. 408-27.)

cross-national design. The systematic gathering and comparison of data from two or more countries. (Ernest W. Burgess. *Aging in Western Societies*. Chicago: University of Chicago Press, 1960; Ethel Shanas et al. *Old People in Three Industrial Societies*. New York: Atherton Press, 1968.)

crossover phenomenon. The contention that there is a reversal of life expectancy* between blacks and whites with blacks outliving whites after a certain age. Some writers place this "crossover" after age 75 and others after age 80. (Kenneth Manton, Sharon S. Poss, and Steve Wing. "The Black/White Mortality Crossover: Investigation from the Perspective of the Components of Aging." *The Gerontologist*, 1979, 19, pp. 291-300; Jacquelyne J. Jackson. "Race, National Origin, and Ethnicity and Aging." In Robert H. Binstock and Ethel Shanas, eds., *Handbook of Aging and the Social Sciences*. New York: Van Nostrand Reinhold, 1985, pp. 264-303.)

cross-sectional design. The comparison of two or more groups of people at one point in time. The data are obtained only once rather than several times, as in a longitudinal design.* This was the earliest and still is the most frequently used method for studying aging.* It involves comparing two or more age groups* at one point in time to measure age differences.* A major

problem with the cross-sectional method is that it confounds the age effect*
and the cohort effect.* Also referred to as the synchronic method. (Paul B.
Baltes, Hayne W. Reese, and John R. Nesselroade. *Life Span Developmental Psychology: Introduction to Research Methods*. Belmont, Calif.:
Brooks/Cole, 1977.)

cross-sequential design. A comparison of two or more cohorts at two or
more points in time. A combination of the cross-sectional and longitudinal
methods, this design was originally proposed by K. Warner Schaie to distinguish between the effects of age, period, and cohort. (K. W. Schaie. "A
General Model for the Study of Developmental Change." *Psychological
Bulletin*, 1965, 64, pp. 92-107; Erdman B. Palmore. "When Can Age,
Period, and Cohort Be Separated?" *Social Forces*, 1978, 57, pp. 282-95.)

crude birthrate. The number of births in a year per 1,000 of the mid-year
population. The crude birthrate is the most frequently used measure of
fertility* and is often referred to as simply the birthrate. (Henry S. Shryock,
Jacob S. Siegel, and Associates. *The Methods and Materials of Demography*. New York: Academic Press, 1976.)

crude death rate. The number of deaths in a year per 1,000 of the mid-year
population. The crude death rate is the most commonly used measure of
mortality and is often referred to as simply the death rate. Generally, the
higher the proportion of elderly persons in the population, the higher the
death rate will be. (Henry S. Shryock, Jacob S. Siegel, and Associates. *The
Methods and Materials of Demography*. New York: Academic Press, 1976.)

cryobiology. The scientific study of living organisms at low temperatures.
Some researchers have demonstrated that lowered body temperature results
in increased longevity in some organisms. (B. L. Strehler. "Studies on the
Comparative Physiology of Aging: On the Mechanism of Temperature
Life-Shortening in Drosophila Melanogaster." *Journal of Gerontology*,
1961, 16, pp. 2-12; Nathan Shock. *Perspectives in Experimental
Gerontology*. Springfield, Ill.: Charles C. Thomas, 1966; R. K. Liu and
R. L. Walford. "The Effect of Lowered Body Temperature on Lifespan
and Immune and Non-Immune Processes." *Gerontologia*, 1972, 18, pp.
363-88.) *See also* hypothermia.

cryonics. Human cold storage; the belief of renewed life after death on this
planet by freezing and placing a person in suspension at the time of death
until reanimation is possible. (Arlene Sheskin. *Cryonics: A Sociology of
Death and Bereavement*. New York: Irvington, 1979; George P. Smith.
Medical-Legal Aspects of Cryonics: Prospects for Mortality. Port Washington, N.Y.: Associated Faculty Press, 1983.)

crystallized intelligence. The skills one acquires through education (formal and informal), the socialization* process, and other past experiences. These skills include vocabulary, factual information, and numerical skills. Crystallized intelligence tends to increase throughout life in healthy, active people, while fluid intelligence* is assumed to decline. The concept was introduced by Raymond B. Cattell and elaborated by John L. Horn. (J. L. Horn and R. B. Cattell. "Age Differences in Primary Mental Ability Factors." *Journal of Gerontology*, 1966, 21, pp. 210-20; J. L. Horn and R. B. Cattell. "Age Differences in Fluid and Crystallized Intelligence." *Acta Psychologica*, 1967, 26, pp. 107-79; J. L. Horn. "The Theory of Fluid and Crystallized Intelligence in Relation to Concepts of Cognitive Psychology and Aging in Adulthood." In F. J. M. Craik and S. Tehub, eds., *Aging and Cognitive Processes*. New York: Plenum, 1982.)

cultural anthropology. *See* anthropology.

cultural relativism. A concept that implies that all patterns of behavior must be analyzed in light of the cultural context in which they are found. It emphasizes cultural diversity and open-mindedness. Used as an antonym for ethnocentrism.* Old age and the solutions to its problems are relative to the cultural setting in which they occur. (Ralph Linton. *The Study of Man*. New York: D. Appleton-Century, 1936; M. J. Herskovits. *Cultural Relativism*. New York: Random House, 1972; L. W. Simmons. *The Role of the Aged in Primitive Society*. New Haven, Conn.: Yale University Press, 1945; Lowell D. Holmes. *Other Cultures, Elder Years: An Introduction to Cultural Gerontology*. Minneapolis: Burgess, 1983.)

cultural universals. Certain broad characteristics and general categories that all societies have in common; for example, age-grading, bodily adornment, and funeral rites. Leo W. Simmons was one of the first to list the cultural universals associated with aging. These include to live a long life, to rest, to remain an active participant in the group, and to die as honorably and as comfortably as possible. (George P. Murdock. "The Common Denominator of Culture. In Ralph Linton, ed., *The Science of Man in the World Crisis*. New York: Columbia University Press, 1945; Leo W. Simmons. *The Role of the Aged in Primitive Society*. New Haven, Conn.: Yale University Press, 1945; Donald O. Cowgill and Lowell D. Holmes. *Aging and Modernization*. New York: Appleton-Century-Crofts, 1972.)

culture. The social heritage of a society* that is transmitted to each generation;* socially learned and shared behavior. Most sociological and anthropological definitions are modifications of Edward B. Tylor's classic definition: "that complex whole which includes knowledge, belief, art, morals, law, custom, and any other capabilities and habits acquired by man as a member of society.'' The attitudes and values toward the aged, the definitions of old age,* the roles that are appropriate for the elderly, how the elderly should be treated, and so on are all determined by one's culture. (E. B. Tylor. *Primitive Culture.* Vol. 1. London: John Murray, 1871; A. L. Kroeber and Clyde Kluckhohn. ''Culture: A Critical Review of Concepts and Definitions.'' *Papers of the Peabody Museum,* 1952, 47, pp. 643-44, 656; Margaret Clark and Barbara G. Anderson. *Culture and Aging: An Anthropological Study of Older Americans.* Springfield, Ill.: Charles C. Thomas, 1967; Diana K. Harris and William E. Cole. *Sociology of Aging.* Boston: Houghton Mifflin, 1980. *See* ''Culture and Adult Socialization,'' pp. 49-122; Lowell D. Holmes. *Other Cultures, Elder Years: An Introduction to Cultural Gerontology.* Minneapolis: Burgess, 1983.)

custodial care facility. *See* residential care facility.

custodial institutions. *See* total institutions.

cytogerontology. The study of cell aging. (Leonard Hayflick. ''Cell Aging.'' In Carl Eisdorfer, ed., *Annual Review of Gerontology and Geriatrics.* Vol. 1. New York: Springer, 1980, pp. 26-67.)

D

dawdling. The tendency of older residents in institutions to return from an activity so slowly that they require supervision. (Robert G. Riedel. "Behavior Therapies." In Carl Eisdorfer, ed., *Annual Review of Gerontology and Geriatrics.* Vol. 2. New York: Springer, 1981, pp. 160-95.)

day-care center/geriatric day hospital. These programs provide group care during the day for handicapped and slightly disoriented elderly persons. Rehabilitative, medical, and personal care services, as well as social and recreational opportunities, are offered by a professional and paraprofessional staff. These five-day-a-week programs help older persons to remain independent and reduce unnecessary institutionalization.* In addition, they provide a respite care* service during the day for family members. (Brahna Trager. "Adult Day Facilities for Treatment, Health Care, and Related Services." *A Working Paper for the U.S. Senate Committee on Aging,* Washington, D.C.: U.S. Government Printing Office, September 1976; E. J. Lorenze, C. M. Hamill, and R. C. Oliver. "The Day Hospital: An Alternative to Institutional Care." *Journal of American Geriatrics Society,* 1974, 22, pp. 316-20; D. R. Matlock. "The Case for Geriatric Day Hospitals." *The Gerontologist,* 1975, 15, pp. 109-13; P. G. Weiler and Eloise Rathbone-McCuan. *Adult Day Care: Community Work with the Elderly.* New York: Springer, 1978.)

death. (1) The United Nations defines death as "the total and permanent disappearance of all evidence of life at any time after birth has taken place." (2) The irreversible absence of brain function. (3) "The transition from the state of being alive to the state of being dead" (L. R. Kass). (United Nations. *Handbook of Vital Statistics Methods.* Studies in Methods, Series F, No. 7, 1955; Herman Feifel. *The Meaning of Death.* New York: McGraw-Hill, 1959; Glenn M. Vernon. *Sociology of Death.* New York: Ronald Press, 1970; L. R. Kass. "Death as an Event: A Commentary on Robert Morison." *Science,* 1971, 173, pp. 698-702; Richard A. Kalish. "The Social Context of Death and Dying." In Robert H. Binstock and Ethel Shanas, eds., *Handbook of Aging and the Social Sciences.* New York: Van Nostrand Reinhold, 1985, pp. 149-70.) *See also* brain death, psychological death, social death, thanatology.

Death Anxiety Scale (DAS). A 15-item scale that measures both verbalized and nonverbalized anxiety about or fear of death.* (D. I. Templer. "The Construction and Validation of a Death Anxiety Scale." *Journal of Genetic Psychology*, 1970, 82, pp. 165-77.)

death-dip hypothesis. A notion which asserts that death-rate statistics drop prior to a meaningful event; for example, birthdays, elections, and so on. (David P. Phillips and Kenneth A. Feldman. "A Dip in Deaths before Ceremonial Occasions: Some New Relationships between Social Integration and Mortality." *American Sociological Review*, 1973, 38, pp. 678-96.)

death rate. *See* crude death rate.

death survival guilt. Guilt from outliving others. (P. C. Chodoff. "Late Effects of the Concentration Camp Syndrome." *Archives of General Psychiatry*, 1969, 20, pp. 323-33.)

death with dignity. To withhold or withdraw heroic measures* and allow a person to die naturally when recovery is impossible and death* is imminent. The first "death with dignity" law was passed in California in 1976. (Derek Humphry and Ann Wickett. *The Right to Die: Understanding Euthanasia.* New York: Harper and Row, 1986.) *See also* Concern for Dying, living will.

decrement-with-compensation model. This model, proposed by K. Warner Schaie, suggests that while decline with aging is to be expected, intervention may compensate for some of the losses. For example, hearing and vision decline may be helped by glasses and hearing aids, and muscular and cardiovascular decline by an exercise program. (K. Warner Schaie. "Methodological Problems in Descriptive Developmental Research in Adulthood and Aging." In J. R. Nesselroade and H. W. Reese, eds., *Life-Span Developmental Psychology: Methodological Issues.* New York: Academic Press, 1973.) *See also* irreversible decrement model.

decubitus ulcers. Sores resulting from constant pressure on the skin from prolonged sitting or lying in one position. Other risk factors include moisture from perspiration or incontinence,* diet, and medication sensitivity. Commonly referred to as bed sores or pressure sores. (T. Husain. "An Experimental Study of Some Pressure Effects in Tissues, with Reference to the Bedsore Problem." *Journal of Pathological Bacteriology*, 1953, 66, pp. 347-58; A. N. Exton-Smith and J. G. Evans, eds., *Care of the Elderly: Meeting the Challenge of Dependency.* New York: Grune and Stratton, 1977; Annette B. Natow and Jo-Ann Heslin. *Nutritional Care of the Older Adult.* New York: Macmillan, 1986.)

defense mechanisms. Techniques that operate at an unconscious level to relieve anxiety* and emotional conflict. (Anna Freud. *The Ego and Mechanisms of Defense.* New York: International Universities Press, 1946; Laurance F. Shaffer and Edward J. Shoben, Jr. *The Psychology of Adjustment.* Boston: Houghton Mifflin, 1956; George E. Vaillant. *Adaptation to Life.* Boston: Little, Brown, 1977.) *See also* compensation, counterphobia, denial, displacement, projection, rationalization, regression, repression.

degenerative disease. A chronic disease characterized by deterioration of the body or a part of the body that results in progressive disability; for example, arthritis* is a chronic degenerative disease that affects the joints. (Molly S. Wantz and John E. Gay. *The Aging Process: A Health Perspective.* Cambridge, Mass.: Winthrop, 1981, pp. 171-227.)

deinstitutionalization movement. This movement stresses community support systems as an alternative to institutionalization.* Efforts are made to avoid putting persons in institutions and to help release those already in them, especially those in mental hospitals. Placement for the deinstitutionalized mentally ill elderly has been mainly in foster homes and boarding homes. In major cities many elderly mental patients have been absorbed by residential hotels; this has created what Wilma Donahue terms "psychiatric ghettos." (Barry Siegel and Judith Lasher. "Deinstitutionalizing Elderly Patients: A Program of Resocialization." *The Gerontologist*, 1978, 18, pp. 293-300; W. Donahue. "What about Our Responsibility toward the Abandoned Elderly?" *The Gerontologist*, 1978, 18, pp. 102-11; Albert J. E. Wilson. *Social Services for Older Persons.* Boston: Little, Brown, 1984.) *See also* institution.

delirium. A reversible organic mental disorder that is charactrized by disturbances of attention, memory, and orientation with altered levels of consciousness ranging from mild confusion to stupor. Delusions, illusions, and/or hallucinations may be present. Delirium can result from a number of conditions including malnutrition, congestive heart failure, head trauma, hypoglycemia,* and drug ingestion. The incidence of delirium is much higher among the elderly than in other age groups. (M. Roth. "The Psychiatric Disorders of Later Life." *Psychiatric Annals*, 1976, 6, pp. 57-98.) *See also* delusion, dementia, hallucination, organic mental disorder.

delusion. A false belief that persists despite logical argument and contradictory evidence. Two major types are grandeur (an exaggerated belief of one's identity or importance) and persecution (the belief that one is being talked about or plotted against). Delusions may occur in senile dementia* or depression.* (R. W. White and N. F. Watt. *The Abnormal Personality.* New York: Ronald Press, 1973.)

dementia. An organic mental disorder that usually results in a deterioration of intellectual functions. It is characterized by memory disturbance, an impairment of judgment, abstract, and rational thought, and personality change. The most common types of dementia among the elderly are senile dementia* and multi-infarct dementia.* It is often inaccurately termed "senility."* (C. E. Wells. *Dementia.* Philadelphia: F. A. Davis Co., 1977; Lissy F. Jarvik. "Diagnosis of Dementia in the Elderly: A 1980 Perspective." In Carl Eisdorfer, ed., *Annual Review of Gerontology and Geriatrics.* Vol. 1. New York: Springer, 1980, pp. 180-203.) *See also* delirium.

demographic transition theory. The theory that population* growth tends to change with industrialization.* In preindustrial societies birth rates and death rates are high and population growth is slow, resulting in a stable population size. As industrialization takes place, death rates decline but birth rates remain high and population growth is rapid. After a society* has become industrialized, birth rates and death rates decline and population growth is again slow, resulting in a stable population size. The final stage results in larger numbers and proportions of older persons in a society. (Kingsley Davis. "The World Demographic Transition." *The Annals of the American Academy of Political and Social Science,* 1945, Vol. 273. pp. 1-11; David M. Heer. *Society and Population.* Englewood Cliffs, N.J.: Prentice-Hall, 1975; Jay Weinstein. *Demographic Transition and Social Change.* Morristown, N.J.: General Learning, 1976.)

Figure 2
Diagram of the Demographic Transition

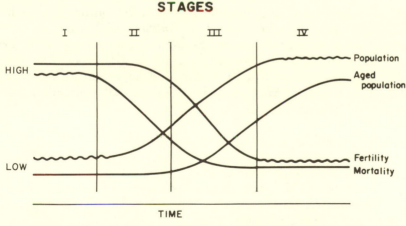

Source: George C. Myers. "Aging and Worldwide Population Change." In Robert H. Binstock and Ethel Shanas, eds., *Handbook of Aging and the Social Sciences.* New York: Van Nostrand Reinhold Co., Inc., 1985, p. 179. Courtesy of the publisher.

demography. The scientific study of the size, compositon, distribution, and changes in human populations. It is generally regarded as a subfield of sociology. The term "demography" was coined by Achille Guillard, a Belgian statistician, in 1855. (Mortimer Spiegelman. *Introduction to Demography*, Cambridge, Mass.: Harvard University Press, 1968; Roland Pressat. *Demographic Analysis: Methods, Results, Applications*. Chicago: Aldine-Atherton, 1972; Henry S. Shryock, Jacob S. Siegel, and Associates. *The Methods and Materials of Demography*. New York: Academic Press, 1976; Jacob S. Siegel "On the Demography of Aging." *Demography*, 1980, 17, pp. 345-64.)

denial. A defense mechanism* in which one unconsciously refuses to face painful feelings, emotions, or thoughts. Some persons refuse to deal with the reality of growing old and pretend that it is not happening to them. Denial not only interferes with the acceptance of aging, but it is promoted in a society that values youth and devalues old age. (Anna Freud. *The Ego and Mechanisms of Defense*. New York: International Universities Press, 1946; Gordon L. Bultena and Edward A. Powers. "Denial of Aging: Age Identification and Reference Group Orientation." *Journal of Gerontology*, 1978, 33, pp. 748-54; Robert N. Butler and Myrna I. Lewis. *Aging and Mental Health*. St. Louis: C. V. Mosby, 1982.) *See also* counterphobia, Peter Pan syndrome.

dependence. The need to rely on one or more persons for physical, economic, mental, and/or social support on a regular basis to maintain life and living arrangements. Anyone who lives to old age eventually becomes dependent on others. This need may arise from ill health, frailty of old age, or for mental health reasons. Senile dementia* of the Alzheimer's type (SDAT) is one of the most frequent causes of dependence in later life. (Margaret Clark and Barbara Anderson. *Culture and Aging: An Anthropological Study of Older Americans*. Springfield, Ill.: Charles C. Thomas, 1967; Richard A. Kalish, ed., *The Dependencies of Old People*. Occasional Papers in Gerontology, No. 6, University of Michigan: Institute of Gerontology, 1969.) *See also* Activities of Daily Living, Index of; Instrumental Activities of Daily Living Scale.

dependency ratio. *See* age dependency ratio.

dependent variable. The variable* that is assumed to be affected by the occurrence or change in the independent variable.* In experimental research the experimenter varies the independent variable and measures the effect on the dependent variable. (Elliot Aronson and J. Merrill Carlsmith. "Experimentation in Social Psychology." In Gardner Lindzey and E. Aronson, eds., *Handbook of Social Psychology*. Vol. 2. Reading, Mass.: Addison-Wesley, 1968, pp. 1-79.)

depression. (1) A serious emotional or affective disorder characterized by loss of appetite, insomnia, lethargy, and feelings of guilt, worthlessness, and a reduction and loss of interest in almost all usual activities. It is the most common mental disorder found in the elderly. (2) A normal variation in mood characterized by sadness, unhappiness, and having "the blues." The term "depression" originally referred to psychotic states, which were also known as "involutional melancholia." (Asser Stenback. "Depression and Suicidal Behavior in Old Age." In James E. Birren and R. Bruce Sloan, eds., *Handbook of Mental Health and Aging.* Englewood Cliffs, N.J.: Prentice-Hall, 1980, pp. 616-51; Dan G. Blazer. *Depression in Late Life.* St. Louis: C. V. Mosby, 1982; Lawrence D. Breslau and Marie R. Haug, eds. *Depression and Aging: Causes, Care, and Consequences.* New York: Springer, 1983.)

depth interview. An unstructured interview designed to allow the respondent complete freedom in discussing a particular topic. It involves the use of extensive probing by the interviewer in order to get the respondent to elaborate further on a response. (William Banaka. *Training in Depth Interviewing.* New York: Harper and Row, 1971; H. W. Smith. *Strategies of Social Research.* Englewood Cliffs, N.J.: Prentice-Hall, 1981.)

Detroit syndrome. A phrase to describe the way our society "scrap piles" the elderly who are considered nonproductive and dependent. This term was originated by Maggie Kuhn. (Dieter T. Hessel. *Maggie Kuhn on Aging.* Philadelphia: Westminster Press, 1977.)

developmental psychology. *See* life-span developmental psychology.

deviance. Behavior that is censured, stigmatized, or penalized for breaking social rules or norms; a lack of conformity to social norms. The incidence of deviance among older persons is relatively low because most types of deviant behavior decrease as one ages with the exception of male suicide.* (Howard Becker. *Outsiders: Studies in the Sociology of Deviance.* New York: Free Press, 1963; Leo Miller. "Toward a Classification of Aging Behaviors." *The Gerontologist*, 1979, 19, pp. 283-89; Douglas C. Kimmel. "Life-History Interviews of Aging Gay Men." *International Journal of Aging and Human Development*, 1979-1980, 10, pp. 239-48.) *See also* age deviance, labeling theory, sick role.

diabetes mellitus. A chronic condition in which there is an overabundance of blood sugar. There are two major kinds of diabetes: juvenile and adult-onset. Juvenile diabetes is usually due to a deficiency of insulin from the pancreas in which the person is insulin dependent. In adult-onset diabetes, this condition may be due to a resistance or inability of the body to use insulin instead of a deficiency. Adult-onset diabetes is a common disorder among older persons and may lead to visual problems and defects in the nervous system. (Kenneth L. Minaker, Graydon S. Meneilly, and John W. Rowe. "Endocrine Systems." In Caleb E. Finch and Edward L. Schneider, eds., *Handbook of the Biology of Aging.* New York: Van Nostrand Reinhold, 1985, pp. 433-56; A. Goldberg, R. Andres, and E. Bierman. "Diabetes Mellitus in the Elderly." In R. Andres, E. Bierman, and W. Hazzard, eds., *Principles of Geriatric Medicine.* New York: McGraw-Hill, 1985, pp. 750-64; Annette B. Natow and Jo-Ann Heslin. *Nutritional Care of the Older Adult.* New York: Macmillan, 1986, pp. 115-27.) *See also* hypoglycemia.

diachronic method. *See* longitudinal design.

diachronic solidarity. A term used by Martha Baum and Rainer C. Baum to describe a type of intergenerational solidarity.* They define it as "a social identity shared with successive generations that always connects the younger with the older in a perpetual chain of community lasting through time, indefinitely." (M. Baum and R. C. Baum. *Growing Old: A Societal Perspective.* Englewood Cliffs, N.J.: Prentice-Hall, 1980.)

diagnosis-related groups (DRGs). A list of 471 specific medical conditions or combinations of illnesses with preset amounts used by Medicare to reimburse hospitals. The concept was developed at Yale University by a group of medical researchers.' (Robert S. Mudge, ed. *Social Security and Retirement: Private Goals, Public Policy.* Washington, D.C.: Congressional Quarterly, 1983; U.S. Senate. *Developments in Aging: 1986.* Vol. 1. A Report of the Special Committee on Aging. Washington, D.C.: U.S. Government Printing Office, 1987.) *See also* prospective payment system, Medicare.

Diagnostic and Statistical Manual of Mental Disorders (DSM). A manual prepared by the Task Force on Statistics and Nomenclature of the American Psychiatric Association, DSM is the official classification system to aid clinicians and researchers in diagnosing, treating, and communicating about mental disorders. The first edition, DSM-I, was published in 1952, DSM-II, the second edition, was published in 1968, and DSM-III, the third edition, was published in 1980 and revised in 1987 (DSM-III R). (The Task Force on Nomenclature and Statistics of the American Psychiatric Association. *Diagnostic and Statistical Manual of Mental Disorders.* Washington, D.C.: American Psychiatric Association, 1987.)

differential disengagement. The withdrawal of older persons from some activities while continuing or increasing their involvement in others; for example, at retirement* one may increase the time spent with family* and friends and at church. (Gordon Streib and Clement Schneider. *Retirement in American Society*. Ithaca, N.Y.: Cornell University Press, 1971.) *See also* disengagement theory.

differential gerontology. The wide variation among elderly persons of the same chronological age* in their social competence, functional capacity, lifestyles, and so on. (George L. Maddox. "The Social and Cultural Context of Aging." In Gene Usdin and Charles K. Hofling, eds., *Aging: The Process and the People*. New York: Brunner/Mazel, 1978, pp. 20-46.)

differential mortality. Differences in the death rates in a population* at a certain time or between different cohorts by such factors as sex, race, and social class. (E. Kitagawa and Philip Hauser. *Differential Mortality in the United States: A Study in Socioeconomic Epidemiology*. Cambridge, Mass.: Harvard University Press, 1973.) *See also* differential mortality.

digit preference. *See* age heaping.

disability. Any reduction in functional capacity that results from physiological, psychological, or social impairments. Short-term disability refers to a reduction in functional capacity as a result of an acute condition. Long-term disability refers to a reduction in functional capacity as a result of a chronic condition. (Saad Z. Nagi. "Some Conceptual Issues in Disability and Rehabilitation." In Marvin B. Sussman, ed., *Sociology and Rehabilitation*. Washington, D.C.: American Sociological Association, 1965.) *See also* impairment.

discontinuity of socialization. A lack of preparation or consistency in training for a role* that one will take on at the next consecutive life stage; experience at one life stage that does not aid or may even hinder the transition to a later stage. An example would be the lack of preparation as one moves from the role of worker to that of a retiree. (Irving Rosow. *Socialization to Old Age*. Berkeley: University of California Press, 1976.)

discrimination. (1) The unfavorable treatment of individuals or groups on the basis of their membership in a category or group of people. (2) Superordinate group members using their power to deny subordinate group members access to social rewards. Discrimination against the elderly occurs in many sectors of our society including employment and delivery of health and mental health services. (3) The process by which one distinguishes between two closely related stimuli or items. (James W. Vander Zanden. *American Minority Relations*. New York: Ronald Press, 1972; Jack Levin and William C. Levin. *Ageism: Prejudice and Discrimination against the Elderly*. Belmont, Calif.: Wadsworth, 1980.) *See also* ageism, prejudice, racism, sexism.

disease. A medically determinable physical or mental disorder that may impair one's functioning and/or be life-threatening. (Henry P. Brehm and Rodney·M. Coe. *Medical Care for the Aged: From Social Problem to Federal Problem.* New York: Praeger, 1980.) *See also* acute disease, chronic disease.

disengagement theory. This theory maintains that as persons grow older, a decreased amount of social interaction* occurs between them and other members of society.* A mutual withdrawal of social interaction takes place in which the elderly withdraw from society and society withdraws from them. It is an inevitable and gradual process. The disengagement theory is considered to be the first explicitly stated social psychological theory of aging to appear in the social gerontological literature. It is set in the framework of functionalist theory and was first described by Elaine Cumming and her associates in 1960. (E. Cumming, Lois Dean, and Isabel McCaffrey. "Disengagement: A Tentative Theory of Aging." *Sociometry*, 1960, 23, pp. 25-35; E. Cumming and William Henry. *Growing Old.* New York: Basic Books, 1961; Arlie R. Hochschild. "Disengagement Theory: A Critique and Proposal." *American Sociological Review*, 1975, 40, pp. 553-69.)

disorientation. To lose one's sense of position in relation to time, space, and other aspects of the environment.* Disorientation that may occur as a result of dementia* and delirium* in older persons tends to be most evident late in the day and at night and is sometimes referred to as the "sundown syndrome." (Irene M. Burnside. "Symptomatic Behaviors in the Elderly." In James E. Birren and R. Bruce Sloane, eds., *Handbook of Mental Health and Aging.* Englewood Cliffs, N.J.: Prentice-Hall, 1980, pp. 719-44.) *See also* reality orientation.

displaced homemakers. Women, frequently in midlife, who have lost their source of income due to separation, divorce, or the death of a husband. (Displaced Homemakers Network, 1411 K Street N.W., Washington, D.C. 20005.)

displacement. (1) A defense mechanism* in which one shifts the blame from the real source of one's anxieties* or difficulties onto another person, object, or situation. (2) Substituting one response for another. (Anna Freud. *The Ego and Mechanism of Defense.* New York: International Universities, 1946; Laurance F. Shaffer and Edward J. Shoben. *The Psychology of Adjustment.* Boston: Houghton Mifflin, 1956; Robert N. Butler and Myrna I. Lewis. *Aging and Mental Health.* St. Louis: C. V. Mosby, 1982.)

dissynchronized retirement. A situation in which both husband and wife work and one retires before the other, usually the husband. (Timothy H.

Brubaker. *Later Life Families*. Beverly Hills, Calif.: Sage, 1985.) *See also* synchronized retirement.

divorce. A type of marital dissolution in which the marriage relationship is legally terminated. At the present time, there is a low incidence of divorce among persons age 65 and over. However, the divorce rate of elderly persons is expected to increase substantially in the next few decades. (Peter Uhlenberg and Mary A. P. Myers. "Divorce and the Elderly." *The Gerontologist*, 1981, 21, pp. 276-82.)

domiciliary-care facilities. Homes that provide mainly custodial and domiciliary-care facilities and some personal care for those persons who do not require medical or nursing supervision but may need some assistance with activities of daily living because of a physical or mental disability. A variety of terms are used to describe domiciliary-care facilities including board-and-care homes, personal-care homes, foster-care homes,* and sheltered-care homes. This category not only includes homes of a residential type but also some homes that are more institutional, such as homes for the aged* and rest homes. (M. Powell Lawton. *Environment and Aging*. Monterey, Calif.: Brooks/Cole, 1980; Kenneth J. Reichstein and Linda Bergofsky. "Domiciliary Care Facilities for Adults: An Analysis of State Regulations." *Research on Aging*, 1983, 5, pp. 25-44; J. K. Eckert and Mary I. Murrey. "Alternative Modes of Living for the Elderly." In I. Altman, M. P. Lawton, and J. F. Wohlwill, eds., *Elderly People and the Environment*. New York: Plenum Press, 1984, pp. 95-128.)

double-blind. A study in which one or more drugs and a placebo* are administered in such a way that neither the subject nor the experimenter knows which preparation is being given. A triple-blind refers to the use of an outside party to administer the drug or drugs and the placebo. (Elliot Aronson and J. Merrill Carlsmith. "Experimentation in Social Psychology." In Gardner Lindzey and Elliot Aronson, eds., *Handbook of Social Psychology*. Vol. 2. Reading, Mass.: Addison-Wesley, 1968, pp. 1-79.)

double jeopardy. (1) The status of being old and black. T. Talley and Jerome Kaplan first introduced the concept in 1956 to refer to the black elderly whose lifetime of racial prejudice and discrimination was compounded by old age. In addition to being old and black (double jeopardy), Jacquelyne J. Jackson in 1971 added being female and poor to coin quadruple jeopardy. (2) Originally used only for blacks, the term has become more broadly used in recent years to include nonblack minorities as well. (T. Talley and Jerome Kaplan. "The Negro Aged." *Newsletter*, (Dec.) Gerontological Society, 1956, p. 6; James J. Dowd and Vern L. Bengtson. "Aging in a Minority Population: An Examination of the Double Jeopardy Hypothesis." *Journal of Gerontology*, 1978, 33, pp. 427-36; Jacquelyne J.

Jackson. "Race, National Origin, Ethnicity and Aging." In Robert Binstock and Ethel Shanas, eds., *Handbook of Aging and the Social Sciences.* New York: Van Nostrand Reinhold, 1985, pp. 281-84.)

double standard of aging. A phrase used to describe how aging takes different forms for men and women in our society. For example, women are defined as "old" earlier than men and become sexually ineligible at a much younger age than men. Also, it is not considered out of the ordinary for an old man to marry a young woman but when the situation is reversed, the woman is often severely criticized. (Inge P. Bell. "The Double Standard: Age." *Trans-Action*, 1970, 8, pp. 75-80; Susan Sontag. "The Double Standard of Aging." *Saturday Review*, September 1972, pp. 29-39.)

dowager's hump. A stooped posture resulting from vertebrae collapse that is a characteristic sign of osteoporosis. The name originated because the condition was most prevalent among older, upper-class women who were apt not to exercise. (Isadore Rossman. "Bodily Changes with Aging." In Ewald W. Busse and Dan G. Blazer, eds., *Handbook of Geriatric Psychiatry.* New York: Van Nostrand Reinhold, 1980, pp. 125-46.) *See also* osteoporosis.

drug interaction. Two or more drugs taken together that may result in serious side effects. For example, alcohol and barbituates taken together have a much greater depressing effect than when taken separately. Also referred to as drug potentiation. Drug interaction is more likely to occur in the elderly than other age groups because of the larger number of medications that they take. (Paul R. Raffoul, James K. Cooper, and David W. Love. "Drug Misuse in Older People." *The Gerontologist*, 1981, 21, pp. 146-50; William Simonson. *Medications and the Elderly.* Rockville, Md.: Aspen Systems, 1984; Robert E. Vestal and Gary W. Dawson. "Pharmacology and Aging." In Caleb E. Finch and Edward L. Schneider, eds., *Handbook of the Biology of Aging.* New York: Van Nostrand Reinhold, 1985, pp. 744-819.) *See also* drug reaction (adverse).

drug reaction (adverse). "Any unintended or undesired consequences of drug therapy" (William Simonson). The elderly tend to experience more adverse reactions to drugs than do younger persons. (D. M. Peterson and C. W. Thomas. "Acute Drug Reactions among the Elderly." *Journal of Gerontology*, 1975, 30, pp. 552-56; William Simonson. *Medications and the Elderly.* Rockville, Md.: Aspen Systems, 1984.) *See also* drug interaction, iatrogenic disorder.

Duke Longitudinal Studies. This project consisted of three distinct longitudinal studies that focused on the normal aging process in middle-aged and older persons. The subjects, who resided in Durham, North Carolina, were given periodic physical, mental, and social examinations at the Duke Medical Center. The first study (1955-1976) examined persons aged 60-90, the second study (1968-1976) persons aged 46-70, and the last study (1972-1983) persons aged 65 and over. (Erdman B. Palmore, ed. *Normal Aging*. Durham, N.C.: Duke University Press, 1970; Erdman B. Palmore, ed. *Normal Aging II*. Durham, N.C.: Duke University Press, 1974; Ewald W. Busse and George L. Maddox. *The Duke Longitudinal Studies of Normal Aging: 1955-1980*. New York: Springer, 1985.)

dyad. A two-person group; for example, a husband and wife. (Georg Simmel. *The Sociology of Georg Simmel*. Translated by Kurt Wolf. Glencoe, Ill.: Free Press, 1950.)

dying. (1) "A process which eventuates in death" (Richard A. Kalish). (2) A nonscheduled status passage in which one passes from the status of being alive to the status of being dead (Barney G. Glaser and Anselm L. Strauss). (B. G. Glaser and A. L. Strauss. "Temporal Aspects of Dying as a Non-Scheduled Status Passage." *American Journal of Sociology*, 1965, 71, pp. 48-59; B. G. Glaser and A. L. Strauss. *Time for Dying*. Chicago: Aldine, 1968; Victor Marshall. *Last Chapters: A Sociology of Aging and Dying*. Monterey, Calif.: Brooks/Cole, 1980; Richard A. Kalish. "The Social Context of Death and Dying." In Robert Binstock and Ethel Shanas, eds., *Handbook of Aging and the Social Sciences*. New York: Van Nostrand Reinhold, 1985, pp. 149-70.) *See also* death, rites of passage, thanatology.

dying trajectory. This term was introduced by Barney G. Glaser and Anselm L. Strauss to describe the stages in the process of going from normal health to the downhill pattern of dying.* The trajectory has two major characteristics: shape and duration. Shape refers to the fact that the trajectory can be charted, and duration means that the trajectory of dying takes place over time. Because dying trajectories depend on the nature of the disease or the condition that the patient suffers from, generally, the dying trajectory of older persons is different from that of younger persons. (Barney G. Glaser and Anselm L. Strauss. *Awareness of Dying*. Chicago: Aldine, 1965.)

dysthanasia. Refers to a painful and undignified death;* deliberate postponement of a merciful death. (Glenn M. Vernon. *The Sociology of Death*. New York: Ronald Press, 1970.)

E

early retirement. Retirement* before the age of 65. The trend toward early retirement has become increasingly popular since the 1960s. (Richard Barfield and James N. Morgan. *Early Retirement: The Decision and the Experience.* Ann Arbor: Institute of Social Research, University of Michigan, 1969; William A. Pollman. "Early Retirement: Relationship to Variations in Life Satisfaction." *The Gerontologist*, 1974, 11, pt. 1, pp. 43-47.)

early retirement benefits (social security). A person may begin drawing social security benefits at age 62, but the amount is permanently reduced by 20 percent to take into account the longer period over which social security* must be paid. (James H. Schulz. *The Economics of Aging.* Belmont, Calif.: Wadsworth, 1985.)

earnings test. *See* retirement test.

ECHO Housing. *See* Elder Cottage Housing Opportunities.

ecological model of aging. Proposed by M. Powell Lawton and L. Nahemow, this model suggests that behavior is a function of the competence of the individual and the environmental press* of the situation. (M. P. Lawton and L. Nahemow. "Ecology and the Aging Process." In C. Eisdorfer and M. P. Lawton, eds., *The Psychology of Adult Development and Aging.* Washington, D.C.: American Psychological Association, 1973, pp. 619-74; M. P. Lawton. "Competence, Environmental Press, and the Adaptation of Older People." In M. Powell Lawton, Paul G. Windley, and Thomas O. Byerts, eds., *Aging and the Environment: Theoretical Approaches.* New York: Springer, 1982, pp. 33-59.)

ecology. *See* ecology of aging.

ecology of aging. "A system of continual adaptation in which both the organism and the environment* change over time in a nonrandom manner" (M. Powell Lawton and L. Nahemow). The term "ecology" is borrowed from biology, where it refers to the study of the interrelationships between organisms and their environment. (M. P. Lawton and L. Nahemow. "Ecology and the Aging Process." In C. Eisdorfer and M. P. Lawton, eds., *The Psychology of Adult Development and Aging.* Washington, D.C.: Ameri-

Figure 3
Diagram of the Ecological Model of Aging

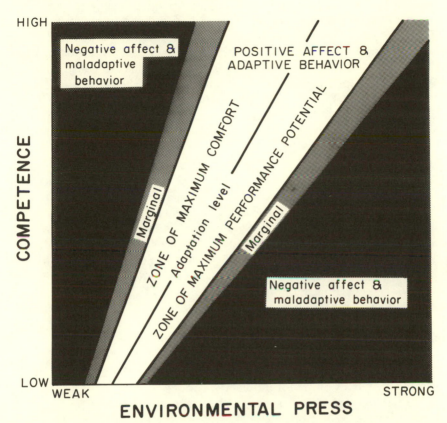

Source: M. Powell Lawton and L. Nahemow. "Ecology and the Aging Process." In C. Eis-
dorfer and M. Powell Lawton, eds., *The Psychology of Adult Development and
Aging*. Washington, D.C.: American Psychological Association, 1973, pp. 619-74.
Courtesy of the authors and the publisher.

can Psychological Association, 1973, pp. 619-74; Rick J. Scheidt and Paul
G. Windley. "The Ecology of Aging." In James E. Birren and K. Warner
Schaie, eds., *Handbook of the Psychology of Aging*. New York: Van
Nostrand Reinhold, 1985, pp. 245-58.)

economic aging. Changes in the financial status of the elderly that alter their
lifestyles (Morris Rockstein and Marvin Sussman). (M. Rockstein and M.
Sussman. *Biology of Aging*. Belmont, Calif.: Wadsworth, 1979; Yung-Ping
Chen. "Economic Status of the Aging." In Robert H. Binstock and Ethel
Shanas, eds., *Handbook of Aging and the Social Sciences*. New York: Van
Nostrand Reinhold, 1985, pp. 641-65.) *See also* pension, social security.

economics. The scientific study concerned with the ways in which goods and services are produced, distributed, and consumed. Older persons tend to spend a larger proportion of their income for housing, food, and health services than do younger persons. (Robert L. Clark and Joseph J. Spengler. *The Economics of Individual and Population Aging*. New York: Cambridge University Press, 1980; Robert L. Clark et al. *Inflation and the Economic Well-being of the Elderly*. Baltimore: Johns Hopkins University Press, 1984; Yung-Ping Chen. "Economic Status of the Aging." In Robert H. Binstock and Ethel Shanas, eds., *Handbook of Aging and the Social Sciences*. New York: Van Nostrand Reinhold, 1985, pp. 641-65; James H. Schulz. *The Economics of Aging*. Belmont, Calif.: Wadsworth, 1985.)

education. (1) A formal set of processes for the transmission of values, knowledge, and skills. The educational level of the older population has been steadily increasing. Since 1970 the median level of education for the elderly has increased from 8.7 years to 11.4 years. (2) Any activity in which learning takes place. (Jeanne H. Ballantine. *The Sociology of Education: A Systematic Analysis*. Englewood Cliffs, N.J.: Prentice-Hall, 1983; Herbert C. Covey. "An Exploratory Study of the Acquisition of a College Student Role by Older People." *The Gerontologist*, 1980, 20, pp. 173-81; Howard Y. McClusky. "Education for Older Adults." In Carl Eisdorfer, ed., *Annual Review of Gerontology and Geriatrics*. Vol. 3. New York: Springer, 1982, pp. 403-28; Louis Lowy and Darlene O'Connor. *Why Eduation in the Later Years?* Lexington, Mass.: Lexington Books, 1986.)

educational gerontology. This term refers to the practice and study of improving the quality of life for the elderly through education.* It includes not only the education of older people, but also educating the public about older people as well as professionals and practitioners who will work with them. (David A. Peterson.) The term was first used at the University of Michigan in 1974 as a title for a course. (D. A. Peterson. "Educational Gerontology: The State of the Art." *Educational Gerontology*, 1976, 1, pp. 61-73; D. A. Peterson, "Toward a Definition of Educational Gerontology." In R. Sherron and D. B. Lumsden, eds., *Introduction to Educational Gerontology*. Washington, D.C.: Hemisphere, 1985, pp. 1-29. Howard Y. McClusky. "Education for Older Adults." In Carl Eisdorfer, ed., *Annual Review of Gerontology and Geriatrics*. Vol. 3. New York: Springer, 1982, pp. 403-28.) *See also* gerontology education.

egalitarian family. A type of family organization in which the authority is almost equally divided between husband and wife. (William J. Goode. *The Family*. Englewood Cliffs, N.J.: Prentice-Hall, 1982.) *See also* matriarchal family, patriarchal family.

ego. In psychoanalytic theory one of the three basic personality structures that serves to mediate between the id (primitive, instinctual drives) and the superego (the conscience). The ego represents the part of the personality that interacts with the outside world, is governed by the reality principle, and may be thought of as the self. Age-related stresses, such as the death of a spouse, retirement, or illness, may cause the ego to function less effectively and strain its capacity to adapt. According to Bernice L. Neugarten, "with increasing old age, ego functions are turned inward." (Sigmund Freud. "The Ego and the Id." In J. S. Trachey, ed., *The Standard Edition of the Complete Psychological Works of Sigmund Freud*. Vol. 19. New York: Norton: 1961; B. L. Neugarten. "Adult Personality." In B. L. Neugarten, ed., *Middle Age and Aging*. Chicago: University of Chicago Press, 1968, pp. 137-47.) *See also* interiority (of personality).

ego integrity. *See* integrity.

egoistic suicide. One of the types of suicide distinguished by Emile Durkheim in 1897 in which individuals lack emotional attachments and psychological support provided by being deeply involved and integrated into group life. In times of emotional crises, these individuals are thrown on their own resources and have no one to fall back on. As a result, they are not constrained against self-destruction. Suicide among the elderly is often of this type. (E. Durkheim. *Suicide*. Translated by J. A. Spaulding and G. Simpson. Glencoe, Ill.: Free Press, 1951; Asser Stenback. "Depression and Suicidal Behavior in Old Age." In James E. Birren and R. Bruce Sloane, eds., *Handbook of Mental Health and Aging*. Englewood Cliffs, N.J.: Prentice-Hall, 1980, pp. 616-52; Nancy C. Osgood. *Suicide in the Elderly*. Rockville, Md.: Aspen Systems Corp., 1985.) *See also* altruistic suicide, anomic suicide.

elder abuse. The mistreatment of older persons through physical or psychological injury or financial exploitation by their caretakers. Elder abuse differs from elder neglect in that neglect refers to the failure of caretakers to fulfill important needs of older persons when resources are available to do so. (Eloise Rathbone-McCuan. "Elderly Victims of Family Violence and Neglect." *Social Casework*, 1980, 61, pp. 296-304; Tom Hickey and Richard S. Douglass. "Neglect and Abuse of Older Family Members: Professionals' Perspectives and Care Experiences." *The Gerontologist*, 1981, 2, 171-76; Mary Jo Quinn and Susan K. Tomita. *Elder Abuse and Neglect*. New York: Springer, 1986; Margaret F. Hudson and Tanya F. Johnson. "Elder Neglect and Abuse: A Review of the Literature." In Carl Eisdorfer, ed., *Annual Review of Gerontology and Geriatrics*. Vol. 6. New York: Springer, 1986, pp. 81-134.) *See also* battered old person syndrome.

Elder Cottage Housing Opportunities (ECHO). Small, freestanding, removable housing units. They are typically placed in the side or backyard of a single-family home to provide housing for elderly parents so that they can be near their adult children for mutual aid and support but still live independently. In Australia, where they originated, they are called "granny flats." In Hawaii they are called "Ohana," and in Denmark they are referred to as "kangaroo housing." (Patrick H. Hare and Linda H. Hollis. *ECHO Housing: A Review of Zoning Issues and Other Considerations.* Washington, D.C.: American Association of Retired Persons, 1983; U.S. Senate. *Developments in Aging: 1984.* Vol. 1. A Report of the Special Committee on Aging. Washington, D.C.: U.S. Government Printing Office, 1984, pp. 231-32.)

elder function. The natural tendency that older persons have to share their experience and knowledge with the young. (Robert N. Butler and Myrna I. Lewis. *Aging and Mental Health.* St. Louis: Mosby, 1982.)

Elderhostel. An international network of colleges and universities that offer short-term residential, campus-based educational programs to persons age 60 and over at a modest cost on a year-round basis. Courses offered are usually in the liberal arts and sciences. The Elderhostel Program, which began in the summer of 1975 with a network of five colleges in New Hampshire, has grown from 200 to over 120,000 participants. (M. P. Knowlton. "Liberal Arts: The Elderhostel Plan for Survival." *Educational Gerontology*, 1977, 2, pp. 87-93.)

eldering. *See* social aging.

elderly. *See* older person.

elder neglect. *See* elder abuse.

elders. (1) Older persons. (2) Governing officers of the church. (3) In anthropology,* a group of older men to whom the tribal government is entrusted. Also referred to as a council of elders. (Leo W. Simmons. *The Role of the Aged in Primitive Society.* New Haven, Conn.: Yale University Press, 1945.) *See also* gerontocracy.

Employee Retirement Income Security Act (ERISA). This legislation, which was passed in 1974, regulates and supervises private pension plans and provides basic protection against the loss of retirement benefits as well as establishing standards for vesting.* (William Greenough and Francis King. *Pension Plans and Public Policy.* New York: Columbia University Press, 1976; U.S. Senate. *Developments in Aging: 1984.* Vol. 1. A Report of the

Special Committee on Aging. Washington, D.C.: U.S. Government Printing Office, 1984, pp. 46-50.) *See also* private pensions.

empty nest. The period in the family life cycle* after the children have left home. (D. Spence and T. Lonner. "The Empty Nest: A Transition in Motherhood." *Family Coordinator*, 1971, 20, 369-76; Marjorie F. Lowenthal and D. Chiriboga. "Transitions to the Empty Nest: Crisis, Change or Relief?" *Archives of General Psychiatry*, 1972, 26, pp. 8-14.) *See also* postparental period.

enculturation. *See* socialization.

endogenous death. Death* that is due to genetic makeup or from conditions occurring before or during birth. Endogenous death includes death from degenerative diseases that usually occur in later life such as heart disease and diabetes. (Roland Pressat. *Demographic Analysis: Methods, Results, Applications*. Chicago: Aldine-Atherton, 1972; Henry S. Shryock, Jacob S. Siegel, and Associates. *The Methods and Materials of Demography*. New York: Academic Press, 1976.) *See also* exogenous death.

End Poverty in California (EPIC). A social movement* in California in the early 1930s led by Upton Sinclair, the novelist, which proposed some solutions to poverty,* including an old-age pension of $50 per month. (Upton Sinclair. *The EPIC Plan for California*. New York: Farrar, 1934; Jackson K. Putnam. *Old-Age Politics in California: From Jackson to Reagan*. Stanford, Calif.: Stanford University Press, 1970.)

environment. The sum of the external conditions and factors that are capable of influencing and stimulating the behavior of individuals and groups.* M. Powell Lawton has proposed the following classification of environments: personal, suprapersonal, social, and physical. (M. P. Lawton. *Environment and Aging*. Monterey, Calif.: Brooks/Cole, 1980; M. P. Lawton, Paul C. Windley and Thomas O. Byerts, eds. *Aging and the Environment: Theoretical Approaches*. New York: Springer, 1982.)

environmental press. The level of behavioral demands that the environment makes on the individual (M. Powell Lawton and L. Nahemow). The press may be positive, negative, or neutral. The term was first used by Henry Murray in 1938 and redefined in 1973 by M. P. Lawton and L. Nahemow. (H. A. Murray. *Exploration in Personality*. New York: Oxford University Press, 1938; M. P. Lawton and L. Nahemow. "Ecology and the Aging Process." In C. Eisdorfer and M. P. Lawton, eds., *The Psychology of Adult Development and Aging*. Washington, D.C.: American Psychological Association, 1973, pp. 619-74; M. P. Lawton; "Competence, Environmental Press, and the Adaptation of Older People." In M. Powell Lawton, Paul G. Windley, and Thomas O. Byerts, eds., *Aging and the Environment: Theoretical Approaches*. New York: Springer, 1982, pp. 33-59.)

epidemiology. The study of the incidence and distribution of diseases in the human population and the factors that influence this distribution. (D. E. Lilienfeld. "Definitions of Epidemiology." *American Journal of Epidemiology*, 1978, 107, pp. 87-90; David W. Kay and Klaus Bergmann. "Epidemiology of Mental Disorders among the Aged in the Community." In James E. Birren and R. Bruce Sloane, eds., *Handbook of Mental Health and Aging*. Englewood Cliffs, N.J.: Prentice-Hall, 1980, pp. 34-56; L. White et al. "Geriatric Epidemiology." In Carl Eisdorfer, ed., *Annual Review of Gerontology and Geriatrics*. Vol. 6. New York: Springer, 1986.) *See also* health, disease, medical sociology.

error catastrophe theory. This biological theory of aging, elaborated by Leslie Orgel, holds that random errors occurring in protein synthesis lead to other errors of protein synthesis that result in cell decline and death. (Leslie Orgel. "The Maintenance of the Accuracy of Protein Synthesis and Its Relevance to Aging." *Proceedings of the National Academy of Sciences*, 1963, 49, pp. 517-21.)

escort services. The provision of companions for older persons to accompany them when walking or traveling either because of physical impairments or for protection from criminal victimization. (A. S. Harbert and L. H. Ginsberg. *Human Services for Older Adults: Concepts and Skills*. Belmont, Calif.: Wadsworth, 1979.)

ethnic group. A group differentiated by a shared feeling of peoplehood and distinguished by characteristics that differ from the dominant group in religion, national origin, race, language, or customs. Examples of ethnic groups in the United States include Hispanics, blacks, and Japanese-Americans. Ethnicity shapes one's life chances and in turn the situation of the ethnic aged. (Milton M. Gordon. *Assimilation in American Life*. New York: Oxford University Press, 1964; Milton J. Yinger. "Ethnicity in Complex Societies: Structural, Cultural, and Characteriological Factors." In Lewis A. Coser and Otto N. Larsen, eds., *The Uses of Controversy in Sociology*. New York: Free Press, 1976; Donald E. Gelfand. *Aging: The Ethnic Factor*. Boston: Little, Brown, 1982; Kyriakos S. Makrides and Charles H. Mindel. *Aging and Ethnicity*. Newbury Park, Calif.: Sage Publications, 1987.) *See also* Asian-American and Pacific-Islander elderly, Hispanic elderly, minority group, Native American elderly.

ethnocentrism. The tendency to regard one's own culture* as superior to all others. The term was introduced by William G. Sumner in 1906 as that "view of things in which one's own group is the center of everything, and all others are scaled and rated with reference to it." An antonym for cultural relativity.* The Eskimo practice of leaving their aged parents in igloos to freeze to death seems barbaric to us, whereas our practice of placing old people in nursing homes until they die would probably seem barbaric to the Eskimo. (W. G. Sumner. *Folkways*. Boston: Ginn, 1906.) *See also* cohort-centrism.

ethnogerontology. Jacquelyne J. Jackson defines this term as the "study of the causes, processes, and consequences of race, national origin, and culture on individual and population aging." (J. J. Jackson. "Race, National Origin, Ethnicity and Aging." In Robert Binstock and Ethel Shanas, eds., *Handbook of Aging and the Social Sciences*. New York: Van Nostrand Reinhold, 1985, p. 265.)

ethos. The dominant, unifying theme in a culture;* the basic character of a society* that is likely to be found in its major value* orientations. To understand aging* and the treatment of the aged in a society,* it is important to study the ethos of the people and their value system. (Walter Goldschmidt. *Ways of Mankind*. Boston: Beacon Press, 1954.)

euthanasia. Permitting persons who are terminally ill to die. The term is derived from the Greek meaning "good death." (A. Verwoerdt. "Euthanasia: A Growing Concern for Physicians." *Geriatrics*, 1967, 22, pp. 44-60; Olive R. Russell. *Freedom to Die: Moral and Legal Aspects of Euthanasia*. New York: Human Sciences Press, 1975; Robert F. Weir. *Ethical Issues in Death and Dying*. New York: Columbia University Press, 1977; Russell A. Ward. "Age and Acceptance of Euthanasia." *Journal of Gerontology*, 1980, 35, pp. 421-31.) *See also* active euthanasia, involuntary euthanasia, passive euthanasia, voluntary euthanasia.

evaluation study. A study that attempts to determine the effects of a program or policy. (M. J. Mack. "An Evaluation of a Retirement Planning Program." *Journal of Gerontology*, 1958, 13, pp. 198-202.)

exact age. Determining an individual's age by taking the difference between a person's birth date and the date on which the calculation is made; for example, someone born on August 10, 1900, will be exactly 88 years, 3 months, and 10 days old on November 20, 1988. Also referred to as absolute age. (Roland Pressat. *Demographic Analysis: Methods, Results, Applications*. Chicago: Aldine-Atherton, 1972.) *See also* age in completed years.

exchange theory (of aging). This theory is based on the premise that persons or groups will continue to interact* as long as each finds sufficient rewards (money, knowledge, services, social position, etc.) to make the interaction* profitable. If a person is able to provide more rewards than his or her exchange partner can return, this creates an imbalance in power,* which allows the partner with the most rewards to gain control over the other. According to James J. Dowd, much of the decreased amount of social interaction among older people is a result of a series of exchange relationships in which the power of the aged becomes diminished. Thus older people become increasingly unable to enter into a balanced exchange relationship with other individuals or groups because of their limited resources and because the costs in compliance and self-respect become too high. As a result of this imbalance, the elderly withdraw from relationships. Dowd offers the above adaptation of the exchange theory as an explanation for the disengagement that occurs in some older persons. The exchange theory was first developed by George C. Homans and Peter Blau. (George C. Homans. *Social Behavior: Its Elementary Forms*. New York: Harcourt, Brace, and World, 1961; Peter Blau. *Exchange and Power in Social Life*. New York: John Wiley, 1964; J. David Martin. "Power, Dependence, and the Complaints of the Elderly: A Social Exchange Perspective." *Aging and Human Development*, 1971, 2, pp. 108-12; J. J. Dowd. "Aging as Exchange: A Preface to Theory." *Journal of Gerontology*, 1975, 30, pp. 584-94.)

exogeneous death. Death that is basically due to environmental or external causes such as infectious diseases and accidents. (Roland Pressat. *Demographic Analysis: Methods, Results, Applications*. Chicago: Aldine-Atherton, 1972; Henry S. Shryock, Jacob S. Siegel, and Associates. *The Methods and Materials of Demography*. New York: Academic Press, 1976.) *See also* endogenous death.

expectation of life. *See* life expectancy.

experimental design. A research method in which the investigator controls or manipulates at least one variable* (the independent variable*) and then makes precise measurements or observations to see what changes occur (in the dependent variable*). (Elliot Aronson and J. Merrill Carlsmith. "Experimentation in Social Psychology." In Gardner Lindzey and Elliot Aronson, eds., *Handbook of Social Psychology*. Vol. 2. Reading, Mass.: Addison-Wesley, 1968, pp. 1-79; Susan G. Philliber, Mary R. Schwab, and G. Sam Sloss. *Social Research*. Itasca, Ill.: Peacock, 1980; Donald H. Kausler. *Experimental Psychology and Human Aging*. New York: Wiley, 1982.)

experimental group. A group of subjects that is given an experimental treatment and is then compared with a control group* that has not received the treatment. (Bernard S. Phillips. *Social Research: Strategy and Tactics*. New York: Macmillan, 1976.)

ex post facto study. A study conducted after an event has occurred. The researcher either uses data already recorded or must rely on the respondents' memories. The term is from the Latin meaning "after the fact." Also called "retrospective study." (Bernard S. Phillips. *Social Research: Strategy and Tactics*. New York: Macmillan, 1976.)

expressive role (family). The affection and emotional support within the nuclear family that is functional for the maintenance of the family unit and is generally assigned to women in most societies. (Talcott Parsons and Robert Bales. *Family, Socialization, and Interaction Process*. Glencoe, Ill.: Free Press, 1955.) *See also* instrumental role (family).

extended care facility (ECF). A facility that provides short-term convalescent care to patients from hospitals. It offers nursing and medical care as well as supportive and rehabilitation services. (E. Cohen. "An Overview of Long-Term Care Facilities." In E. Brody, ed., *A Social Work Guide for Long-Term Care Facilities*. Rockville, Md.: National Institute of Mental Health, 1974; Barbara B. Manard, Cary S. Kart, and Dirk W. L. Van Gils. *Old Age Institutions*. Lexington, Mass.: Lexington Books, 1975; Donald E. Gelfand. *Aging Network: Programs and Services*. New York: Springer, 1984.) *See also* skilled nursing facility, intermediate care facility.

extended family. (1) A family* that includes three or more generations that live together under one roof. (2) The network of relatives not living in the same household but maintaining close ties with the nuclear family. Used in this sense, it refers more specifically to a modified extended family. (George Murdock. *Social Structure*. New York: Macmillan, 1949; R. M. Kessing. *Kin Groups and Social Structure*. New York: Holt, Rinehart and Winston, 1975; Eugene A. Friedmann. "The Impact of Aging on the Social Structure." In Clark Tibbitts, ed., *Handbook of Social Gerontology*. Chicago: University of Chicago Press, 1960.) *See also* modified extended family, nuclear family, stem family.

extraordinary measures. *See* heroic measures.

extraversion. A tendency for one's interests to be oriented toward the external world and social values. Carl G. Jung used a biopolar personality dimension in which he divided individuals into extraversion (outward-directed) and introversion (inward-directed) types. Some researchers maintain that with age there is a tendency to move away from extraversion. Sometimes incorrectly spelled "extroversion." (C. G. Jung. *Psychological Types*. New York: Harcourt, Brace, 1933; Bernice L. Neugarten and Associates, eds. *Personality in Middle and Late Life*. New York: Atherton, 1964.) *See also* introversion.

F

family. The United Nations defines a family "as those members of the household* who are related, to a specified degree, through blood, adoption, or marriage." The family is a basic unit of social organization that is found in some form in all known societies and is the setting for the allocation of roles by generation.* (United Nations. *Principles and Recommendations for Population and Housing Censuses*. Statistical Papers. Series M, No. 67. New York: Department of International Economic and Social Affairs, 1980; William J. Goode. *The Family*. Englewood Cliffs, N.J.: Prentice-Hall, 1982; Lillian E. Troll. "The Family of Later Life: A Decade Review." *Journal of Marriage and the Family*, 1971, 33, pp. 263-90; Lillian E. Troll, Sheila J. Miller, and Robert C. Atchley. *Families in Later Life*. Belmont, Calif.: Wadsworth, 1979.) *See also* extended family, modified extended family, nuclear family, stem family.

family alienation myth. The misconception in our society that older persons have infrequent contact with their families. Also referred to as the "family abandonment" myth. (Ethel Shanas. "Social Myth as Hypothesis: The Case of the Family Relations of Old People." *The Gerontologist*, 1979, 19, pp. 3-9.)

family institution. One of the basic social institutions of a society* consisting of a system of roles and norms organized around the regulation of sexual relationships, and the rearing of children. (William J. Goode. *The Family*. Englewood Cliffs, N.J.: Prentice-Hall, 1982.) *See also* institution.

family life cycle. The sequence of events beginning with the husband-wife pair, the birth of the first to last child, the launching of the last child, the postparental period,* to the death* of one spouse. (Reuben Hill. "Methodological Issues in Family Development Research." *Family Process*, 1964, 3, pp. 186-206; J. Deutscher. "Socialization for Post-Parental Life." In J. K. Hadden and M. L. Borgatta, eds., *Marriage and the Family*. Itasca, Ill.: Peacock, 1969; Paul C. Glick. "Updating the Life Cycle of the Family." *Journal of Marriage and the Family*, 1977, 39, pp. 5-13; Steven L. Nock. "The Family Life Cycle: Empirical or Conceptual Tool?" *Journal of Marriage and the Family*, 1979, 41, pp. 15-26.)

family solidarity. The interaction* between family members involving affection, association, and consensus. (Vern L. Bengtson, Edward B. Olander, and Annes A. Haddad. "The 'Generation Gap' and Gaining Family Members." In Jaber F. Gubrium, ed., *Time, Roles, and Self in Old Age*. New York: Human Sciences Press, 1976, pp. 237-63.)

farsightedness. *See* presbyopia.

fecundity. The physiological capacity to bear chlidren; the maximum number of children a woman is able to bear. (T. Lynn Smith and Paul E. Zopf. *Demography: Principles and Methods*. Port Washington, N.Y.: Alfred, 1976; H. Leridon. *Human Fertility: The Basic Components*. Chicago: University of Chicago Press, 1977.) *See also* fertility.

Federal Council on Aging. Established under Title II of the 1973 Amendments to the Older Americans Act,* this fifteen-member council is appointed by the president. It is charged with advising and assisting the president, the secretary of health and human services, and the commissioner of the Administration on Aging on federal programs and policies, as well as on special needs and problems concerning the elderly. (Federal Council on Aging, 300 Independence Ave., S.W., Room 4620, North Building, Washington, D.C. 20201.)

fertility. The actual birth performance; the number of children a woman actually bears. (T. Lynn Smith and Paul E. Zopf. *Demography: Principles and Methods*. Port Washington, N.Y.: Alfred, 1976; H. Leridon. *Human Fertility: The Basic Components*. Chicago: University of Chicago Press, 1977.) *See also* fecundity.

field research. Research that is conducted in the subjects' natural setting instead of a laboratory. It may involve observation, participant observation,* and/or interviews. (John Lofland. *Doing Social Life*. New York: Wiley, 1976; Arlie Hochschild. *The Unexpected Community*. Berkeley: University of California Press, 1973.)

filial maturity. A stage of development in which adult children, as they reach middle age, are depended on by their parents and are seen as being dependable. This term was introduced by Margaret Blenkner. (Margaret Blenkner. "Social Work and Family Relationships in Later Life with Some Thoughts on Filial Maturity." In Ethel Shanas and Gordon Streib, eds., *Social Structure and the Family: Generational Relations*. Englewood Cliffs, N.J.: Prentice-Hall, 1965.) *See also* filial responsibility.

filial piety. An ethic based on Confucian teachings and the ancient practice of ancestor worship. Filial piety is expressed in respect, reverence, and obedience to one's parents. It is believed that it is a child's duty to support his or her parents in their old age even at the expense of one's own children. Examples of the practice of filial piety include the classical Chinese family and families in pre-World War II Japan. (Donald O. Cowgill. *Aging around the World*. Belmont, Calif.: Wadsworth, 1986.)

filial responsibility. The obligation of adult children to help their aged parents when they are in need of assistance. Filial responsibility may consist of caregiving, financial aid, emotional support, and so on. Although this responsibility is supported by our values, norms, and customs, many states have laws requiring children to provide financial support to their needy parents. (Alvin L. Schorr. *Filial Responsibility in the Modern American Family*. Washington, D.C.: Social Security Administration, 1960; Wayne C. Seelback and William J. Sauer. "Filial Responsibility Expectations and Morale among Aged Parents." *The Gerontologist*, 1977, 17, pp. 492-99; Timothy H. Brubaker. *Later Life Families*. Beverly Hills, Calif.: Sage, 1985.) *See also* filial maturity.

flexible retirement. Voluntary retirement by the worker at whatever age he or she chooses within certain limits; the individualization of retirement* so that the employee may work beyond the normal retirement age. (Fred Slavick. *Compulsory and Flexible Retirement in the American Economy*. Ithaca, N.Y.: Cornell University Press, 1966; Erdman B. Palmore. "Compulsory versus Flexible Retirement: Issues and Facts." *The Gerontologist*, 1972, 12, pp. 324-48.) *See also* mandatory retirement.

fluid intelligence. A type of intelligence that is related to the functioning of the central nervous system. In fluid intelligence, innate capacity or native mental ability is more important than past learning experience. It is assessed on one's ability to solve novel problems such as figure analogies, number series, and nonsense equations. Fluid intelligence tends to decline with age, and older persons tend to compensate by relying more on crystallized intelligence. The concept was introduced by Raymond B. Cattell in 1943. (J. L. Horn and R. B. Cattell. "Age Differences in Fluid and Crystallized Intelligence." *Acta Psychologica*, 1967, 26, pp. 107-29; J. L. Horn. "The Theory of Fluid and Crystallized Intelligence in Relation to Concepts of Cognitive Psychology and Aging in Adulthood." In F. J. M. Craik and S. Tehub, eds., *Aging and Cognitive Processes*. New York: Plenum, 1982.) *See also* crystallized intelligence.

focused interview. An interview* that concentrates on the effect of a given situation or event experienced by the respondent.* The term was introduced by Robert K. Merton and his associates in 1956. (R. K. Merton, Marjorie Fiske, and Patricia L. Kendall. *The Focused Interview*. New York: Free Press, 1956.)

folkways. Norms* that govern the conventions and routines of everyday life. When folkways are violated, mild disapproval follows, whereas strong disapproval occurs when the mores* are violated. Examples of folkways would include helping elderly persons across the street, opening doors for them, or giving them a seat on a bus. The term was introduced by William G. Sumner in 1906. (W. G. Sumner. *Folkways*. Boston: Ginn, 1906.)

formal organization. A highly organized, impersonal group that operates according to formally stated policies and procedures and is designed to pursue specific objectives. Examples of formal organizations include hospitals, government agencies, and voluntary associations. (James March, ed. *Handbook of Organizations*. Chicago: Rand McNally, 1965.) *See also* bureaucracy, voluntary association.

formal support systems. Assistance provided within the context of the helping professions; for example, therapy groups for widows, counseling programs for older persons, suicide hotlines, and various other organizations. (Charles Froland et al. "Linking Formal and Informal Support Systems." In Benjamin H. Gottleib, ed., *Social Networks and Social Support*. Beverly Hills, Calif.: Sage, 1981.) *See also* informal support systems.

foster care home. Housing that provides a support system within a family setting for no more than three or four paying residents who are given some supervision but are not in need of institutionalization.* (Susan R. Sherman and E. S. Newman. "Foster Family Care for the Elderly in New York State." *The Gerontologist*, 1977, 17, pp. 513-20.) *See also* domiciliary-care facilities.

Foster Grandparent Program (FGP). Established in 1965, this program is designed to provide part-time volunteer opportunities to low-income persons 60 years of age and older. The volunteers provide companionship and guidance to children with physical, emotional, and mental disabilities and to children who are abused, neglected, or have other special needs. Foster grandparents serve in various settings including public schools, day-care centers, residential facilities, and hospitals for mentally retarded, physically handicapped, and emotionally disturbed children; in correctional facilities, and in homes of abused and/or neglected children. Volunteers serve 20 hours a week, devoting two hours daily to each of two children, and receive a small hourly stipend. (U.S. Senate. *Developments in Aging: 1984*. Vol. 1. A Report of the Special Committee on Aging. Washington,

D.C.: U.S. Government Printing Office, 1985, p. 291; Rosalyn Saltz. "Aging Persons as Child Care Workers in a Foster Grandparent Program." *Aging and Human Development*, 1971, 2, pp. 314-40; Foster Grandparent Program/ACTION, 806 Connecticut Ave., N.W., Washington, D.C. 20525.) *See also* ACTION.

fountain theme. This legend, which dates back over a thousand years, refers to the belief that there is some unusual substance that will bring about rejuvenation. Ponce de Leon's Fountain of Youth is an example of this theme. Sometimes referred to as the "rejuvenation theme." (Gerald J. Gruman. "A History of Ideas about the Prolongation of Life: The Evolution of Prolongevity Hypotheses to 1800." *Transactions of the American Philosophical Society*, 1966, vol. 56, pt. 9, pp. 1-102.) *See also* antediluvian theme, hyperborean theme.

401(k) plan. A plan created in 1978 by Congress to encourage employees to save for retirement. It allows them to set aside a portion of their salary for deposit into the plan each year on which no income tax is paid. The money is subject to tax only at withdrawal. There is also a 10 percent tax on early withdrawals. Also referred to as a salary reduction plan and cash-or-deferred arrangements. (Gary L. Klott. *The New York Times Complete Guide to the New Tax Law*. New York: Times Books, 1986.)

403(b) plan. A retirement plan for teachers, workers at religious organizations, and other tax-exempt institutions. This plan allows employees to set aside a portion of their salary to purchase a tax-sheltered annuity on which no income tax is paid. The money is not subject to tax until retirement benefits are received. (Gary L. Klott. *The New York Times Complete Guide to the New Tax Law*. New York: Times Books, 1986.)

4 percent fallacy. A widely accepted estimate is that about 4 to 5 percent of elderly persons in the United States are in nursing homes. But in a study done by Robert J. Kastenbaum and Sandra E. Candy in 1973, they found that 20 percent of all deaths of elderly persons occurred in nursing homes. Kastenbaum and Candy note that the four percent estimate is misleading because knowing how many elderly persons are in nursing homes at one particular time does not tell us how many people will have lived in nursing homes at some point in their lives. (R. Kastenbaum and S. E. Candy. "The Four Percent Fallacy: A Methodological and Empirical Critique of Extended Care Facility Population Statistics." *International Journal of Aging and Human Development*, 1973, 4, pp. 15-21; H. J. Wershow. "The Four Percent Fallacy: Some Further Evidence and Policy Implications." *The Gerontologist*, 1976, 16, pp. 52-55.)

frail elderly. Older persons with mental, physical, and/or emotional disabilities that limit their independence and necessitate continuing assistance; persons 75 years or older. (Barbara Silverstone and Ann Burack-Weiss. *Social Work Practice with the Frail Elderly and Their Families: The Auxiliary Function Model*. Springfield, Ill.: Charles C. Thomas, 1983; Bob Knight and Deborah L. Walker. "Toward a Definition of Alternatives to Institutionalization for the Frail Elderly." *The Gerontologist*, 1985, 25, pp. 358-63; Amy Horowitz. "Famly Caregiving to the Frail Elderly." In Carl Eisdorfer, ed., *Annual Review of Gerontology and Geriatrics*. Vol. 5. New York: Springer, 1985, pp. 194-246.)

Framingham Study. A longitudinal study that began in 1948 to investigate cardiovascular disease in a sample of community residents of Framingham, Massachusetts. One of the findings from the study is that cardiovascular diseases are the major cause of death and disability in the elderly. (W. B. Kannel. "Recent Findings of the Framingham Study." *Resident and Staff Physician*, 1978, 24, pp. 56-61, 64-66, 71.)

free radicals. *See* free radical theory.

free radical theory. A biological theory of aging proposed by Denham Harman which asserts that aging* and cell death occur from the damaging effects of the formation of free radicals. Free radicals are elements in cells that have molecular fragments and are produced during metabolism. They have one unpaired electron and are attracted to the electrons of other molecules. According to this theory, this union or molecular collision results in damage and eventually death to the cell. (Denham Harman. "Aging: A Theory Based on Free Radical and Radiation Chemistry." *Journal of Gerontology*, 1956, 11, pp. 298-300.)

Friendly Visitors. This program provides volunteers to visit frail, isolated, homebound persons and institutionalized persons on a regular basis. Visitors write letters, play cards, offer companionship, and provide other services to elderly persons who have no friends or relatives to fill this need. Friendly Visitors began in Chicago in 1946. Similar programs date back as far as the late 1800s. (Mary Anne Mulligan and Ruth Bennett. "Assessment of Mental Health and Social Problems during Multiple Friendly Visits." *International Journal of Aging and Human Development*, 1977-1978, 8, pp. 43-66.) *See also* telephone reassurance service.

functional age. (1) The calculation of age as it affects the competency or proficiency of older workers. (2) The calculation of age in terms of physical decline; the functioning of the vital organ systems that contribute to the individual's survival. (3) The determination of "the interrelationship of behavioral and biological characteristics across the adult life span*" (Timothy A. Salthouse). The term was first introduced by R. A. McFarland in 1943. (R. A. McFarland. "The Older Worker in Industry." *Harvard Business Review*, Summer 1943, pp. 505-20; R. A. McFarland. "The Need for Functional Age Measurements." *Industrial Gerontology*, 1973, 19, pp. 1-19; Timothy A. Salthouse. "Functional Age: Examination of a Concept." In James E. Birren, Pauline K. Robinson, and Judy E. Livingston, eds., *Age, Health, and Employment*. Englewood Cliffs, N.J.: Prentice-Hall, 1986, pp. 78-92.) *See also* biological age, chronological age, GULHEMP profile, psychological age, social age.

functional disorders. Physical disturbances in which there is no known organic basis and whose origins appear to be emotional. Often elderly persons who develop functional disorders have also experienced emotional disturbances when they were younger. (Ewald W. Busse and Eric Pfeiffer. "Functional Psychiatric Disorders in Old Age." In E. W. Busse and E. Pfeiffer, eds., *Behavior and Adaptation in Late Life*. Boston: Little, Brown, 1969, pp. 183-235; Robert N. Butler and Myrna I. Lewis. *Aging and Mental Health*. St. Louis: C. V. Mosby, 1982.) *See also* organic disorders.

G

general adaptation syndrome (GAS). Introduced by Hans Selye, this concept postulates that external stimuli that arouse an individual's physiological system produce stress. Failure to adapt to a stressful state results in exhaustion, disease,* and ultimately death.* With age one experiences a wide variety of stressors including grief* and bereavement.* (Hans Selye. *The Stress of Life*. New York: McGraw-Hill, 1956.) *See also* Social Readjustment Rating Scale.

generation. (1) Kinship lineage such as the position of a child, parent, or grandparent in the ranked descent within a family.* Children having a common parent or parents constitute a single stage of descent. (2) Commonly used to identify a group of individuals who are linked by age, world view, or lifestyle;* for example, "World War II babies," the "beat" generation, and the "Pepsi" generation. In this sense, generation is used synonymously with cohort.* (Karl Mannheim. "The Problems of Generations." In Paul Kesskemeti, ed., *Essays on the Sociology of Knowledge*. New York: Oxford University Press, 1952, pp. 276-320; David I. Kertzer. "Generation as a Sociological Problem." In Ralph H. Turner, ed., *Annual Review of Sociology*. Vol. 9. Palo Alto, Calif.: Annual Reviews, 1983, pp. 125-49; Vern L. Bengtson et al. "Generations, Cohorts, and Relations between Age Groups." In Robert H. Binstock and Ethel Shanas, eds., *Handbook of Aging and the Social Sciences*. New York: Van Nostrand Reinhold, 1985, pp. 304-38.)

generation gap. Differences in values, norms, or lifestyles between individuals or groups of different ages. (Vern L. Bengtson. "The 'Generation Gap': A Review and Typology of Social-Psychological Perspectives." *Youth and Society*, 1970, 2, pp. 7-32; Lillian E. Troll. "The 'Generation Gap': An Introductory Discussion and Some Preliminary Findings." *Sociological Focus*, 1971, 5, pp. 18-28; Alfred P. Fengler and Vivian Wood. "The Generation Gap: An Analysis of Attitudes on Contemporary Issues." *The Gerontologist*, 1972, 12, pp. 124-28.)

geriatric day-care center. *See* day-care center/geriatric day hospital.

geriatric ghetto. An inner-city area on the fringes of the downtown and the commercial district that is inhabited by large numbers of the aged poor. (Margaret Clark. "Patterns of Aging among the Elderly Poor of the Inner City." *The Gerontologist*, 1971, 11, pp. 58-66.)

geriatric psychiatry. A subspeciality of psychiatry concerned with the treatment of mental disorders of older persons; psychiatry for the elderly. Also referred to as psychogeriatrics, geropsychiatry, and gerontopsychiatry. (Ewald W. Busse and Dan G. Blazer, eds.. *Handbook of Geriatric Psychiatry*. New York: Van Nostrand Reinhold, 1980; K. Gunnar Gotestam. "Behavioral and Dynamic Psychotherapy with the Elderly." In James E. Birren and R. Bruce Sloane, eds., *Handbook of Mental Health and Aging*. Englewood Cliffs, N.J.: Prentice-Hall, 1980, pp. 775-805.)

geriatrics (geriatric medicine). A branch of medical science devoted to the preventive, remedial, and research aspects of diseases of the elderly. This term was coined in 1909 by Ignatz L. Nascher, an Austrian-born physician who practiced medicine in New York City. He decided to call this new branch of medicine "geriatrics," a combination of two Greek words *geras* meaning "old" and *iatrikos* meaning "medical." (I. L. Nascher. *Geriatrics*. Philadelphia: P. Blakiston's Son & Co., 1914; Joseph T. Freeman. "Nascher: Excerpts from His Life, Letters, and Works." *The Gerontologist*, 1961, 1, pp. 17-26; Richard W. Besdine. "Geriatric Medicine: An Overview." In Carl Eisdorfer, ed., *Annual Review of Gerontology and Geriatrics*. Vol. 1. New York: Springer, 1980, pp. 135-53.)

gericide. *See* gerontocide.

gerocomeia. A system of old age homes established by the Romans in Constantinople and throughout the Mediterranean. (D. J. Constantelos. *Byzantine Philanthropy and Social Welfare*. New Brunswick, N.J.: Rutgers University Press, 1968.)

gerocomy. The belief and practice that an old man may absorb youth from young women. (Alex Comfort. *The Process of Aging*. London: Weidenfeld and Nicolson, 1965; Gerald J. Gruman. "A History of Ideas about the Prolongation of Life: The Evolution of Prolongevity Hypotheses to 1800." *Transactions of the American Philosophical Society*, 1966, vol. 56, pt. 9, pp. 1-102.

geronting. *See* psychological aging.

gerontocide. The killing of the old. Also referred to as "gericide," "senicide," and "senilicide." (Leo W. Simmons. *The Role of the Aged in*

Primitive Societies. New Haven, Conn.: Yale University Press, 1945; A. P. Glascock and S. L. Feinman. "Social Asset or Social Burden: Treatment of the Aged in Non-Industrial Societies." In C. L. Fry, ed., *Dimensions: Aging, Culture and Health.* New York: J. F. Bergin, 1981, pp. 13-32; Lowell D. Holmes. *Other Cultures, Elder Years: An Introduction to Cultural Gerontology.* Minneapolis, Minn.: Burgess, 1983.)

gerontocracy. This term refers to a society* in which the political system is in the hands of the oldest community members. Literally, the term means "rule by old men." Some writers (e.g., Jennie Keith, 1982) distinguish two types of gerontocracy: ascribed and achieved. Ascribed gerontocracy occurs when all political power is based on age and held by the elderly. Achieved gerontocracy occurs when most of the political power is held by the elderly, not because of age but because of their greater accessibility to it. The term "gerontocracy" was coined by Jean-Jacques Fazy in a political tract he wrote in Paris in 1828. (Leo W. Simmons. *The Role of the Aged in Primitive Societies.* New Haven, Conn.: Yale University Press, 1945; P. Spencer. *The Samburn: A Study of Gerontocracy in a Nomadic Tribe.* Berkeley: University of California Press, 1965; Frederick R. Eisele. "Origins of Gerontocracy." *The Gerontologist,* 1979, 19, pp. 403-7; Jennie Keith. *Old People as People: Social and Cultural Influences on Aging and Old Age.* Boston: Little, Brown, 1982, p. 106.)

gerontogamy. The control of women by older men as wives for themselves and as potential wives for others. (Peter M. Gardner. "Gerontocracy and Polygyny." In Richard B. Lee and Irven DeVore, eds., *Man the Hunter.* Chicago: Aldine, 1968.) *See also* polygyny.

gerontolinguistics. A subfield of psycholinguistics dealing with the linguistic systems used by the elderly and problems with communication that are associated with aging. (Hede Helfrich. "Age Markers in Speech." In K. R. Scherer and H. Giles, eds., *Social Markers in Speech.* Cambridge: Cambridge University Press, 1979; Donna Cohen and Suzanne Wu. "Language and Cognition during Aging." In Carl Eisdorfer, ed., *Annual Review of Gerontology and Geriatrics.* Vol. 1. New York: Springer, 1980, pp. 71-96.)

Gerontological Society of America. Established in 1945 for the purpose of promoting the scientific study of aging, this organization consists of researchers, practitioners, and educators concerned with aging and the aged. Since 1946 it has published the *Journal of Gerontology* and since 1961 *The Gerontologist.* (Marjorie Adler. "History of the Gerontological Society, Inc." *Journal of Gerontology,* 1958, 13, pp. 94-102; Gerontological Society of America, 1411 K St., N.W., Washington, D.C. 20005.)

gerontology. The scientific study of the biological, psychological, and social aspects of aging. Elie Metchnikoff, a biologist, coined the term in 1903 from the Greek word *geront* meaning "old man" and *logos* meaning "study of." (Elie Metchnikoff. *The Nature of Man*. New York: Putnam, 1903; Gordon F. Streib and Harold L. Orbach, "Aging." In P. F. Lazarsfeld, W. H. Sewell, H. L. Wilensky, eds., *The Uses of Sociology*. New York: Basic Books, 1967; Caleb E. Finch and Edward L. Schneider, eds. *Handbook of the Biology of Aging*. New York: Van Nostrand Reinhold, 1985; James E. Birren and K. Warner Schaie, eds. *Handbook of the Psychology of Aging*. New York: Van Nostrand Reinhold, 1985; Robert H. Binstock and Ethel Shanas, eds. *Handbook of Aging and the Social Sciences*. New York: Van Nostrand Reinhold, 1985.) *See also* social gerontology.

gerontology education. An aspect of educational gerontology that deals with instruction at the undergraduate and graduate levels. It focuses primarily on the study of the elderly population and the processes of aging. (David A. Peterson and Christopher R. Bolton. *Gerontology Instruction in Higher Education*. New York: Springer, 1980.) *See also* educational gerontology.

gerontophilia. Veneration and honoring of the elderly. (David H. Fischer. *Growing Old in America*. New York: Oxford University Press, 1978.)

gerontophobia. (1) Fear and/or hatred of the elderly. (2) A pathological fear of aging. The term was coined by Alex Comfort. Sometimes spelled gerophobia. (Alex Comfort. "On Gerontophobia." *Medical Opinion & Review*, 1967, 3, pp. 30-37; Joseph H. Bunzel. "Note on the History of a Concept—Gerontophobia." *The Gerontologist*, 1972, 12, pp. 116-203.) *See also* ageism.

gerontophratria. Defined by David H. Fischer as "a fraternity of age and youth, a brotherhood of generations." (D. H. Fischer. *Growing Old in America*. New York: Oxford University Press, 1978, p. 199.)

Gerovital-H3 (GH3). A specially formulated 2 percent solution of procaine hydrochloride that has been touted by researchers, especially Ana Aslan at the Geriatric Institute of Bucharest, Romania, since 1945 as an effective treatment for the aging process as well as a number of degenerative diseases. While it is highly questionable if this compound has any effect on the aging process or degenerative diseases, it may have some use as an antidepressant. (A. Ostfeld, C. M. Smith, and B. A. Stotsky. "The Systematic Use of Procaine in the Treatment of the Elderly: A Review." *Journal of American Geriatrics Society*, 1977, 25, pp. 1-19.)

glaucoma. A condition that involves a buildup of pressure inside the eye which eventually results in a loss of vision if untreated. Its prevalence increases from ages 60 to 85. (A. L. Kornzweig. "The Prevention of Blindness in the Aged." *Journal of American Geriatric Society*, 1972, 20, pp. 383-86.)

Golden Age clubs. A name commonly used for voluntary associations composed of older persons. The specific content and sponsorship of these groups varies from place to place. However, most include some volunteer work and recreational activities in their programs. They are based on a model developed in Cleveland in 1949. (O. Schulze. "Recreation for the Aged." *Journal of Gerontology*, 1949, 4, pp. 310-13; Arnold M. Rose. "The Impact of Aging on Voluntary Associations." In Clark Tibbitts, ed., *Handbook of Social Gerontology*. Chicago: University of Chicago Press, 1960, pp. 666-97.) *See also* voluntary association.

"golden age" myth. The belief that in the past the elderly were honored and revered in the family and in the community. (P. N. Stearns, ed. *Old Age in Pre-Industrial Societies*. New York: Holmes and Meier, 1982.)

Gompertz curve. This curve shows the exponential increase in the probability of death* with advancing age. For example, after age 30, the likelihood of dying* doubles every seven years. After age 35, the death rate doubles every 8½ years. Introduced by the English actuary Benjamin Gompertz in 1825, this curve is used often in the construction of life tables. (B. Gompertz. "On the Nature of the Function Expressive of the Law of Human Mortality on a New Mode of Determining Life Contingencies." *Philosophical Transactions of the Royal Society* (London), 1825, Series A, 11, pp. 513-85; Mortimer Spiegelman. *Introduction to Demography*. Cambridge, Mass.: Harvard University Press, 1968; James F. Fries and Lawrence M. Crapo. *Vitality and Aging*. San Francisco: W. H. Freeman, 1981.) *See also* life table.

gradual retirement. Giving an employee increasing amounts of time away from the job in the form of extended vacations or shorter hours. This method allows individuals to experience retirement* in small doses and make the transition from full-time employment to full-time leisure* less traumatic. Also referred to as phased retirement. Closely related to gradual retirement is rehearsal for retirement, which allows employees to take unpaid leave up to six months to try out retirement before making a decision to stop work. (Lawrence S. Root. "Corporate Programs for Older Workers." *Aging*, 1985, No. 351, pp. 12-16.)

granny flats. *See* Elder Cottage Housing Opportunities.

graying of America. Refers to the changes in the age composition* of the population of the United States, which is characterized by an increasing percentage of elderly persons and a rising median age.* (Beth J. Soldo and Kenneth G. Manton. "Demographic Challenges for Socio-Economic Planning." *Socio-Economic Planning Sciences*, 1985, 19, pp. 227-47.)

graying of suburbia. This phrase refers to the changing age composition* of the average American suburb that is a result of aging-in-place* as well as the migration of young people. Since 1980, a larger number of persons age 65 and over have lived in the suburbs than in central cities. (Michael Gutowski and Tracey Field. *The Graying of Suburbia*. Washington, D.C.: The Urban Institute, 1979; Stephen M. Golant. "Residential Concentrations of the Future Elderly." *The Gerontologist*, 1975, 15, pt. 2, pp. 16-23.)

gray lobby. A group that tries to influence legislation on behalf of older persons. It includes aging-based organizations, professionals who work with the elderly, and adult children concerned with the care of their aged parents. The term was coined by Henry J. Pratt. (H. J. Pratt. *The Gray Lobby*. Chicago: University of Chicago Press, 1976.) *See also* aging-based interest group, aging-based organization.

Gray Panthers. A social activist consciousness-raising group of both young and old persons whose primary objective is to change society's outdated concept of age and to fight against ageism.* The group was founded in Philadelphia in 1970 by Maggie Kuhn, who continues to be its national convener. The original name for the Gray Panthers was the Consultation of Older and Younger Adults for Social Change. A television program director dubbed the group the Gray Panthers in 1971 and the name stuck. ("Statement of Principles." In Beth B. Hess, ed., *Growing Old in America*. New Brunswick, N.J.: Transaction Books, 1976, pp. 462-65; Ruth H. Jacobs and Beth B. Hess. "Panther Power: Symbol and Substance." *Long Term Care and Health Services Administration Quarterly*, Fall 1978, pp. 238-44; C. Clearwater. *Gray Panther History: 1970-1981*. Philadelphia: Gray Panther National Office, 1981.)

Green Thumb. A program sponsored by the National Farmers Union and funded under Title V of the Older Americans Act, that provides part-time employment for low-income persons age 55 or older. Originally developed in rural areas to beautify public parks and roadsides, its projects have been expanded to include employment in such areas as education, transportation, health care, and weatherization. (Louis Lowy. "Mental Health Services in the Community." In James E. Birren and R. Bruce Sloane, eds.,

Handbook of Mental Health and Aging. Englewood Cliffs, N.J.: Prentice-Hall, 1980, pp. 827-53; Green Thumb, 511 Leesburg Pike, Falls Church, Va. 22041.)

grief. The psychological response to the loss of a loved person or object. (Erich Lindemann. "Symptomology and Management of Acute Grief." *American Journal of Psychiatry*, 1944, 101, pp. 141-48; Richard A. Kalish. "The Social Context of Death and Dying." In Robert H. Binstock and Ethel Shanas, eds., *Handbook of Aging and the Social Sciences*. New York: Van Nostrand Reinhold, 1985, pp. 149-70.) *See also* bereavement, mourning.

grief work. A process by which survivors grieve, free themselves from the relationship that existed with the deceased, and review and rebuild their lives. (Erich Lindemann. "Symptomology and Management of Acute Grief." *American Journal of Psychiatry*, 1944, 101, pp. 141-48; Helena Z. Lopata. *Widowhood in an American City*. Cambridge, Mass.: Schenkman, 1973.) *See also* anticipatory grief.

group. (1) In strict sociological usage a group consists of two or more persons who interact with one another in a standardized pattern and who have a sense of common identity. (2) Any collectivity of persons who are together in the same place. (3) People who have some common characteristic; for example, all persons age 65 and over. In this sense, group is used interchangeably with category. (George C. Homans. *The Human Group*. New York: Harcourt Brace and World, 1950; Howard L. Nixon. *The Small Group*. Englewood, Cliffs, N.J.: Prentice-Hall, 1979; John E. Dono et al. "Primary Groups in Old Age: Structure and Function." *Research on Aging*, 1979, 1, pp. 403-33.) *See also* interaction, primary group, reference group, secondary group.

group residences. Homes or apartments for about 3 to 15 persons in which each resident has a private bedroom but shares common areas such as the living room and kitchen. Group residences provide an alternative housing option for older persons, are usually sponsored by a community organization, and vary in their management. Also referred to as group shared housing. (Dennis Day-Lower. *Shared Housing for Older People: A Planning Manual for Group Residences*. Philadelphia: Shared Housing Resource Center, 1983.) *See also* Share-A-Home.

guardianship. A type of protective service in which a guardian manages the person and property of another who is found to be legally incompetent. The incompetent, referred to as a "ward," is stripped of all his or her rights including the right to resist admission to a nursing home or mental hospital.

(Winsor C. Schmidt. "Guardianship: Public and Private." In Marshall B. Kapp, Harvey E. Pies, and A. Edward Doudera, eds., *Legal and Ethical Aspects of Health Care for the Elderly*. Ann Arbor: Health Administration Press, School of Public Health, University of Michigan, 1985, pp. 198-211.) *See also* protective services.

GULHEMP profile. A method to measure and rate job applicants to determine their functional age.* Seven components are tested: general physique, upper extremities, lower extremities, hearing, eyesight, mentality, and personality. The name is derived from the first letter of each component. (E. L. Meier and E. A. Kerr. "Capabilities of Middle-Aged and Older Workers." *Industrial Gerontology*, 1976, 3, pp. 147-56; L. F. Koyl. *Employing the Older Workers: Matching the Employee to the Job*. Washington, D.C.: National Council on the Aging, 1974.)

H

hallucination. A false perception believed to be real that occurs in the absence of adequate sensory experience. Hallucinations may occur in multi-infarct dementia* and delirium.* (R. W. White and N. F. Watt. *The Abnormal Personality*. New York: Ronald Press, 1972.) *See also* delusion.

Ham and Eggs Movement. Founded by Robert Noble in 1937, this plan proposed that money in the form of a stamp scrip be given to everyone in California who was 50 and over and unemployed. However, the money was to be spent by a certain date. The original slogan "Twenty-five dollars every Tuesday" was later changed to "Thirty dollars every Thursday." Also referred to as the California Pension Plan. (Frank A. Pinner, Paul Jacobs, and Philip Selznick. *Old Age and Political Behavior: A Case Study*. Berkeley, Calif.: University of California Press, 1959; Jackson K. Putnam. *Old Age Politics in California: From Richardson to Reagan*. Stanford: Stanford University Press, 1970.) *See also* social movement.

Hayflick limit. The barrier to indefinite proliferation of the cells. Leonard Hayflick and his associates studied human fibroblast cells maintained in tissue culture and found that they are limited to about 50 divisions and no more. (L. Hayflick and P. S. Moorhead. "The Serial Cultivation of Human Diploid Cell Strains." *Experimental Cell Research*, 1961, 25, pp. 585, 621; L. Hayflick. "The Cellular Basis for Biological Aging." In L. Hayflick and Caleb E. Finch, eds., *Handbook of the Biology of Aging*. New York: Van Nostrand Reinhold, 1977, pp. 159-86.)

health. (1) As defined by the World Health Organization, health is "a state of complete physical, mental, and social well-being and not merely the absence of disease or infirmity." (2) Health in older persons may be defined on the basis of the presence or absence of disease (medical model) or on the basis of how well one is functioning (functional model). According to the World Health Organization Advisory Group: "Health in the elderly is best measured in terms of function; . . . degree of fitness rather than extent of pathology may be used as a measure of the amount of services the aged will require from the community." (World Health Organization. *The First Ten Years of World Health Organization*. Geneva: World Health Organization, 1958; World Health Organization. *The Public Health Aspects of the Aging*

Figure 4
Growth Characteristics of Human Cells in Tissue Culture

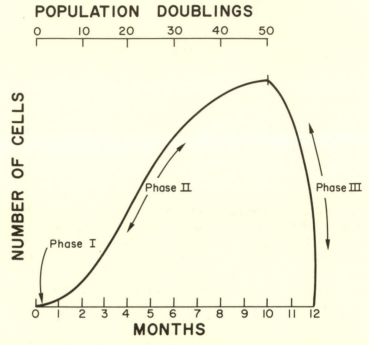

Source: James F. Fries and Lawrence M. Crapo. *Vitality and Aging: Implications of the Rectangular Curve*. San Francisco: W. H. Freeman, 1981, p. 49. Copyright © 1981 W. H. Freeman and Company. Reprinted with permission.

of the Population. Report of an Advisory Group. Copenhagen: World Health Organization, 1959; Ethel Shanas and George L. Maddox. "Health, Resources, and the Utilization of Care." In Robert H. Binstock and Ethel Shanas, eds., *Handbook of Aging and the Social Sciences*. New York: Van Nostrand Reinhold, 1985, pp. 696-726; George L. Maddox. "Self Assessment of Health Status: A Longitudinal Study of Selected Elderly Subjects." *Journal of Chronic Diseases*, 1964, 17, pp. 449-60.)

Health Maintenance Organization (HMO). A type of medical group practice that provides to an enrolled group of subscribers for a fixed advanced payment all necessary health services including hospitalization, which are obtained either directly or through specialists under contract. (H. Luft. *Health Maintenance Organizations: Dimensions of Performance*. New York: Wiley, 1981; George L. Maddox. "The Continuum of Care: Movement toward the Community." In Ewald W. Busse and Dan G. Blazer, eds., *Handbook of Geriatric Psychiatry*. New York: Van Nostrand Reinhold, 1980, pp. 501-20; Susan B. Eve. "Older Americans' Use of Health Maintenance Organizations." *Research on Aging*, 1982, 4, pp. 179-204.)

healthy worker effect. This phrase refers to the favorable health status of the employed population as compared to the general population, which includes those persons who are unemployed, hospitalized, and institutionalized. (A. J. McMichael, S. Haynes, and H. A. Tyroler. "Observations on the Evaluation of Occupational Mortality Data." *Journal of Occupational Medicine*, 1975, 17, pp. 128-31; C. P. Wen, S. P. Tsai, and R. L. Gibson. "Anatomy of the Healthy Worker Effect: A Critical Review." *Journal of Occupational Medicine*, 1983, 25, pp. 283-89.)

heart attack. *See* myocardial infarction.

heart disease. *See* angina pectoris, congestive heart failure, coronary artery disease.

heroic measures. Treatments to maintain or preserve life (which include artificial respiration, nasogastric tubes, intravenous infusions, etc.) that make intense therapeutic demands on the patient and often on the health-care staff as well. Used interchangeably with extraordinary or aggressive measures. (Robert Veatch. *Death, Dying and the Biological Revolution*. New Haven, Conn.: Yale University Press, 1976; Douglas N. Walton. *Ethics of Withdrawal of Life-Support Systems: Case Studies on Decision Making in Intensive Care*. Westport, Conn.: Greenwood Press, 1983.) *See also* Concern for Dying, death with dignity, living will.

hidden elderly. Older persons who have become withdrawn or have been isolated from the mainstream of society.* This label is commonly applied to those older persons who live in inner-city hotels (SROs). (Anita S. Harbert and Leon H. Ginsberg. *Human Services for Older Adults: Concepts and Skills*. Belmont, Calif.: Wadsworth, 1979.) *See also* single-room occupancy hotels.

hidden patients. Caregivers, usually older wives or husbands, who care for their physically and/or mentally disabled spouses. (A. P. Fengler and N. Goodrich. "Wives of Elderly Disabled Men: The Hidden Patients." *The Gerontologist*, 1975, 19, pp. 175-83.) *See also* caregiver.

hidden poor. Those older persons who are poor but are not included in the census figures as being poor because they live in institutions or they live with others (usually relatives) whose incomes are sufficient to raise them above the poverty* level. (Margaret Clark. "Patterns of Aging among the Elderly Poor of the Inner City." *The Gerontologist*, 1971, 11, pp. 58-66.)

high blood pressure. *See* hypertension.

Hispanic elderly. The Hispanic population, which is composed of persons of Cuban, Mexican, Puerto Rican and other Spanish origin, is the second largest ethnic group* in the United States. A major problem for the Hispanic elderly is the language barrier. Of all the ethnic elderly, the Hispanics are the least educated. (Ron C. Manuel, ed. *Minority Aging: Sociological and Social Psychological Issues*. Westport, Conn.: Greenwood Press, 1982; Carmela G. Lacayo. "Hispanics." In Erdman B. Palmore, ed., *Handbook on the Aged in the United States*. Westport, Conn.: Greenwood Press, 1984, pp. 253-67.) *See also* minority group.

historical design. The gathering of data from records, newspapers, letters, diaries, and documents as well as artifacts to obtain knowledge about the past. (Bernard S. Phillips. *Social Research: Strategy and Tactics*. New York: Macmillan, 1976.) *See also* historical sociology of aging, oral history.

historical sociology of aging. The study of how the aging process and the elderly's position have changed over time. The major sources of historical information on aging are birth, death, and marriage records; census information, and literary and plastic materials (Peter Laslett). (David H. Fischer. *Growing Old in America*. New York: Oxford University Press, 1978; W. Andrew Achenbaum. *Old Age in the New Land*. Baltimore: Johns Hopkins University Press, 1978; P. Laslett. "Societal Development and Aging." In Robert H. Binstock and Ethel Shanas, eds., *Handbook of Aging and the Social Sciences*. New York: Van Nostrand Reinhold, 1985, pp. 199-230.)

holistic health care. A health model that emphasizes the treatment of the whole person physically, emotionally, mentally, and spiritually in the context of his or her environment.* Also spelled "wholistic." (Lynda J. Moore. *The Complete Handbook of Holistic Health*. Englewood Cliffs, N.J.: Prentice-Hall, 1983.)

holocultural design. *See* cross-cultural design.

holographic will. A will that is handwritten by the testator and may be either witnessed or unwitnessed. Holographic wills are not recognized in some states. Also referred to as an olographic will. (Robert A. Farmer and Associates. *How to Avoid Problems with Your Will*. New York: Arco, 1968.)

home-delivered meals program. A program that provides for the delivery of a hot noon meal to older persons who are homebound and unable to cook and shop or obtain help to do so. The federal meal program is funded through the Older Americans Act,* but additional meal programs are funded by the state, the county, and privately funded organizations. The first home-delivered meals program in the United States was started in Philadelphia in 1954. The idea originated in England in 1939. Also called "Meals-on-Wheels", and "mobile meals." (Annette B. Natow and Jo-Ann Heslin. *Nutritional Care of the Older Adult*. New York: Macmillan, 1986.) *See also* congregate meals program.

home health services. These services provide aides who perform such nursing duties as dispensing and supervising medication, changing of dressings, giving rehabilitation therapy, and providing personal hygiene services. (W. M. Beattie. "Aging and the Social Services." In Robert H. Binstock and Ethel Shanas, eds., *Handbook of Aging and the Social Sciences*. New York: Van Nostrand Reinhold, 1976, pp. 619-42; Louis Lowy. *Social Policies and Programs on Aging*. Lexington, Mass.: Lexington Books, 1980.)

homemaker services. These services provide professionally supervised and specially trained personnel, usually women, to do light housekeeping, shop for food, prepare meals, and offer companionship primarily to older persons who are temporarily or permanently disabled. Homemaker services began in England and came to the United States during the 1920s. (W. M. Beattie. "Aging and the Social Services." In Robert H. Binstock and Ethel Shanas, eds., *Handbook of Aging and the Social Sciences*. New York: Van Nostrand Reinhold, 1976, pp. 619-42; Louis Lowy. *Social Policies and Programs on Aging*. Lexington, Mass.: Lexington Books, 1980.)

homes for the aged. Nonprofit institutions that are usually sponsored by a church or a fraternal organization. They are operated for people who are relatively physically and mentally healthy but because of social dependency or poverty need such a facility. Very few homes of this type remain today. (M. Powell Lawton. *Environment and Aging*. Monterey, Calif.: Brooks/ Cole, 1980.) *See also* domiciliary-care facilities.

homestead exemptions. A property tax relief program for low-income elderly homeowners that exempts a dollar amount or percent share of property valuation from property taxes. (Sandra J. Newman, James Zais, and Raymond Struyk. "Housing Older America." In I. Altman, M. P. Lawton, and J. Wohlwill, eds., *Elderly People and the Environment*. New York: Plenum Press, 1984, pp. 17-55.) *See also* circuit breakers.

hospice. An independent facility or a hospital unit that is devoted specifical- ly to the care of the dying.* Terminally ill patients are helped through the dying process by careful management of pain and maximum social support. Family support is given during the patient's illness and continues through the bereavement* period. Some hospice programs are also carried out in the home. Cicely A. Saunders founded the first hospice, St. Christopher's, outside of London in the 1950s. The first American hospice was started in 1976 at Branford, Connecticut. Originally, the term hospice referred to a way-station for travelers. (C. A. Saunders. "A Therapeutic Community: St. Christopher's Hospice." In B. Schoenberg, ed., *Psychosocial Aspects of Terminal Care*. New York: Columbia University Press, 1972; Theodore H. Koff. *Hospice: A Caring Community*. Cambridge, Mass.: Winthrop, 1981.)

hot flash. A symptom of menopause* in which there is a sudden sensation of heat in the face that spreads down the neck and trunk. Often this is followed by sweating and/or a slight chill. Clinically known as the vasomotor symptom complex. (Nan Corby and Robert L. Solnick. "Psychosocial and Physiological Influences on Sexuality in the Older Adult." In James E. Birren and R. Bruce Sloane, eds., *Handbook of Mental Health and Aging*. Englewood Cliffs, N.J.: Prentice-Hall, 1980, pp. 893-921; G. W. Bates. "On the Nature of the Hot Flash." *Clinical Obstetrics and Gynecology*, 1981, 24, pp. 231-41.)

household. This concept is based on the arrangements that a person or persons make for the provision of food and other living essentials. According to the United Nations, in a one-person household a person provides for his or her own food and other living essentials without combining with anyone else. In a multiperson household two or more persons commonly provide for food and other living essentials. They may pool their incomes and have a common budget. Also they may be related, unrelated, or a combination of both. (United Nations. *Principles and Recommendations for Population and Housing Censuses*. Statistical Papers, Series M, No. 67. New York: Department of International Economic and Social Affairs, 1980; Marvin Sussman. "The Family Life of Old People." In Robert H. Binstock and Ethel Shanas, eds., *Handbook of Aging and the Social Sciences*. New York: Van Nostrand Reinhold, 1985, pp. 415-49.) *See also* Share-A-Home.

house sharing. *See* shared housing.

Hutchinson-Gilford Syndrome. *See* progeria.

hyperborean theme. This theme asserts that there are people in some remote place that live an extremely long time. The idea originated with the Greek legend of the Hyperboreans and reappeared in recent times in James

Hilton's imaginary Shangri-La. (Gerald J. Gruman. "A History of Ideas about the Prolongation of Life: The Evolution of Prolongevity Hypotheses to 1800." *Transactions of the American Philosophical Society*, 1966, vol. 56, pt. 9, pp. 1-102.) *See also* antediluvian theme, fountain theme.

hyperglycemia. *See* diabetes milletus.

hyperopia. *See* presbyopia.

hypertension. An elevated resting blood pressure that is commonly referred to as high blood pressure. The arterioles constrict and cause the heart to pump harder to circulate the blood throughout the body resulting in an elevation of the blood pressure.* It is a leading risk factor in heart attacks (myocardial infarctions) and may also cause strokes (cerebrovascular accidents). (Michael Tuck and James Sowers. "Hypertension and Aging." In Stanley G. Korenman, ed., *Endocrine Aspects of Aging*. New York: Elsevier, 1982, pp. 89-117; William B. Kannel. "Hypertension and Aging." In Caleb E. Finch and Edward L. Schneider, eds., *Handbook of the Biology of Aging*. New York: Van Nostrand Reinhold, 1985, pp. 859-77.) *See also* blood pressure, cerebrovascular accident, myocardial infarction.

hypoglycemia. A condition resulting from too much insulin. Commonly referred to as low blood sugar. Generally defined as a blood glucose concentration below 50 milligrams per deciliter. A hypoglycemic reaction includes trembling, rapid heartbeat, impaired vision, weakness, incoordination, perspiration, and confusion. (R. H. Williams, ed. *Textbook of Endocrinology*. Philadelphia: W. B. Saunders, 1974.) *See also* diabetes.

hypothermia. *See* accidental hypothermia.

hypothesis. A tentative statement asserting the relationship between two or more variables; a statement of the expected outcome of research. (Earl R. Babbie. *The Practice of Social Research*. Belmont, Calif.: Wadsworth, 1983.) *See also* null hypothesis, variable.

I

IADL. *See* Instrumental Activities of Daily Living Scale.

iatrogenic disorder. A disorder caused by physicians or the drugs that they prescribe. Some of the major causes of iatrogenic disorders in the elderly are improper prescriptions and taking of medications. (D. M. Peterson and C. W. Thomas. "Acute Drug Reactions among the Elderly." *Journal of Gerontology*, 1975, 30, pp. 552-56; William Simonson. *Medications and the Elderly*. Rockville, Md.: Aspen Systems, 1984.) *See also* drug reaction (adverse).

id. In psychoanalytic theory one of the three basic personality structures. The id is the primitive, instinctual element of the mind that is entirely unconscious. It is governed by the pleasure principle (seeking of gratification and avoidance of pain) and restrained by the ego.* In old age there may be a weakening of the id. (Laurance F. Shaffer and Edward J. Shoben. *The Psychology of Adjustment*. Boston: Houghton Mifflin, 1956; Sigmund Freud. "The Ego and The Id." In J. Strachey, ed., *The Standard Edition of the Complete Psychological Works of Sigmund Freud*. Vol. 19. New York: Norton, 1961.) *See also* superego.

identity crisis. A loss of the sense of one's identity and self-continuity as well as the ability to take on a role* that is offered or expected by society. For example, Stephen J. Miller contends that at retirement* one loses his or her occupational identity and a functional role in society. In place of work, the individual is offered leisure.* But our society has not yet legitimized leisure as a full-time pursuit, and this results in an identity crisis for the retiree. The concept of the identity crisis was developed by Erik Erikson. (Stephen J. Miller. "The Social Dilemma of the Aging Leisure Participant." In Arnold M. Rose and Warren A. Peterson, eds., *Older People and Their Social World*. Philadelphia: F. A. Davis, 1965; Erik H. Erikson. *Identity: Youth and Crisis*. New York: Norton, 1968.)

identity review. *See* life review.

impairment. Any anatomical, physiological, or psychological abnormality or loss. Not all impairments result in disabilities. An elderly person, for example, with a severe hearing impairment may still be able to live independently. (Saad Z. Nagi. *Disability and Rehabilitation*. Columbus: Ohio State University Press, 1969; Ethel Shanas and George L. Maddox. "Health, Health Resources, and the Utilization of Care." In Robert H. Binstock and Ethel Shanas, eds., *Handbook of Aging and the Social Sciences*. New York: Van Nostrand Reinhold, 1985, pp. 696-726.) *See also* disability.

impressionistic study. An informal and descriptive account of some phenomena that is based on organized and purposeful observations. (Earl R. Babbie. *The Practice of Social Research*. Belmont, Calif.: Wadsworth 1983.)

incontinence. The inability to control the release of urine and feces. Urinary incontinence (enuresis) is more common than fecal incontinence. Either condition may be temporary or permanent. Incontinence in the elderly is both a medical and a social problem. (B. Isaacs, "A Survey of Incontinence in the Elderly." *Gerontologica Clinica*, 1964, 6, pp. 8-22; F. L. Willington. *Incontinence in the Elderly*. New York: Academic Press, 1976.)

independent variable. A variable* that occurs prior to the dependent variable* and whose occurrence or change affects the dependent variable. In experimental research it is the variable that is directly manipulated by the experimenter so its effect upon the dependent variable may be studied. Also referred to as the experimental variable or the explanatory variable. (Elliot Aronson and J. Merrill Carlsmith. "Experimentation in Social Psychology." In Gardner Lindzey and Elliot Aronson, eds., *Handbook of Social Psychology*. Vol. 2. Reading, Mass.: Addison-Wesley, 1968, pp. 1-79. James A. Black and Dean J. Champion. *Methods and Issues in Social Research*. New York: John Wiley, 1976.)

Individual Retirement Account (IRA). A custodial account in which deposits can increase and compound tax-free until withdrawn. The custodian can be a bank, brokerage firm, mutual fund, or some other financial institution that invests an individual's funds according to the plan he or she has selected, or one may set up a "self-directed" plan. In this type of plan the individual makes his or her own investment decisions but the custodian still handles the account. Funds in IRAs may be placed in such financial instruments as certificates of deposits, stocks, bonds, and mutual funds. Since 1981 the contribution limit for an IRA has been $2,000 a year for a worker and $2,250 for a worker with a nonworking spouse. The tax law imposes a 10 percent penalty for withdrawals before age 59½ except in cases of disability. Beginning with the 1987 tax returns, the law was changed so that individuals over a certain income or who were covered by a retirement plan at work no longer were able to claim an IRA deduction on their returns. (Bernard Greisman, ed. *J. K. Lasser's All You Should Know about IRA, Keogh, and Other Retirement Plans.* New York: Simon and Schuster, 1985; Gary L. Klott. *The New York Times Complete Guide to the New Tax Law.* New York: Times Books, 1986.)

individual retirement annuity. A contract issued by an insurance company that pays a specified monthly amount beginning at age 59½ or at retirement* and continuing for life. The contract may be only on the insured individual's life or it may contain a joint and survivor option.* (Bernard Greisman, ed., *J. K. Lasser's All You Should Know about IRA, Keogh, and Other Retirement Plans.* New York: Simon and Schuster, 1985; Gary L. Klott. *The New York Times Complete Guide to the New Tax Law.* New York: Times Books, 1986.)

industrial gerontology. The scientific study of the employment and retirement problems of middle-aged and older workers. It draws upon the fields of adult education,* industrial psychology, industrial and occupational sociology, industrial medicine, industrial and labor relations, management science, and economics* (Norman Sprague). (Harold L. Sheppard. *Industrial Gerontology: An Introduction to a New Field of Applied Research and Service.* Cambridge, Mass.: Schenkman, 1970.) *See also* older adult worker.

industrialization. This term refers to the change in a predominantly agrarian society from human to inanimate sources of energy resulting in the rise of the factory system. The number of people employed in agriculture decreases as the number of people employed in industry increases. Some writers maintain that the status of the elderly has declined with industrialization. However, there is some evidence that the status of the elderly is beginning to improve in postindustrial societies. (Erdman B. Palmore. "The Future Status of the Aged." *The Gerontologist,* 1976, 16, pp. 297-303; Gerhard Lenski and Jean Lenski. *Human Societies: An Introduction to Macrosociology.* New York: McGraw-Hill, 1982.) *See also* modernization.

informal support systems. The network of family,* friends, neighbors, and other nonprofessionals who provide social support or social care. It is to these informal systems that the elderly turn first and most often. (Marjorie H. Cantor. "The Informal Support System: Its Relevance in the Lives of the Elderly." In Edgar F. Borgatta and Neil G. McCluskey, eds., *Aging and Society: Current Research.* Beverly Hills, Calif.: Sage, 1980, pp. 131-44; Margaret J. Penning and Neena L. Chappell. "Ethnicity and Informal Supports among Older Adults." *Journal of Aging Studies,* 1987, 1, pp. 145-60.) *See also* formal support systems.

information and referral services. These services link the needs of the elderly with the resources available to them in their community.* The major objectives of information and referral programs are to develop and maintain files of all the services for the elderly in the community and to make this information easily accessible to them. It is also responsible for identifying the elderly's unmet needs in the community as well as discovering gaps and duplications in the services available to them. (J. E. Burkhart. "Evaluating Information and Referral Services." *The Gerontologist*, 1979, 19, pp. 28-33; Louis Lowy. "Mental Health Services in the Community." In James E. Birren and R. Bruce Sloane, eds., *Handbook of Mental Health and Aging*. Englewood Cliffs, N.J.: Prentice-Hall, 1980, pp. 827-53.)

Institute for Retired Professionals. Allied with the New School for Social Research in New York City, this institute, which began in 1962, is specifically designed for retired professionals and executives who wish to explore new interests in their retirement years. The New School for Social Research was the first adult education university in the United States and also the first to sponsor a special program for retirees. (Frances Tenenbaum. *Over 55 Is Not Illegal: A Resource Book for Active Older People*. Boston: Houghton Mifflin, 1979; The New School for Social Research, 66 West 12th Street, New York, N.Y. 10011.)

Institutes of Lifetime Learning. Sponsored by the American Association of Retired Persons (AARP)* and the National Retired Teachers Association (NRTA), these institutes offer a wide variety of courses through extension learning centers in more than a dozen locations across the country as well as working with universities and colleges to promote educational opportunities for older persons. (Frances Tenenbaum. *Over 55 Is Not Illegal: A Resource Book for Active Older People*. Boston: Houghton Mifflin, 1979; Institutes of Lifetime Learning. 1909 K St., N.W., Washington, D.C. 20049.)

institution. (1) In sociological usage an institution refers to a stable cluster of norms and roles that is designed to meet the needs of a society.* The basic institutions in a society include the family,* economy, religion, government, and education.* (2) An established pattern or custom that is valued by a group* or society; for example, Mother's Day or professional football. (3) An organized social group (Pitirim A. Sorokin). (4) An organization; for example, a nursing home. Also, the building occupied by such an organization. (P. A. Sorokin. *Society, Culture, and Personality*. New York: Harper and Row, 1947; Peter L. Berger and Thomas Luckmann. *The Social Construction of Reality*. New York: Doubleday, 1963; Shmuel N. Eisenstadt. "Social Institutions: The Concept." In David L. Sills, ed.,

International Encyclopedia of the Social Sciences. Vol. 5. New York: Macmillan, 1968, pp. 228-34; Eva Kahana, "The Humane Treatment of Old People in Institutions." *The Gerontologist*, 1973, pp. 282-89; Barbara B. Manard, Cary S. Kart, and Dirk W. L. van Gils. *Old-Age Institutions.* Lexington, Mass.: Lexington Books, 1975.) *See also* total institution.

institutional effects. The view that institutional life has harmful consequences on individuals because of its depersonalizing and dehumanizing environment. (Morton A. Lieberman. "Institutions of the Aged: Effects on Behavior." *Journal of Gerontology*, 1969, 24, pp. 330-40.) *See also* institutional personality syndrome.

institutional inmates. Persons who live in group quarters usually for long periods of time; for example, prisons, mental hospitals, and nursing homes. (Henry S. Shryock, Jacob S. Siegel, and Associates. *Methods and Materials of Demography.* New York: Academic Press, 1976.)

institutionalization. (1) The process of the gradual emergence and permanent establishment of values, norms, and patterns of behavior; for example, retirement* has become normatively defined as a proper pattern of behavior and is now spoken of as being institutionalized. (2) To live in an institutional setting; for example, a nursing home. (Erdman B. Palmore. "Total Chance of Institutionalization among the Aged." *The Gerontologist*, 1976, 16, pp. 504-7; John Myles. "Institutionalization and Sick Role Identification among the Elderly." *American Sociological Review*, 1978, 43, pp. 508-21; Kristen F. Smith and Vern L. Bengtson. "Positive Consequences of Institutionalization: Solidarity between Elderly Parents and Their Middle-aged Children." *The Gerontologist*, 1979, 19, pp. 438-47.) *See also* deinstitutionalization movement, institutional personality syndrome, nursing home.

institutional personality syndrome. This phrase refers to the traditional view that elderly patients in long-term care facilities tend to develop certain personality characteristics. These characteristics include being disoriented, depressed, withdrawn, submissive, and apathetic. Also referred to as "institutional neurosis." (Morton A. Lieberman. "Institutionalization of the Aged: Effects on Behavior." *Journal of Gerontology*, 1969, 24, pp. 330-40; Sheldon S. Tobin and Morton A. Lieberman. *Last Home for the Aged: Critical Implications of Institutionalization.* San Francisco: Jossey-Bass, 1976.) *See also* institutional effects.

Instrumental Activities of Daily Living Scale (IADL). A scale that assesses an older person's ability to do activities needed for independent living. These activities include using the telephone, preparing food, shopping, and handling finances. Each task is rated on the degree of success in its completion and the amount of help needed. (M. Powell Lawton and Elaine Brody. "Assessment of Older People: Self Maintaining and Instrumental Activities of Daily Living." *The Gerontologist*, 1969, 9, pp. 179-86.) *See also* Activities of Daily Living, Index of; Older Americans Resources and Services Multidimensional Functional Assessment Questionnaire.

instrumental role (family). A role,* usually the work role, which involves relationships between the nuclear family* and the outside world and is generally assigned to men in most societies. (Talcott Parsons and Robert Bales. *Family, Socializaton, and Interaction Process*. Glencoe, Ill.: Free Press, 1955.) *See also* expressive role (family).

integrity vs. despair crisis. The last of Erik H. Erikson's eight stages of self-development, which he introduced in 1950. In this stage persons review their lives to decide whether or not they were meaningful and productive. Those who are content with their lives approach the end of their days with satisfaction, while those who are not approach the end with feelings of frustration and despair. (E. H. Erikson. *Childhood and Society*. New York: Norton, 1950; E. H. Erikson. *The Life Cycle Completed: A Review*. New York: Norton, 1982.)

interaction. The process by which one person acts toward another person who then interprets the act and responds to it; mutual influence. Social interaction in older persons sometimes becomes limited because of health and mobility. (Talcott Parsons and Edward A. Shils, eds. *Toward a General Theory of Action*. Cambridge, Mass.: Harvard University Press, 1951; M. I. Knapp. *Nonverbal Communication in Human Interaction*. New York: Holt, Rinehart and Winston, 1978; Marjorie F. Lowenthal and Clayton Haven. "Interaction and Adaptation Intimacy as a Critical Variable." *American Sociological Review*, 1968, 33, pp. 20-30; Jay Sokolovsky and Carl Cohen. "Measuring Social Interaction of the Urban Elderly: A Methodological Synthesis." *International Journal of Aging and Human Development*, 1981, 13, pp. 233-44.)

interdisciplinary research. A cooperative effort in which individuals from two or more scientific disciplines work together on different parts of a research project. (Bernice L. Neugarten and Associates, eds. *Personality in Middle and Late Life*. New York: Atherton Press, 1964; Margaret Clark and Barbara G. Anderson. *Culture and Aging*. Springfield, Ill.: Charles C. Thomas, 1967.) *See also* multidisciplinary research.

interest group. *See* aging-based interest group.

intergenerational solidarity. The extent to which family members like each other, do things together, and have similar values and opinions. (Vern L. Bengtson and Judith Treas. "The Changing Family Context." In James E. Birren and R. Bruce Sloane, eds., *Handbook of Mental Health and Aging.* Englewood Cliffs, N.J.: Prentice-Hall, 1980, pp. 400-28.)

intergeneration mobility. A vertical change in the social position of children in comparison with their parents. (Peter M. Blau and Otis D. Duncan. *The American Occupational Structure.* New York: Wiley, 1967.)

interiority (of personality). This term refers to the change that is believed to accompany old age* in which there is a movement away from the external world and a turning inward and preoccupation with oneself. (Bernice L. Neugarten. "A Developmental View of Adult Personality." In James E. Birren, ed., *Relations of Development and Aging.* Springfield, Ill.: Charles C. Thomas, 1964; Bernice L. Neugarten. "Personality Change in Late Life: A Developmental Perspective." In Carl Eisdorfer and M. Powell Lawton, eds., *The Psychology of Adult Development and Aging.* Washington, D.C.: American Psychological Association, 1973.) *See also* introversion.

intermediate care facility (ICF). A facility that provides health-related care and services to those who need less care than a skilled nursing facility, but more than custodial or residential care. (Barbara B. Manard, Cary S. Kart, and Dirk W. L. van Gils. *Old Age Institutions.* Lexington, Mass.: Lexington Books, 1975; R. Glasscote et al. *Old Folks at Homes.* Washington, D.C.: American Psychiatric Association and the Mental Health Association, 1976.) *See also* skilled nursing facility, extended care facility.

intervening variable. A variable* that is considered to be the link between the correlation* of two other variables. (Bernard S. Phillips. *Social Research: Strategies and Techniques.* New York: Macmillan, 1976.)

interview. A conversation in which the interviewer seeks to obtain attitudes, opinions, beliefs, or information from the respondent.* (Charles F. Cannell and Robert L. Kahn. "Interviewing." In Gardner Lindzey and Elliot Aronson, eds., *Handbook of Social Psychology.* Vol. 2. Reading, Mass.: Addison-Wesley, 1968.) *See also* attitude, depth interview, focused interview.

interview schedule. When the interviewer asks questions from a questionnaire* and records the respondent's answers. (Charles F. Cannell and Robert L. Kahn. "Interviewing." In Gardner Lindzey and Elliot Aronson, eds., *Handbook of Social Psychology*. Vol. 2. Reading, Mass.: Addison-Wesley, 1968.) *See also* interview, respondent, survey.

intestinal putrefaction theory. Proposed by Elie Metchnikoff in 1908, this theory asserts that the toxins that arise from intestinal putrefaction are one of the principal causes of aging. He advocated drinking fermented milk which contains acid-producing bacteria to prevent the breeding of "noxious microbes." (Olga Metchnikoff. *Life of Elie Metchnikoff*. Boston: Houghton Mifflin, 1921.)

intimacy at a distance. Older persons that desire to live apart from their children and relatives but still live near enough to exchange services on a daily basis. This phrase was introduced by Leopold Rosenmayr and Eva Kockeis in 1963. (L. Rosenmayr and E. Kockeis. "Propositions for a Sociological Theory of Aging and the Family." *International Social Science Journal*, 1963, 15, pp. 410-26.) *See also* modified extended family.

intracohort study. A type of longitudinal design* in which samples of individuals from a cohort* are studied at two or more points in time. While the same cohort is studied, it is not likely the same individuals will be. (Norval Glenn. *Cohort Analysis*. Beverly Hills, Calif.: Sage, 1977.) *See also* panel study, sample.

introversion. A tendency for one's interests to be oriented inward and to be preoccupied with one's own thoughts and feelings. Carl G. Jung used a bipolar personality dimension in which he divided individuals into introversion (inward-directed) and extraversion* (outward-directed). Some researchers maintain that with age there is a movement toward increased introversion. Commonly misspelled "intraversion" (C. G. Jung. *Psychological Types*. New York: Harcourt, Brace, 1933; Bernice L. Neugarten and Associates, eds. *Personality in Middle and Late Life*. New York: Atherton, 1964; P. Cameron. "Introversion and Egocentricity among the Aged." *Journal of Gerontology*, 1967, 22, pp. 465-68.) *See also* disengagement theory, interiority.

involuntary euthanasia. Passive or active euthanasia imposed upon a patient who is incapable of giving consent. (Wayne Sage. "Choosing the Good Death." *Human Behavior*, June 1974, pp. 16-23; Ruth O. Russell. *Freedom to Die: Moral and Legal Aspects of Euthanasia*. New York: Human Sciences Press, 1975.) *See also* voluntary euthanasia.

irreversible decrement model. This model, proposed by K. Warner Schaie, refers to a progressive, biological decline that occurs in the later part of life.

(K. Warner Schaie. "Methodological Problems in Descriptive Developmental Research on Adulthood and Aging." In J. R. Nesselroade and H. W. Reese, eds., *Life-Span Developmental Psychology: Methodological Issues.* New York: Academic Press, pp. 253-80.) *See also* decrement-with-compensation model, Gompertz curve.

isolation. *See* social isolation.

J

joint and survivor option. A pension plan option that provides income to the surviving spouse at the same rate or some reduced rate from when the insured spouse was alive. (James H. Schulz. *The Economics of Aging.* Belmont, Calif.: Wadsworth, 1985.)

K

Kansas City Studies of Adult Life. Two studies that investigated the social-psychological aspects of aging* and were conducted in Kansas City, Missouri. The studies began in 1952 and extended over a ten-year period under the direction of Robert J. Havighurst, William E. Henry, and Bernice Neugarten of the University of Chicago. One study was cross-sectional and interviewed persons aged 40 to 70; the other was longitudinal and interviewed persons aged 50 to 90 over a six-year period. (Elaine Cumming and William Henry. *Growing Old: The Process of Disengagement*. New York: Basic Books, 1961; Bernice L. Neugarten, ed. *Personality in Middle and Late Life*. New York: Atherton, 1964; Richard H. Williams and Claudine G. Wirths. *Lives through the Years*. New York: Atherton, 1965.) *See also* activity theory, disengagement theory.

Keogh plan. A retirement plan for persons who earn income from self-employment either from their main occupation or from a sideline business. Deposits are tax-deductible and money is allowed to increase and compound tax-free until withdrawn. (Bernard Griesman, ed. *J. K. Lasser's All You Should Know about IRA, Keogh, and Other Retirement Plans*. New York: Simon and Schuster, 1985; Gary L. Klott. *The New York Times Complete Guide to the New Tax Law*. New York: Times Books, 1987.)

kinship. Social relationships based on blood ties (descent) and marriage (affinity). (George P. Murdock. *Social Structure*. New York: Macmillan, 1949; Ira L. Reiss. *The Family System in America*. New York: Holt, Rinehart and Winston, 1971; R. M. Keesing. *Kin Groups and Social Structure*. New York: Holt, Rinehart and Winston, 1975.) *See also* bilateral descent, extended family, matrilineal descent, nuclear family, patrilineal descent.

Kutner Interaction Scale. This scale was designed to measure frequency of interaction* with friends, especially close friends, and the formation of new friendships. (B. Kutner et al. *Five Hundred over Sixty: A Community Survey on Aging*. New York: Russell Sage, 1956.)

kyphosis. A condition in which there is a backward curvature of the spine. Shoulders are often rounded, the back hunched, and the chest has a caved-in appearance. Kyphosis may be due to a lifelong stooping posture or a disease such as osteoporosis.* (D. Grob. "Common Disorders of Muscles in the Aged." In A. B. Chinn, ed., *Working with Older People: Clinical Aspects of Aging*. Washington, D.C.: Department of Health, Education and Welfare, 1971.) *See also* dowager's hump.

L

labeling theory. A theory that explains deviance* in terms of the process by which members of a group* define someone as deviant. Much deviant behavior goes unnoticed but once a deviant act is discovered, an individual is labeled by others as a deviant and people begin to respond to the offender in terms of this label. The offender then accepts the label and begins to behave in a deviant way. Labeling theory has also been applied to aging; for example, labeling an older person as incompetent may represent a significant step in the process of that person becoming incompetent. (Edwin Lemert. *Social Pathology*. McGraw-Hill, 1951; Judith Rodin and Ellen Langer. "Aging Labels: The Decline of Control and the Fall of Self-Esteem." *Journal of Social Issues*, 1980, 36, pp. 12-29.) *See also* self-fulfilling prophecy, social breakdown syndrome (SBS).

lactose intolerance. A deficiency of lactase, which is an intestinal enzyme needed to break down milk sugar (lactose) into glucose and galactose so it can be absorbed in the body. When a deficiency is present, the milk sugar remains in the intestine and begins to ferment. This condition results in bloating, gas, cramping, and diarrhea. With age the lactase enzyme often becomes deficient. (Annette B. Natow and Jo-Ann Heslin. *Nutritional Care of the Older Adult*. New York: Macmillan, 1986.)

latent function. A consequence that is unintended and unrecognized. An example would be the federal nutrition program, which provides large numbers of elderly persons with a hot, midday meal at a congregate feeding site. While the intended purpose (manifest function) of the nutrition program is to provide a hot, nutritious meal for older persons, it also provides an occasion for the elderly to meet and talk with others, which in many cases is more important than the meal itself (latent function). The term was introduced by Robert K. Merton, who adapted it from use in another context by Sigmund Freud. (R. K. Merton. *Social Theory and Social Structure*. New York: Free Press, 1968.) *See also* manifest function.

later life family. A married couple in the post child-rearing years who have begun to launch their children. (Lillian Troll, Sheila J. Miller, and Robert C. Atchley. *Families in Later Life*. Belmont, Calif.: Wadsworth, 1979; Timothy H. Brubaker. *Later Life Families*. Beverly Hills, Calif.: Sage, 1985.)

later maturity. *See* old age.

Lawton's Morale Scale. A scale that assesses morale, adjustment, and well-being in older persons. (M. Powell Lawton. "The Philadelphia Geriatric Center Morale Scale: A Revision." *Journal of Gerontology*, 1975, 30, pp. 85-89.)

learned helplessness. A fatalistic, passive attitude* of accepting whatever comes along and a belief that all is hopeless. Some elderly persons because of their diminished ability to control the environment feel a loss of control over their lives and that all self-assertion is futile. This feeling may result in a helplessness set. This term was coined by Martin E. P. Seligman in 1975 in his experiments with dogs. (M. E. P. Seligman. *Helplessness: On Depression, Development and Death.* San Francisco: Freeman, 1975; L. Y. Abramson, M. E. P. Seligman, and J. D. Teasdale. "Learned Helplessness in Humans: Critique and Reformulation." *Journal of Abnormal Psychology*, 1978, 87, pp. 49-74; Kenneth Soloman. "Social Antecedents of Learned Helplessness in the Health Care Setting." *The Gerontologist*, 1982, 22, pp. 282-87.)

leisure. Max Kaplan defines leisure as "free time that is seen as leisure by participants, that is psychologically pleasant in anticipation and recollection, that potentially covers the whole range of commitment and intensity, that contains the characteristic norms* and constraints, and that provides opportunities for recreation, personal growth, and service to others." Today's elderly have been described as the new leisure class. (M. Kaplan. *Leisure: Lifestyle and Lifespan.* Philadelphia: W. B. Saunders, 1979, p. 26; Robert W. Kleemeier. *Aging and Leisure.* New York: Oxford University Press, 1961; Lei Lane Burrus-Bammel and Gene Bammel. "Leisure and Recreation." In James E. Birren and K. Warner Schaie, eds., *Handbook of the Psychology of Aging.* New York: Van Nostrand Reinhold, 1985, pp. 848-63; M. Powell Lawton. "Activities and Leisure." In Carl Eisdorfer, ed., *Annual Review of Gerontology and Geriatrics.* Vol. 5. New York: Springer, 1985, pp. 127-64.)

lentigenes. Harmless, flat, brown spots that appear with age at the exposed areas of the skin due to an accumulation of lipofuscin* in the tissue. They are found in greatest concentration on the backs of the hands. Commonly referred to as liver spots, although they have no relation to the liver. Also called age spots. (Molly S. Wantz and John E. Gay. *The Aging Process: A Health Perspective.* Cambridge, Mass.: Winthrop, 1981.)

Leonard Davis School of Gerontology. This school began in 1975 at the University of Southern California and is the first gerontology school in the United States. It offers an undergraduate and a master's degree program to prepare students for careers in aging. The school was named for Davis, an insurance specialist who worked closely with Ethel P. Andrus in founding the American Association of Retired Persons. ("The Story of AARP." *Modern Maturity*, August-September 1976, pp. 57-64; David A. Peterson and Christopher R. Bolton. *Gerontology Instruction in Higher Education*. Springer: New York, 1980.)

levirate. A custom in which a widow automatically becomes the wife of her deceased husband's brother. Practiced by many patrilineal groups. This custom was prevalent among ancient Greeks and Hebrews. (John J. Honigmann. *The World of Man*. New York: Harper and Row, 1959.) *See also* patrilineal descent.

life care communities. Communities that provide a type of combined health, housing, and social care insurance for older persons. A person signs a contract and agrees to pay an entrance fee (fees range from $20,000 to $100,000) and a monthly service fee in exchange for a living unit, health care, and lifetime nursing care if needed. The contract remains in effect as long as the person lives. (U.S. Senate. *Developments in Aging, 1984*. Special Committee on Aging. Washington, D.C.: U.S. Government Printing Office, 1985.)

life course. The predictable sequence of stages (e.g., infancy, childhood, youth, adolescence, middle age, and old age) that individuals follow as they go through life, which roughly coincide to a series of life events* beginning with birth and ending with death.* For example, life events that one may experience in the old-age stage of the life course would be retirement* and widowhood. Used interchangeably with life cycle. (Leonard D. Cain. "Life Course and Social Structure." In Robert E. Faris, ed., *Handbook of Modern Sociology*. Chicago: Rand McNally, 1964, pp. 272-309; Glen H. Elder. "Age Differentiation and the Life Course." In Alex Inkeles, J. Coleman, and Neil Smelser, eds., *Annual Review of Sociology*. Palo Alto, Calif.: Annual Reviews, 1975; Gunhild O. Hagestad and Bernice L. Neugarten. "Aging and the Life Course." In Robert H. Binstock and Ethel Shanas, eds., *Handbook of Aging and the Social Sciences*. New York: Van Nostrand Reinhold, 1985, pp. 35-61.) *See also* age grade.

life cycle. *See* life course.

life cycle education. The teaching of personal, psychological, familial, occupational, and other tasks that are related to specific stages of the life course* (Robert N. Butler). An example of this type of education would be preretirement planning programs.* (R. N. Butler. *Why Survive? Being Old in America*. New York: Harper and Row, 1975; B. J. Turock. *Serving the Older Adult*. New York: Bowker, 1983.)

life events. Significant changes in an individual's life that take place at definite points in time; for example, graduation from college, entry into the labor force, marriage, retirement, and so on. Life events often serve as turning points or markers at which persons change some direction in the course of their lives. Change, whether it is pleasant or unpleasant, can be stressful and may make a person more susceptible to illness. (David A. Chiriboga. "An Examination of Life Events as Possible Antecedents to Change." *Journal of Gerontology*, 1982, 37, pp. 595-601; Orville G. Brim. "Types of Life Events." *Journal of Social Issues*, 36, pp. 148-57; David F. Hultsch and J. K. Plemmons. "Life Events and Life Span Development." In Paul B. Baltes and Orville G. Brim, eds. *Life-Span Development and Behavior*. Vol. 2. New York: Academic Press, 1979.) *See also* Social Readjustment Rating Scale, general adaptation syndrome.

life expectancy. (1) The average number of years of life remaining at any specified age. (2) The most commonly used indicator of mortality is life expectancy at birth: the expected number of years to be lived. For example, a baby born in 1900 could be expected to live an average of 47.3 years, while a baby born in 1984 could be expected to live nearly 75 years. As mortality has decreased, life expectancy has increased. Used synonymously with expectation of life. Not to be confused with life span.* (Philip M. Hauser. "Aging and World-Wide Population Change." In Robert H. Binstock and Ethel Shanas, eds., *Handbook of Aging and the Social Sciences*. New York: Van Nostrand Reinhold, 1976, pp. 59-86; J. F. Fries and L. M. Crapo. *Vitality and Aging*. San Francisco: W. H. Freeman, 1981.)

life history method. A complete account of the experiences and sequences of events in an individual's life from birth until death.* Usually this information is gained from interviews in which the respondent* relates his or her life story and also from such sources as questionnaires, autobiographies, letters, and diaries. (D. Bertaux. *Biography and Society: The Life History Approach in the Social Sciences*. Beverly Hills, Calif.: Sage, 1981; Gelya Frank. "Life Histories in Gerontology: The Subjective Side to Aging." In Christine Fry and Jennie Keith, eds., *New Methods for Old Age Research*. New York: Praeger, 1982.) *See also* interview, oral history, questionnaire.

Lifeline service. A 24-hour service that permits homebound persons to call for instant help with the use of the Lifeline emergency alarm and response system. (S. Sherwood and J. Morris. *A Study of the Effects of an Emergency and Response System for the Aged*. Boston: Department of Social Gerontological Research, Hebrew Rehabilitation Center for the Aged, 1981.)

lifelong learning. Education* and training across the life course.* Education for and of the older adult includes continuing education, adult basic education, job training programs, education for retired persons, and educational activities to upgrade occupational and professional skills. (R. E. Peterson et al. *Lifelong Learning in America*. San Francisco: Jossey-Bass, 1979; David A. Peterson. *Facilitating Education for Older Learners*. San Francisco: Jossey-Bass, 1983; Howard Y. McClusky. "Education for Older Adults." In Carl Eisdorfer, ed., *Annual Review of Gerontology and Geriatrics*. Vol. 3. New York: Springer, 1982, pp. 403-28.) *See also* Elderhostel, Institute for Retired Professionals, Institutes of Lifetime Learning.

life review. A natural, universal mental process in the elderly that is induced by the realization of one's impending death.* It is characterized by returning to past experiences so that these experiences and unresolved conflicts can be thought about and reintegrated. This concept was first described by G. Stanley Hall in 1922 and elaborated by Robert N. Butler. (G. Stanley Hall. *Senescence: The Last Half of Life*. New York: D. Appleton, 1922; R. N. Butler. "The Life Review: An Interpretation of Reminiscence in the Aged." *Psychiatry*, 1963, 26, pp. 65-76; R. N. Butler. "Successful Aging and the Role of the Life Review." *Journal of American Geriatrics Society*, 1974, 22, pp. 529-35.) *See also* reminiscence.

life satisfaction. The attitudes that persons have about their past and present lives as a whole; the extent to which one is content or discontent with his or her life situation. Used interchangeably with morale, adjustment, well-being, and successful aging. (John N. Edwards and David L. Klemmack. "Correlates of Life Satisfaction: A Re-Examination." *Journal of Gerontology*, 1973, 28, pp. 497-502; R. Larson. "Thirty Years of Research on the Subjective Well-Being of Older Americans." *Journal of Gerontology*, 1978, 33, pp. 109-25; Jaber F. Gubrium and Robert J. Lynott. "Rethinking Life Satisfaction." *Human Organization*, 1983, 42, pp. 30-38.) *See also* adaptation, adjustment, attitude.

Life Satisfaction Index (LSIA). A self-reporting instrument that measures life satisfaction* as well as demoralization syndromes in older persons. Five components are defined along with five rating scales. They are (1) zest vs. apathy; (2) resolution vs. blaming oneself; (3) relationships between desired vs. achieved goals; (4) self concept; and (5) mood tone. (Bernice L. Neugarten, Robert J. Havighurst and Sheldon S. Tobin. "The Measurement of Life Satisfaction." *Journal of Gerontology*, 1961, 16, pp. 134-43.)

life span. The average age to which human beings as a species can survive under optimum conditions (free of disease and accident). The maximum life span potential (MLP), the length of life of the longest lived members of a species, appears to be about 115 years for the human species. The verified record is 113 years. Life span is not to be confused with life expectancy.*

(Alex Comfort. *The Biology of Senescence*. New York: Elsevier, 1979; James F. Fries and Lawrence M. Crapo. *Vitality and Aging*. San Francisco: Freeman, 1981.) *See also* life expectancy.

life-span developmental psychology. The study of the sequences of individual change and variation in human development from birth to death* and the affect of historical changes on this development. Also referred to as developmental psychology. (John R. Nesselroade and H. W. Reese, eds. *Life-Span Developmental Psychology: Methodological Issues*. New York: Academic Press, 1973; Nancy Datan and Leon H. Ginsberg, ed. *Life-Span Developmental Psychology: Normative Life Crises*. New York: Academic Press, 1975; Paul B. Baltes, H. W. Reese, and L. P. Lipsitt. "Life-Span Developmental Psychology." *Annual Review of Psychology*. Vol. 31. Palo Alto, Calif.: Annual Review, Inc., 1980, pp. 65-110; Benjamin B. Wolman, ed. *Handbook of Developmental Psychology*. Englewood Cliffs, N.J.: Prentice-Hall, 1982.)

lifestyle. An overall living pattern that persons adopt to meet their biological, psychological, and social needs. (Richard H. Williams and Claudine Wirths. *Lives through the Years*. New York: Atherton, 1965; H. S. Maas and J. A. Kuypers. *From Thirty to Seventy*. San Francisco: Jossey-Bass, 1974.)

life table. A table that gives the death rate and life expectancy* along with other data, for each age* or age group* in a specified population.* An unabridged life table presents data on each age, while an abridged life table presents data by age groups (e.g., 65-70 or 70-80). The life table is the most important tool for the analysis of mortality in a given population. The first scientifically correct life table was done by Joshua Milne in 1815. (Roland Pressat. *Demographic Analysis: Methods, Results, Applications*. New York: Aldine-Atherton, 1972; J. Milne. "A Treatise on the Valuation of Annuities and Assurances on Lives and Survivors." In D. Smith and N. Keyfitz, eds., *Mathematical Demography: Selected Papers*. New York: Springer, 1977, pp. 27-34.)

lipofuscin. Pigment granules that accumulate in various cells with advancing age, especially in the liver, spleen, and myocardium. Often called old-age pigment. (Harold Brody and N. Vijayashankar. "Anatomical Changes in the Nervous System." In Caleb E. Finch and Leonard Hayflick, eds., *Handbook of the Biology of Aging*. New York: Van Nostrand Reinhold, 1977, pp. 241-61; Morris Rockstein and Marvin Sussman. *Biology of Aging*. Belmont, Calif.: Wadsworth, 1979.)

liver spots. *See* lentigenes.

living will. A signed, dated, and witnessed document that recognizes an individual's advance written instructions to withhold or withdraw life-sustaining procedures in the event of a terminal illness. It is prepared while individuals are mentally competent and is intended for future use in the event that they are unable to participate fully in decisions regarding their treatment during a terminal illness. It informs others of their wish not to prolong the inevitability of death by heroic measures.* Between 1976 and 1986, 38 states enacted laws that have made the living will a legally binding document. (R. M. Veatch. *Death, Dying and the Biological Revolution.* New Haven: Yale University Press, 1976; Marshall B. Kapp, Harvey E. Pies, and A. Edward Doudera, eds. *Legal and Ethical Aspects of Health Care for the Elderly.* Ann Arbor, Michigan: Health Administration Press, School of Public Health, University of Michigan, 1985.) *See also* Concern for Dying.

lobbying. *See* aging-based interest group.

longevity. Length of life. (Diana S. Woodruff. *Can You Live to Be 100?* New York: Chatham Square Press, 1977; Ursula M. Lehr. "Social-Psychological Correlates of Longevity." In Carl Eisdorfer, ed., *Annual Review of Gerontology and Geriatrics.* Vol. 3. New York: Springer, 1982, pp. 102-47; Thomas B. L. Kirkwood. "Comparative and Evolutionary Aspects of Longevity." In Caleb E. Finch and Edward L. Schneider, eds., *Handbook of the Biology of Aging.* New York: Van Nostrand Reinhold, 1985, pp. 27-44.) *See also* centenarians.

longevity (total index of ancestral). A measure that predicts the longevity of an individual by totaling the ages at death of an individual's parents and four grandparents divided by six. In the event any of these persons are still alive, then their present ages are used or their expected ages at death are predicted from a life expectancy table. This method was developed by Raymond Pearl. (R. Pearl and R. D. Pearl. *The Ancestry of the Long-Lived.* Baltimore: Johns Hopkins University Press, 1934.)

longitudinal design. (1) A method of study in which repeated measures on the same individuals are made at two or more points in time. (2) The study of the same individuals or different individuals from the same cohort* at two or more points in time. Used in this way, longitudinal design refers to both panel studies and intracohort trend studies. A major problem with longitudinal studies is that they cannot distinguish whether age changes* within individuals are the result of the age effect* or the period effect.* Also referred to as the diachronic method. (Paul B. Baltes, Hayne W. Reese, and John R. Nesselroade. *Life-Span Developmental Psychology: Introduction to Research Methods.* Belmont, Calif.: Brooks/Cole, 1977; Norval Glenn.

Cohort Analysis. Beverly Hills, Calif.: Sage, 1977; K. Warner Schaie and C. Hertzog. "Longitudinal Methods." In Benjamin B. Wolman and George Stricker, eds., *Handbook of Developmental Psychology.* Englewood Cliffs, N.J.: Prentice-Hall, 1982, pp. 91-115; Ewald W. Busse and George L. Maddox. *The Duke Longitudinal Studies of Normal Aging, 1955-1980.* New York: Springer, 1985.) *See also* cross-sectional design, intracohort study, panel study.

long-term care. A range of health and social services that are provided on a sustained basis to those persons who have chronic physical and/or mental impairments so that they may be maintained at their optimum level of functioning. In the past long-term care referred only to care in institutions, but today it also includes community-based care. (E. M. Brody. *Long-Term Care of Older People.* New York: Human Sciences, 1977; M. Powell Lawton. *Environment and Aging.* Monterey, Calif.: Brooks/Cole, 1980; Stanley J. Brody and Saul M. Spivack. "Long-Term Health Care Planning: The State of the Practice." In Carl Eisdorfer, ed., *Annual Review of Gerontology and Geriatrics.* Vol. 2. New York: Springer, 1981, pp. 320-41; Theodore H. Koff. *Long-Term Care: An Approach to Serving the Frail Elderly.* Boston: Little, Brown, 1982.)

long-term care facility. Any facility that provides extended care for patients who do not need an acute care hospital. Long-term care facilities include skilled nursing facilities,* intermediate-care facilities,* chronic disease hospitals, and psychiatric hospitals. (Theodore H. Koff. *Long-Term Care: An Approach to Serving the Frail Elderly.* Boston: Little, Brown, 1982.)

long-term disability. *See* disability.

long-term memory (LTM). The memory system in which information is stored for long periods of time or even permanently, except in cases of brain injury or disease. With age some people experience a substantial decline in the acquisition and retrieval of information stored in long-term memory. Also referred to as secondary memory. (Leonard W. Poon. "Differences in Human Memory with Aging: Nature, Causes, and Clinical Implications." In James E. Birren and K. Warner Schaie, eds., *Handbook of the Psychology of Aging.* New York: Van Nostrand Reinhold, 1985, pp. 427-62; Terence M. Hines and James L. Fozard. "Memory and Aging: Relevance of Recent Developments for Research and Application." In Carl Eisdorfer, ed., *Annual Review of Gerontology and Geriatrics.* Vol. 1. New York: Springer, 1980, pp. 97-117.) *See also* short-term memory.

looking-glass self. The concept of self that a person forms from the reaction of others. The looking-glass self has three principal parts: (1) the way we think we look to others; (2) our perception of their judgment of how we look; and (3) our feelings about these judgments. The role losses that an individual experiences with aging affect his or her concept of self or self-image; for example, at retirement the looking-glass composed of one's former colleagues or co-workers gives back a changed image. This concept was introduced by Charles Horton Cooley in 1902. (C. H. Cooley. *Human Nature and the Social Order*. New York: Scribner, 1902.)

M

McLain Movement. An organization founded in 1940 by George McLain, who played a dominant role in pension politics in California until his death in 1965. He devoted himself to bringing about improvements in California's old-age legislation and liberalizing the aged welfare program in the state. McLain's organization was known successively by various names: Old-Age Payment Campaign Committee, the Citizens' Committee for Old-Age Pensions, the California Institute of Social Welfare, and the California League of Senior Citizens. (Jackson K. Putnam. *Old-Age Politics in California: From Richardson to Reagan.* Stanford: Stanford University Press, 1970.)

malignant neoplasms. *See* neoplasia.

mandatory retirement. The imposition of retirement* at a fixed age upon individuals whether they desire it or not; rules in business, industry, and government agencies that terminate employees by a certain age. Until 1978, 65 was the mandatory retirement age. The basis for this age can be traced back to the Social Security Act of 1935 in which the act set 65 as the age of eligibility for social security* payments. American employees then began using 65 as the age for mandatory retirement so that retirement and the time that social security benefits began would coincide. In 1978, with the amending of the Age Discrimination in Employment Act,* age 70 became the mandatory retirement age in the private sector as well as in state and local governments. The upper age limit for federal employees was removed. In 1986 this act was amended to remove the upper age limit of 70 for all workers. Also referred to as compulsory or forced retirement. (Fred Slavick. *Compulsory and Flexible Retirement in the American Economy.* Ithaca, N.Y.: Cornell University Press, 1966; Erdman B. Palmore. "Compulsory versus Flexible Retirement: Issues and Facts." *The Gerontologist,* 1972, 12, pp. 324-48; James H. Schulz. "The Economics of Mandatory Retirement." *Industrial Gerontology,* 1974, 1, pp. 1-10; Lawrence M. Friedman. *Your Time Will Come: The Law of Age Discrimination and Mandatory Retirement.* New York: Russell Sage, 1984.) *See also* flexible retirement.

manifest function. A consequence that is intended and recognized. The term was introduced by Robert K. Merton, who adapted it from use in another context by Sigmund Freud. (R. K. Merton. *Social Theory and Social Structure*. New York: Free Press, 1968.) *See also* latent function.

master status. The most important of a person's many statuses, usually occupational, and therefore it determines an individual's general social position in society.* At retirement* a person often loses his or her master status. Also referred to as key status. (Everett C. Hughes. "Dilemmas and Contradictions of Status." *American Journal of Sociology*, 1945, 50, pp. 353-59.) *See also* status.

matriarchal family. A rare if not nonexistent type of family organization in which the authority is vested in the hands of females. The oldest living female of the family holds the primary authority. (Meyer F. Nimkoff. *Comparative Family Systems*. Boston: Houghton Mifflin, 1965; William J. Goode. *The Family*. Englewood Cliffs, N.J.: Prentice-Hall, 1982.) *See also* egalitarian family, patriarchal family.

matrilineal descent. A family* in which descent or inheritance is traced through the mother and female line. (David M. Schneider. "The Distinctive Features of Matrilineal Descent Groups." In David M. Schneider and Kathleen Gough, eds., *Matrilineal Kinship*. Berkeley: University of California Press, 1961; Meyer F. Nimkoff. *Comparative Family Systems*. Boston: Houghton Mifflin, 1965; William J. Goode. *The Family*. Englewood Cliffs, N.J.: Prentice-Hall, 1982.) *See also* bilateral descent, patrilineal descent.

matrilocal residence. A family system in which the married couple are expected to live with the wife's family. (Meyer F. Nimkoff. *Comparative Family Systems*. Boston: Houghton Mifflin, 1965; William J. Goode. *The Family*. Englewood Cliffs, N.J.: Prentice-Hall, 1982.) *See also* neolocal residence, patrilocal residence.

maturation effect. *See* age effect.

mature aging populations. *See* aged nations.

maturity. (1) "The capacity of individuals to undergo continual change in order to adapt successfully and cope flexibly with the demands and responsibilities of life" (James W. Vander Zanden). (2) The state of having reached full development or growth. Often used with an adjective preceding it to specify the kind of development; for example, emotional maturity, intellectual maturity, and so on. (Jaber F. Gubrium and David R. Buckholdt. *Toward Maturity: The Social Processing of Human Development*. San Francisco: Jossey-Bass, 1977; Douglas H. Heath. *Maturity and*

Competence: A Transcultural View. New York: Gardner, 1977; J. W. Vander Zanden. *Human Development.* New York: Alfred A. Knopf, 1978.)

maximum life span potential. *See* life span.

Meals-on-Wheels. *See* home delivered meals program.

mean. (μ) A measure of central tendency in which the sum of the values of a variable* for all observations in a data set are divided by the total number of observations; arithmetic average. (Mark Abrahamson. *Social Research Methods.* Englewood Cliffs, N.J.: Prentice-Hall, 1983; Earl R. Babbie. *The Practice of Social Research.* Belmont, Calif.: Wadsworth, 1983). *See also* median, mode.

means test. A requirement of eligibility for financial aid or social services* that is dependent on the amount of income and assets that an individual or a family has. (James H. Schulz. *The Economics of Aging.* Belmont, Calif.: Wadsworth, 1976; Albert J. E. Wilson. *Social Services for Older Persons.* Boston: Little, Brown, 1984.)

median (Md). A measure of central tendency that divides a distribution into two equal parts. (Mark Abrahamson. *Social Research Methods.* Englewood Cliffs, N.J.: Prentice-Hall, 1983; Earl R. Babbie. *The Practice of Social Research.* Belmont, Calif.: Wadsworth, 1983.) *See also* mean, mode.

median age. The age that divides the population into two equal-size segments, one of which is younger than the median, and one of which is older than the median. This term is used for describing a population as "young" or "old." For example, when the median age rises, the population may be said to be aging and when it drops the population may be said to be growing younger. (Henry S. Shryock, Jacob S. Siegel, and Associates. *The Methods and Materials of Demography.* New York: Academic Press, 1976.)

median income. That income value that divides income recipients or families into two equal parts, one higher and one lower than the median.* The median income for the elderly is less than that of younger age groups; for example in 1985 persons age 65 years and over had a median income of $19,117 whereas persons aged 25 to 64 had a median income of $30,504. (Henry S. Shryock, Jacob S. Siegel, and Associates. *The Methods and Materials of Demography.* New York: Academic Press, 1976.)

Medicaid. Enacted in 1965, this comprehensive program, which provides health care for low-income persons of all ages, is jointly financed by the states and the federal government. Unlike Medicare,* it provides for long-term care services for the elderly. It is authorized through Title XIX of the Social Security Act. (Karen Davis. "Health Care Policies and the Aged: Observations from the United States." In Robert H. Binstock and Ethel Shanas, eds., *Handbook of Aging and the Social Sciences*. New York: Van Nostrand Reinhold, 1985, pp. 727-44; John F. Holahan and Joel W. Cohen. *Medicaid: The Trade-off between Cost Containment and Access to Care*. Washington, D.C. The Urban Institute, 1986.) *See also* Medicare.

medical sociology. A subfield of sociology* that deals with the social aspects of illness, the modern health-care system, and the development of health-care institutions. (David Mechanic. *Medical Sociology*. New York: Free Press, 1978; William C. Cockerham. *Medical Sociology*. Englewood Cliffs, N.J.: Prentice-Hall, 1982.) *See also* epidemiology, health, sick role.

medicalization of life. The extension of medical jurisdiction to problems and behavior that previously were not considered as medical; for example, alcoholism and drug addiction. According to Arnold Arluke and John Peterson, today old age is being defined as a medical problem, and medicine is increasingly being used as means to control the behavior of older persons. (Ivan Illich. *Medical Nemesis: The Expropriation of Health*. New York: Pantheon, 1976; A. Arluke and J. Peterson. "Accidental Medicalization of Old Age and Its Social Control Implications." In Christine L. Fry and Contributors, *Dimensions: Aging, Culture and Health*. New York: Praeger, 1981, pp. 271-84.)

Medicare. Enacted in 1965, this federal program provides health insurance for persons 65 and over, people of any age with permanent kidney failure, and certain disabled persons. Medicare consists of two parts: Part A (hospital insurance) helps pay for hospital care, and after hospitalization a stay in a skilled nursing facility* (up to 100 days), home health care, and hospice* care. Part B (medical insurance) helps pay for physicians' services, outpatient hospital services, home health services, as well as a number of other services and items. Part A is supported by the social security payroll tax and Part B is maintained by monthly premiums paid by Medicare enrollees and general revenues. Medicare is authorized through Title XVIII of the Social Security Act. (Theodore Marmor. *The Politics of Medicare*. Chicago: Aldine, 1970; Karen Davis. "Health Care Policies and the Aged: Observations from the United States." In Robert H. Binstock and Ethel Shanas, eds., *Handbook of Aging and the Social Sciences*. New York: Van Nostrand Reinhold, 1985, pp. 727-44.) *See also* Medicaid, diagnosis-related groups, prospective payment system.

Medigap insurance. Insurance policies available from private insurance companies to supplement Medicare coverage. (J. J. Feder. "Health." In J.

L. Palmer and I. V. Sawhill, eds., *The Reagan Experiment*. Washington, D.C.: Urban Institute, 1982.)

memory. *See* long-term memory, short-term memory.

menopause. The permanent cessation of menstruation and the reproductive capacity in women. Menopause is an event that occurs during the climacteric* and generally between the ages of 45 and 55. Commonly referred to as the "change of life." (A. Voder, M. Dinnerstein, and S. O'Donnell, eds. *Changing Perspectives on Menopause*. Austin: University of Texas Press, 1982; Howard L. Judd and Stanley G. Korenman. "Effects of Aging on Reproductive Function in Women." In Stanley G. Korenman, ed., *Endocrine Aspects of Aging*. New York: Elsevier, 1982, pp. 163-97.) *See also* hot flash.

middle age. A period that usually begins between 35 to 40 years and ends somewhere between 60 and 65 years. A relatively recent development in the life course* with the increase of life expectancy.* (Bernice L. Neugarten. *Middle Age and Aging*. Chicago: University of Chicago Press, 1968; K. Warner Schaie and Sherry L. Willis. *Adult Development and Aging*. Boston: Little, Brown, 1986.)

midlife crisis. A period often occurring between the ages of 40 and 50 in which individuals realize the incompatibility of their hopes and dreams with their present life and a growing awareness of their own mortality. The term was introduced by Elliot Jacques in 1965. (E. Jacques. "Death and the Midlife Crisis." *International Journal of Psychoanalysis*, 1965, 46, pp. 502-14; Stanley D. Rosenberg and Michael P. Farrell. "Identity and Crisis in Middle-Aged Men." *International Journal of Aging and Human Development*, 1976, 7, pp. 153-70.)

minority group. A category or group of people who in some way differ from the dominant group in society (e.g., by race or ethnicity) and because of this difference they are the object of prejudice* and discrimination* that results in their being disadvantaged. Some writers argue that the elderly constitute a minority group, while others maintain that elderly persons, especially retirees, have some of the characteristics of minority status. (Louis Wirth. "The Problem of Minority Groups." In Ralph Linton, ed., *The Science of Man in the World Crisis*. New York: Columbia University Press, 1945, pp. 347-72; Milton Barron. "Minority Group Characteristics in the Aged in American Society." *Journal of Gerontology*, 1953, 8, pp. 477-82; Gordon F. Streib. "Are the Aged a Minority Group?" In Alvin W. Gouldner and S. M. Miller, eds., *Applied Sociology*. New York: Free Press, 1965, pp. 311-28; Sharon M. Fujii. "Minority Group Elderly: Demographic

Characteristics and Implications for Public Policy." In Carl Eisdorfer, ed., *Annual Review of Gerontology and Geriatrics*. Vol. 1. New York: Springer, 1980, pp. 261-84; Ron C. Manuel, ed. *Minority Aging: Sociological and Social Psychological Issues*. Westport, Conn.: Greenwood Press, 1982.) *See also* ethnic group.

mobile home. A stationary, detached, freestanding single-family dwelling generally situated on a site in a mobile home park. Mobile homes were introduced into the U.S. in the 1930s. A substantial number of elderly persons live in these units today. (Sheila K. Johnson. *Idle Haven: Community Building among the Working Class Retired*. Berkeley: University of California Press, 1971; Barbara A. Haley. "Are Mobile Homes a Solution to the Housing Problems of Low-Income Elderly?" In R. J. Newcomer, M. P. Powell, and Thomas O. Byertz, eds., *Housing an Aging Society*. New York: Van Nostrand Reinhold, 1986, pp. 217-28.)

mobile meals. *See* home-delivered meals program.

mode (Mo). The value* that appears most often in a series. (Mark Abrahamson. *Social Research Methods*. Englewood Cliffs, N.J.: Prentice-Hall, 1983; Earl R. Babbie. *The Practice of Social Research*. Belmont, Calif.: Wadsworth, 1983.) *See also* mean, median.

modernization. The social and cultural changes brought about by industrialization.* Donald O. Cowgill defines modernization as "the transformation of a total society from a relatively rural way of life based on animate power, limited technology, relatively undifferentiated institutions, parochial and traditional outlook and values, toward a predominantly urban way of life based on inanimate sources of power, highly developed scientific technology, highly differentiated institutions matched by segmented individual roles, and a cosmopolitan outlook which emphasizes efficiency and progress." Sometimes used as a synonym for westernization, and industrialization. (D. O. Cowgill. "Aging and Modernization: A Revision of the Theory." In Jaber F. Gubrium, ed., *Late Life: Communities and Environmental Policy*. Springfield, Ill.: Charles C. Thomas, 1974; Erdman B. Palmore and Kenneth Manton. "Modernization and Status of the Aged: International Correlations." *Journal of Gerontology*, 1974, 29, pp. 205-10.) *See also* acculturation, industrialization, social change.

modernization theory. Proposed by Donald O. Cowgill and Lowell D. Holmes, this theory asserts that with increasing modernization* the status* of the elderly declines. In a revision of the theory, Cowgill points out that "while modernization is detrimental to the status and the interests of the aged in its early stages, this trend may 'bottom out' in later stages of modernization and from then on there is some comparative improvement in the status and condition of older people." (Donald O. Cowgill and Lowell D. Holmes, eds. *Aging and Modernization*. New York: Appleton-Century-Crofts, 1972; Donald O. Cowgill. "Aging and Modernization: A Revision of the Theory." In Jaber F. Gubrium, ed., *Late Life: Communities and Environmental Policy*. Springfield, Ill.: Charles C. Thomas, 1974.)

modified extended family. The organized structure of family networks and their patterns of mutual aid. This structure is composed of partially independent nuclear families that exchange goods, services, and emotional support but maintain separate households from one another. Some writers refer to this type of family form as "intimacy at a distance."* Used interchangeably with extended kin network. (Marvin B. Sussman and Lee Burchinal. "Kin Family Network: An Unheralded Structure in Current Conceptualizations of Family Functioning." *Marriage and Family Living*, 1962, 24, pp. 231-40; Marvin B. Sussman. "Relationships of Adult Children with Their Parents in the United States." In Ethel Shanas and Gordon Streib, eds., *Social Structure and the Family: Generational Relations*. Englewood Cliffs, N.J.: Prentice-Hall, 1965, pp. 62-92.) *See also* extended family, nuclear family, stem family.

morale. *See* life satisfaction.

morbidity. The extent of disease* and disability* in a population.* (Ethel Shanas and George L. Maddox. "Health, Health Resources, and Utilization of Care." In Robert H. Binstock and Ethel Shanas, eds., *Handbook of the Social Sciences and Aging*. New York: Van Nostrand Reinhold, 1985, pp. 696-726; L. White et al. "Geriatric Epidemiology." In Carl Eisdorfer, ed., *Annual Review of Gerontology and Geriatrics*. Vol. 6. New York: Springer, 1986.) *See also* epidemiology, medical sociology.

mores. Norms* that govern the moral standards of a society* and are considered important for the group's welfare. Unlike folkways,* any violation of the mores carries strong disapproval; for example, elder abuse.* The singular of mores is mos. (William G. Sumner. *Folkways*. Boston: Ginn, 1906.)

mortality differentials. *See* differential mortality.

mortality revolution. This phrase refers to the increase in life expectancy,* the low infant death rate, and the control of infectious diseases that have taken place in recent years. (C. Goldscheider. *Population, Modernization and Social Sciences*. Boston: Little, Brown, 1971, pp. 102-34.)

Figure 5
Diagram of Aging and Modernization Theory

SALIENT ASPECTS   INTERVENING VARIABLES

OF

MODERNIZATION

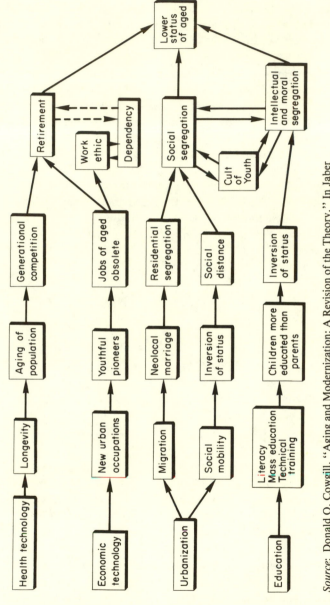

Source: Donald O. Cowgill. "Aging and Modernization: A Revision of the Theory." In Jaber F. Gubrium, ed., *Late Life Communities and Environmental Policy.* Springfield, Ill.: Charles C. Thomas, 1974, p. 141. Courtesy of Charles C. Thomas, Publisher, Springfield, Illinois.

mother-in-law apartments. *See* accessory apartments.

mourning. A process determined by custom in which one expresses grief.* (Robert Fulton. *Death and Identity*. New York: John Wiley, 1965.) *See also* bereavement.

multidisciplinary research. Group research in which individuals from several scientific disciplines work parallel to one another on a common area of interest such as aging. (Marian G. Spencer and Caroline J. Dorr. *Understanding Aging: A Multidisciplinary Approach*. New York: Appleton-Century-Crofts, 1975; Ewald W. Busse and Eric Pfeiffer. *Behavior and Adaptation in Later Life*. Boston: Little, Brown, 1977.) *See also* interdisciplinary research.

multigeneration family households. Older persons living in the home of their adult children and/or grandchildren or adult children and/or grandchildren returning to the parental home to live with the older generation. Two, three, or even four generations may live in the same household. (Joan F. Robertson. "Interaction in Three Generation Families: Parents as Mediators." *International Journal of Aging and Human Development*, 1975, 6, pp. 103-10; C. H. Mindell. "Multigenerational Family Households: Recent Trends and Implications for the Future." *The Gerontologist*, 1979, 19, pp. 456-63; Ethel Shanas. "Older People and Their Families: The New Pioneers." *Journal of Marriage and the Family*, 1980, 42, pp. 9-15; Timothy H. Brubaker. *Later Life Families*. Beverly Hills, Calif.: Sage, 1985.)

multi-infarct dementia. A type of dementia* that results from damage to the cerebral blood vessels. It is characterized by a progressive but uneven loss of intellectual functions and/or some neurological abnormalities. The onset of multi-infarct dementia is usually from middle age* to about age 70. Also referred to as cerebral arteriosclerosis. (Murray A. Raskind and Michael C. Storrie. "The Organic Mental Disorders." In Ewald W. Busse and Dan G. Blazer, eds., *Handbook of Geriatric Psychiatry*. New York: Van Nostrand Reinhold, 1980; Sander Glatt and Robert Katzman. "Multi-Infarct Dementia." In Carl Eisdorfer, ed., *Annual Review of Gerontology and Geriatrics*. Vol. 4. New York: Springer, 1984, pp. 61-86.) *See also* senile dementia.

multiple correlation. A coefficient expressing the relationship between a dependent variable* and a number of independent variables. (Mark Abrahamson. *Social Research Methods*. Englewood Cliffs, N.J.: Prentice-Hall, 1983; Earl R. Babbie. *The Practice of Social Research*. Belmont, Calif.: Wadsworth, 1983.) *See also* correlation, independent variable.

multiple jeopardy. *See* double jeopardy.

multiple stress theory. This theory maintains that mental disorders result from the accumulation of stress throughout life. Some older persons, according to this theory, experience more stress than others, and repeated stress eventually places a strain on one's adaptive capacity, which may eventually result in a breakdown. (Marjorie F. Lowenthal. *Aging and Mental Disorder in San Francisco*. San Francisco: Jossey-Bass, 1967.)

multipurpose senior center. *See* senior center.

multivariate analysis. This technique is employed in statistical research in which two or more variables are involved. It refers to the analysis of the relationships among them. (J. P. Van de Geer. *Introduction to Multivariate Analysis for the Social Sciences*. San Francisco: W. H. Freeman, 1971; H. M. Blalock. *Social Statistics*. New York: McGraw-Hill, 1972.) *See also* variable.

myocardial infarction. Commonly referred to as a heart attack, this condition results in damage to the heart muscle as a result of the circulation of the blood being interrupted in the coronary arteries. Literally, the term means "heart muscle death." Also referred to as a coronary. (F. I. Caird and R. D. Kennedy. "Epidemiology of Heart Disease in Old Age." In F. I. Caird and J.L.C. Dall, and R. D. Kennedy, eds., *Cardiology in Old Age*. New York: Plenum, 1976, pp. 1-10.) *See also* cardiovascular disease, coronary artery disease.

myopia. A condition in which the eyeball becomes somewhat elongated, and as a result, objects viewed at a distance appear blurred. Commonly referred to as nearsightedness. (A. P. Weiss. "Sensory Functions." In James E. Birren, ed., *Handbook of Aging and the Individual*. Chicago: University of Chicago Press, 1959, pp. 505-42; Francis B. Colavita. *Sensory Changes in the Elderly*. Springfield, Ill.: Charles C. Thomas, 1978.) *See also* presbyopia.

National Association of Area Agencies on Aging (N4A). A private, non-profit organization that works toward a responsible national policy on aging* and serves as an advocate for the elderly's needs at the national level, as well as a link to the national network on aging. (National Association of Area Agencies on Aging, West Wing, Suite 208, 600 Maryland Avenue S.W., Washington, D.C. 20042.)

National Association of Retired Federal Employees (NARFE). Founded in 1921, this organization promotes, sponsors, and supports federal legislation on behalf of retired civil servants. It has been a strong advocate of liberalizing the Civil Service Retirement Law and eliminating its restrictions and inequities. (Henry J. Pratt. "Old Age Associations in National Politics." *Annals of the American Academy of Political and Social Sciences.* 1974. Vol. 415. pp. 106-19; Henry J. Pratt. *The Gray Lobby.* Chicago: University of Chicago Press, 1976.)

National Association of State Units on Aging (NASUA). Founded in 1964, this association serves as a channel for the exchange of information on problems of older persons with the State Units on Aging* and with other aging-based organizations. Also, it keeps states informed about federal legislation and policies. Membership is composed mainly of the staff of state units and member agencies. (National Association of State Units on Aging, West Wing, Suite 208, 600 Maryland Ave. S.W., Washington, D.C. 20042.)

National Council of Senior Citizens (NCSC). An educational and action group that is composed of senior centers along with organizations and councils associated with the elderly. The council supports Medicare,* increased social security,* better housing, and a number of other programs and issues concerning older people. Founded in 1961, the NCSC was an outgrowth of the "Seniors for Kennedy" movement. Later it became strongly supported by labor unions and helped push for the passage of Medicare. (Henry J. Pratt. *The Gray Lobby.* Chicago:. University of Chicago Press, 1976.)

National Council on the Aging (NCOA). Founded in 1950, the council cooperates with other organizations to promote concern for the elderly and

to develop ways of meeting their needs. It holds workshops and conferences, provides demonstration programs, and conducts research on the
problems of older persons. The NCOA publishes a quarterly bibliography,
Current Literature on Aging, two magazines, *Perspective on Aging* and
Aging and Work, as well as various books and brochures dealing with
aging. (Henry J. Pratt. *The Gray Lobby*. Chicago: University of Chicago
Press, 1976.)

National Institute on Aging (NIA). The nation's leading research center on
aging,* which was established in 1974 by Congress as a separate institute in
the National Institutes of Health for the "conduct and support of biomedical, social, and behavioral research and training related to the aging
process and the diseases and other special problems and needs of the aged."
Under the leadership of Robert N. Butler, its first director, NIA established
its two major priorities: research on senile dementia* of the Alzheimer's
type and the stimulation of interest in geriatric medicine among medical
schools. (R. N. Butler. "Guest Editorial: Early Directions for the National
Institute on Aging." *The Gerontologist*, 1976, 16, pp. 293-94; National
Institute on Aging, National Institutes of Health, Bethesda, Md. 20205.)

National Retired Teachers Association (NRTA). *See* American Association
of Retired Persons.

National Volunteer Agency. *See* ACTION.

Native American elderly. The Native American population consists of
Indians, Eskimos, and Aleuts. The proportion of elderly persons in this
population has increased more rapidly than in other ethnic groups.
(National Indian Council on Aging. *American Indian Elderly: A National
Profile*. Albuquerque, N.M.: National Indian Council on Aging, 1981.) *See
also* ethnic group, minority group.

natural increase. The number of births minus the number of deaths in a
given population during a certain period of time, usually a year. (T. Lynn
Smith and Paul E. Zopf. *Demography: Principles and Methods*. Port
Washington, N.Y.: Alfred, 1976.)

nearsightedness. *See* myopia.

negative correlation. *See* correlation.

neolocal residence. A family system in which the married couple is expected
to establish a new residence separate from their parents, thus creating a
nuclear family.* (Meyer F. Nimkoff. *Comparative Family Systems*.

Boston: Houghton Mifflin, 1965.) *See also* matrilocal residence, patrilocal residence.

neoplasia. The development of any new and abnormal growth of body tissue; a tumor. The abnormal growth is called a neoplasm. Malignant neoplasms are commonly referred to as cancer, which is the second leading cause of death in the United States for persons aged 65 and over. (Jeffrey Crawford and Harvey J. Cohen. "Aging and Neoplasia." In Carl Eisdorfer, ed., *Annual Review of Gerontology and Geriatrics.* Vol. 4. New York: Springer, 1984, pp. 3-32.)

neurosis. An emotional disturbance in which there is an inability to cope satisfactorily with anxiety* or internal conflict. However, while there is an impairment in psychological functioning, there is no break with reality as in psychosis.* Under the stresses of later life, earlier neurotic behavior may reappear. Most types of neuroses seldom occur for the first time in old age.* Also referred to as psychoneurosis. (James E. Birren and R. Bruce Sloane, eds. *Handbook of Mental Health and Aging.* Englewood Cliffs, N.J.: Prentice-Hall, 1980.)

New School for Social Research. *See* Institute for Retired Professionals.

norms. (1) Shared standards or rules for behavior to which members of a group* are expected to conform. Conformity is enforced by positive and negative sanctions. Mutual aid between aging parents and their adult children is an example. (2) In a statistical sense, norms are baseline measures or scores used for comparison. (William G. Sumner. *Folkways.* Boston: Ginn, 1906; Muzafer Sherif. *The Psychology of Social Norms.* New York: Harper and Row, 1936; Judith Blake and Kingsley Davis. "Norms, Values and Sanctions." In Robert E. L. Faris, ed., *Handbook of Modern Sociology.* Chicago: Rand McNally, 1964; Gordon Bultena and Vivian Wood. "Normative Attitudes toward the Aged Role among Migrant and Non Migrant Retirees." *The Gerontologist*, 1969, 9, pt. 1, pp. 204-8; Vivian Wood. "Age Appropriate Behavior of Older People." *The Gerontologist*, 1971, 2, pt. 2, pp. 74-78.) *See also* age norms, folkways, mores.

nuclear family. A family* unit consisting of husband, wife, and their dependent offspring. Used interchangeably with conjugal family when referring to the family unit. However, the term "conjugal" is preferable when referring to the family system as a whole. The nuclear family is the basic unit of family organization and is the most common form of family in industrialized societies. A nuclear family may be a separate family or part of a larger family such as a polygamous family. (George P. Murdock. *Social Structure.* New York: Macmillan, 1949; William J. Goode. *The Family.*

Englewood Cliffs, N.J.: Prentice-Hall, 1982.) *See also* extended family, modified extended family, stem family.

null hypothesis (Ho). A hypothesis* that states that there is no relationship between two variables or that there is no difference in the groups that are being tested. (Bernard S. Phillips. *Social Research: Strategy and Tactics.* New York: Macmillan, 1976; Earl Babbie. *The Practice of Social Research.* Belmont, Calif.: Wadsworth, 1983.) *See also* variable.

nursing home. A generic term for any residential facility that gives some level of nursing care. (Burton D. Dunlop. *The Growth of Nursing Home Care.* Lexington, Mass.: D. C. Heath, 1979; B. C. Vladeck. *Unloving Care: The Nursing Home Tragedy.* New York: Basic Books, 1980.) *See also* extended care facility, intermediate care facility, skilled nursing facility.

nutrition programs. *See* home-delivered meals program and congregate meals program.

O

OARS. *See* Older Americans Resources and Services Multidimensional Functional Assessment Questionnaire.

Obasute. A recurrent theme throughout Japanese literature dating back to the sixth century in which adult children were supposed to have taken their elderly parents to a mountain and abandoned them. (Simone de Beauvoir. *The Coming of Age.* New York: G. P. Putnam's Sons, 1972; David Plath. " 'Ecstasy Years'—Old Age in Japan." *Pacific Affairs*, 1973, 46, pp. 421-29.)

observational study. A study in which the investigator simply watches, records, and interprets what is happening. (Earl R. Babbie. *The Practice of Social Research.* Belmont, Calif.: Wadsworth, 1983.)

off-time/on-time. A description of one's position within the social time-tables regarding life events.* For example, a person may consider himself or herself "off-time" in starting a family at age 40 but "on-time" in retiring at age 65. (Bernice L. Neugarten. "Adaptation and the Life Cycle." *Journal of Geriatric Psychology*, 1970, 4, pp. 71-87; Gunhild O. Hagestad and Bernice L. Neugarten. "Age and the Life Course." In Robert H. Binstock and Ethel Shanas, eds., *Handbook of Aging and the Social Sciences.* New York: Van Nostrand Reinhold, 1985, pp. 35-61.) *See also* career timetable, social clock.

old age. The last period in the life course.* The definition of old age varies from culture* to culture. In American society we define old age chronologically (the number of years a person has lived) and place the onset of old age at 65. However, this age is purely arbitrary. It has no basis in reality as the point at which a person becomes old. Some nonindustrial societies define old age in terms of the work that a person is capable of doing, and still others define old age socially in terms of role transitions (e.g., becoming a grandparent). Still others use a combination of all of the above. Used interchangeably with late life, later maturity, and senescence. (Margaret Clark and Barbara G. Anderson. *Culture and Aging: An Anthropological Study of Older Americans.* Springfield, Ill.: Charles C. Thomas, 1967; Bernice L. Neugarten and Joan W. Moore. "The Changing Age-Status

System." In B. Neugarten, ed., *Middle Age and Aging*. Chicago: University of Chicago Press, 1968, pp. 5-21; Janet Roebuck. "When Does Old Age Begin? The Evolution of the English Definition." *Journal of Social History*, 1979, 12, pp. 416-28; Anthony P. Glascock and Susan L. Feinman. "Social Asset or Social Burden: Treatment of the Aged in Non-Industrialized Societies." In Christine L. Fry, ed., *Dimensions: Aging, Culture, and Health*. Brooklyn, N.Y.: Praeger, 1981.) *See also* chronological age, functional age, social age.

Old-Age, Survivors, and Disability Insurance (OASDI). *See* social security.

Old Age Assistance (OAA). A federal-state program for financial aid to the needy elderly provided for under the Social Security Act of 1935. OAA was replaced in 1974 by the Supplemental Security Income Program (SSI).* (Margaret S. Gordon. "Aging and Income Security." In Clark Tibbitts, ed., *Handbook of Social Gerontology*. Chicago: University of Chicago Press, 1960, pp. 208-60.)

old age association. *See* aging-based organization.

old-age dependency ratio. *See* age dependency ratio.

old age institutions. A term that includes all types of nursing homes* and domiciliary-care homes* for the elderly. (Barbara B. Manard, Cary S. Kart, and Dirk W. L. van Gils. *Old Age Institutions*. Lexington, Mass.: Lexington Books, 1975; M. Powell Lawton. *Environment and Aging*. Monterey, Calif.: Brooks/Cole, 1980.)

old age movements. *See* End Poverty in California, Gray Panthers, Ham and Eggs Movement, McClain Movement, Townsend Movement.

older adult worker. An individual aged 40 or over. (Harvey L. Sterns. "Training and Retraining Adult and Older Adult Workers." In James E. Birren, Pauline K. Robinson, Judy E. Livingston, eds., *Age, Health, and Employment*. Englewood Cliffs, N.J.: Prentice-Hall, 1986, pp. 93-113.) *See also* Age Discrimination in Employment Act.

Older Americans Act (OAA). Enacted in 1965, this legislation represents the first attempt to establish program objectives and funding to improve the lives of the elderly and to provide for their special needs through federal, state, and local agencies. Title I of the OAA includes the following objectives for the elderly: to provide an adequate income in retirement, suitable housing, employment without discrimination, the best possible physical and mental health, and cultural and recreational activities. (Lorin E.

Baumhover and Joan D. Jones. *Handbook of American Aging Programs.*
Westport, Conn.: Greenwood Press, 1977; Louis Lowy. *Social Policies and
Programs on Aging.* Lexington, Mass.: Lexington Books, 1980; Donald E.
Gelfand. *The Aging Network: Programs and Services.* New York: Springer,
1984.)

**Older Americans Resources and Services (OARS) Multidimensional Func-
tional Assessment Questionnaire.** A two-part instrument that measures
functional status and service use in adults aged 18 and over. However, it has
mainly been used for the elderly. Part A is designed to rate five levels of
functioning: social, economic, mental, physical, and activities of daily
living (ADL). Part B deals with the use and need of services (e.g.,
transportation, social and recreational services, employment, etc.) (Duke
Center. *Multidimensional   Functional   Assessment: The   OARS
Methodology.* Durham, N.C.: Duke University Center for the Study of
Aging and Human Development, 1978; George L. Maddox and D. C.
Dellinger. "Assessment of Functional Status in a Program Evaluation and
Resource Allocation Model." *Annals of the American Academy of
Political and Social Sciences.* Vol. 438. 1978. pp. 59-70.) *See also* Activities
of Daily Living, Index of; Instrumental Activities of Daily Living Scale
(IADL).

Older American Volunteer Programs (OAVP). The Office of the Older
American Volunteer Programs is the largest of the ACTION* program
components and manages the Retired Senior Volunteer Program (RSVP),*
the Foster Grandparent Program (FGP),* and the Senior Companion Program (SCP).* (Action/OAVP, 806 Connecticut Ave. N.W., Washington,
D.C. 20525.)

older person. An individual who is age 65 or older. An older person is
defined in modern Western societies in terms of chronological age (the
number of years a person has lived). Many nonindustrial societies use a different criterion or a combination of criteria to define an older person. The
term "older person" is used interchangeably with aged, old person, older
adult, older American, elderly, senior citizen, senior, golden-ager, and
senescent. (Margaret Clark and Barbara G. Anderson. *Culture and Aging:
An Anthropological Study of Older Americans.* Springfield, Ill.: Charles C.
Thomas, 1967; Anthony P. Glascock and Susan L. Feinman. "Social Asset
or Social Burden: Treatment of the Aged in Non-Industrialized Societies."
In Christine L. Fry, ed., *Dimensions: Aging, Culture, and Health.*
Brooklyn, N.Y.: Praeger, 1981.) *See also* old age.

Older Women's League (OWL). Founded in 1980, this national advocacy
organization focuses exclusively on issues of special concern to midlife and

older women. (Older Women's League, 730 11th St., Suite 300, Washington, D.C. 20001).

oldest-old. Persons aged 85 and over. (R. Suzman and Matilda W. Riley, eds. "The Oldest Old." [Special Issue]. *Milbank Memorial Fund Quarterly*, 1985, 63.) *See also* old-old, young-old.

Old Folks Picnic Association. This association was founded in the 1920s by C. H. Parsons for the purpose of dealing with the psychological and social problems of the elderly in California. (Jackson K. Putnam. *Old-Age Politics in California: From Richardson to Reagan.* Stanford: Stanford University Press, 1970.)

old-old. Persons who are 75 to 84 years of age. Bernice L. Neugarten introduced this term in 1974. (B. L. Neugarten. "Age Groups in American Society and the Rise of the Young-Old." *Annals of the American Academy of Political and Social Science.* Vol. 415. 1974, p. 191; B. L. Neugarten. "The Future of the Young-Old." *The Gerontologist*, 1975, 15, pp. 4-9.) *See also* frail elderly, oldest-old, young-old.

ombudsman program. Mandated and funded by the Older Americans Act amendments of 1975, these programs have been instituted at both local and state levels to receive complaints from nursing home residents. The ombudsman acts as an advocate for the institutionalized elderly by assessing and verifying each complaint and then seeking to resolve it. The ombudsman concept originated in Scandinavia in the nineteenth century. (Howard Litwin. "Ombudsman Services." In Abraham Monk, ed., *Handbook of Gerontological Services.* New York: Van Nostrand Reinhold, 1985, pp. 514-30.)

open-ended question. A question in which the respondent* is free to answer without being restricted to a list of alternatives. (H. W. Smith. *Strategies of Social Research.* Englewood Cliffs, N.J.: Prentice-Hall, 1981; Charles F. Cannell and Robert L. Kahn. "Interviewing." In Gardner Lindzey and Elliot Aronson, eds., *Handbook of Social Psychology.* Vol. 2. Reading, Mass.: Addison-Wesley, 1968, pp. 526-95.) *See also* closed-ended question.

"open window" option. This plan offers the employee an attractive lump-sum benefit and early pension benefits in exchange for his or her early retirement. Also called the "golden handshake" option. (U.S. Senate. *Developments in Aging: 1985.* A Report of the Special Committee on Aging. Washington, D.C.: U.S. Government Printing Office, 1984; Thomas D. Leavitt. *Early Retirement Incentive Programs.* Waltham, Mass.: Policy Center on Aging, Brandeis University, 1983.)

operational definition. A definition that translates an abstract concept into something which can be observed so that it may be measured and tested; a definition that specifies an observable indicator. For example, the operational definition of social life space might be a quantitative estimate of the number of contacts a respondent has in a month. (Elaine Cumming and William Henry. *Growing Old*. New York: Basic Books, 1961, p. 4; Earl R. Babbie. *The Practice of Social Research*. Belmont, Calif.: Wadsworth, 1983.)

oral history. The systematic gathering of the recollections of individuals, usually older persons, through detailed interviews about some past phenomena that they experienced. (P. Thompson. *The Voice of the Past: Oral History*. Oxford University Press, 1978; Carl Ryant. "Comment: Oral History and Gerontology." *The Gerontologist*, 1981, 21, pp. 104-105.) *See also* historical method.

organic brain syndrome. *See* organic mental disorder.

organic disorders. Disturbances that are caused by a known pathological or organic condition. (Robert N. Butler and Myrna I. Lewis. *Aging and Mental Health*. St. Louis: C. V. Mosby, 1982.) *See also* functional disorders.

organic mental disorder. A temporary or permanent dysfunction of the brain in which the origin or cause is known or can be inferred from other information. A general term used to encompass a number of organic mental disorders is organic brain syndrome. The most common organic brain syndromes found in the elderly are delirium* and dementia.* (B. Seltzer and I. Sherwin. "Organic Brain Syndromes: An Empirical Study and Review." *American Journal of Psychiatry*, 1978, 135, pp. 13-21; Richard A. Hussian. *Geriatric Psychology: A Behavioral Perspective*. New York: Van Nostrand Reinhold, 1981; Robert N. Butler and Myrna I. Lewis. *Aging and Mental Health*. St. Louis: C. V. Mosby, 1982.)

osteoporosis. A crippling, disfiguring disease due to bone loss. While it affects both sexes, women are much more likely to be affected by it. After menopause* women lose bone mass six times more rapidly than men. Around age 65 the rate of bone loss slows. (Louis V. Avioli. "Aging, Bone and Osteoporosis." In Stanley G. Korenman, ed., *Endocrine Aspects of Aging*. New York: Elsevier, 1982, pp. 199-230; A. N. Exton-Smith. "Mineral Metabolism." In Caleb E. Finch and Edward L. Schneider, eds., *Handbook of the Biology of Aging*. New York: Van Nostrand Reinhold, 1985, pp. 511-39.)

OWL. *See* Older Women's League.

P

pacemakers. (1) Regulative mechanisms that control the sequence of physiological changes that occur with aging (Caleb E. Finch). Some researchers have postulated that pacemakers may be located in the hypothalamus, thymus, thyroid, or pituitary gland. (2) Artificial devices that help regulate the heartbeat. (C. E. Finch. "Monamine Metabolism in the Aging Male Mouse." In M. Rockstein and M. L. Sussman, eds., *Development and Aging in the Nervous System*. New York: Academic Press, 1973, pp. 199-213; Arthur V. Everitt. "Pacemaker Mechanisms in Aging and the Diseases of Aging." In H. T. Bleumenthal, ed., *Handbook of Diseases of Aging*. New York: Van Nostrand Reinhold, 1983, pp. 93-132.) *See also* aging clock theory.

Pacific-Islander elderly. *See* Asian-American and Pacific-Islander elderly.

PADL. *See* Activities of Daily Living, Index of.

panel study. A type of longitudinal design in which the same individuals are studied at two or more points in time. Often used synonymously with longitudinal design. (Norval D. Glenn. *Cohort Analysis*. Beverly Hills, Calif.: Sage, 1977; K. Warner Schaie and C. Hertzog. "Longitudinal Methods." In Benjamin B. Wolman and George Stricker, eds., *Handbook of Developmental Psychology*. Englewood Cliffs, N.J.: Prentice-Hall, 1982, pp. 19-115.) *See also* intracohort trend study.

paranoia. A functional disorder characterized by delusions of grandeur and/or persecution and jealousy. Paranoid disorders tend to be more frequent in old age. They may stem from such factors as sensory defects, especially hearing loss, social isolation, and living alone. (Carl Eisdorfer. "Paranoia and Schizophrenic Disorders in Later Life." In Ewald W. Busse and Dan G. Blazer, eds., *Handbook of Geriatric Psychiatry*. New York: Van Nostrand Reinhold, 1980, pp. 329-37.) *See also* functional disorders.

participant observation. A type of field research* in which the investigator becomes a participating member of the group he or she is studying. (George J. McCall and J. L. Simmons, eds. *Participant Observation*. Reading, Mass.: Addison-Wesley, 1969; Christine L. Fry. "Participant Observation."

In C. L. Fry and Jennie Keith, eds., *New Methods for Old Age Research*. New York: Praeger, 1982; Arlie R. Hochschild. *The Unexpected Community*. Berkeley: University of California Press, 1973.)

passive euthanasia. To permit a patient whose condition is beyond help to die instead of using heroic measures* to prolong life. (Wayne Sage. "Choosing the Good Death." *Human Behavior*, June 1974, pp. 16-23; John A. Behnke and Sisela Bok, eds. *The Dilemmas of Euthanasia*. Garden City, N.Y.: Anchor Books, 1975.) *See also* active euthanasia.

patriarchal family. A type of family organization in which males have absolute authority. The central authority is usually the oldest living male of the family. (Meyer F. Nimkoff. *Comparative Family Systems*. Boston: Houghton Mifflin, 1965; William J. Goode. *The Family*. Englewood Cliffs, N.J.: Prentice-Hall, 1982.) *See also* egalitarian family, matriarchal family.

patrilineal descent. A family in which descent or inheritance is traced through the father and the male line. Older men and women tend to receive more care and support in a patrilineal than in a matrilineal society (Leo W. Simmons). (L. W. Simmons. *The Role of the Aged in Primitive Society*. New Haven, Conn.: Yale University Press, 1945; Meyer F. Nimkoff. *Comparative Family Systems*. Boston: Houghton Mifflin, 1965; William J. Goode. *The Family*. Englewood Cliffs, N.J.: Prentice-Hall, 1982; Adam Kuper. "Lineage Theory: A Critical Retrospect." In *Annual Review of Anthropology for 1982*. Palo Alto, Calif.: Annual Reviews, 1982.) *See also* bilateral descent, matrilineal descent.

patrilocal residence. A type of residence in which a married couple lives with the husband's parents. (Meyer F. Nimkoff. *Comparative Family Systems*. Boston: Houghton Mifflin, 1965; William J. Goode. *The Family*. Englewood Cliffs, N.J.: Prentice-Hall, 1982.) *See also* matrilocal residence, neolocal residence.

peer group. A group composed of members of the same age and/or equal status that habitually associate with one another. (Mary M. Sequin. "Opportunity for Peer Socialization in a Retirement Community." *The Gerontologist*, 1973, 13, pp. 208-14.)

peer review organizations (PROs). Formal associations of colleagues in scientific fields who evaluate the work of other colleagues. For example, groups of physicians in each state are paid by the federal government to determine if the hospital care of Medicare patients is reasonable and necessary as well as meeting the standards of quality accepted by the medical profession. They also review decisions about hospital stays and investigate patient complaints. (Jean Crichton. *The Age Care Sourcebook: A Resource Guide for the Aging and Their Families.* New York: Simon and Schuster, 1987.)

pension. A plan established and maintained by the employer that regularly provides a fixed dollar amount to employees after their retirement.* (W. Greenough and F. King. *Pension Plans and Public Policy.* New York: Columbia University Press, 1976; Louis Lowy. *Social Policies and Programs on Aging.* Lexington, Mass.: Lexington Books, 1980.)

pension replacement rate. The percentage of a retired worker's previous earnings that is replaced by the pension he or she receives. (James H. Schulz. *The Economics of Aging.* Belmont, Calif.: Wadsworth, 1985.)

period effect. (1) A particular historical event that affects the entire population* for a limited time. For example, the Depression or World War II would be considered a period effect. Also referred to as a historical effect or time-of-measurement effect.* (2) A change in the individual or group being studied that occurs in the interval between measurements and that is thought to be due to a historical event. (Matilda W. Riley, W. Johnson, and A. Foner, eds. *Aging and Society: A Sociology of Age Stratification.* Vol. 3. New York: Russell Sage, 1972.) *See also* age effect, cohort effect.

personal adjustment. (1) An individual's reorientation in response to new or changed situations. (2) Differences between the expressed wishes of a person and the activities that he or she actually performs. (3) General happiness. (Ruth S. Cavan et al. *Personal Adjustment in Old Age.* Chicago: Scientific Research Associates, 1949; Raymond G. Kuhlen. "Aging and Life-Adjustment." In James E. Birren, ed., *Handbook of Aging and the Individual.* Chicago: University of Chicago, 1959, pp. 852-97; Klaus F. Riegel. "History of Psychological Gerontology." In James E. Birren and K. Warner Schaie, eds., *Handbook of the Psychology of Aging.* New York: Van Nostrand Reinhold, 1977, pp. 70-102.) *See also* social adjustment.

personal-care homes. *See* domiciliary-care facilities.

personal competence. (1) The feeling of mastery over oneself and one's environment.* (2) Successful role performance. (3) The capacity to adapt (Kuypers and Bengtson). Many elderly persons experience increasing competence with age while with others there is decline. (M. Powell Lawton. "Assessing the Competence of Older People." In Donald P. Kent, Robert Kastenbaum, and Sylvia Sherwood, eds., *Research Planning and Action for the Elderly.* New York: Behavioral Publications, 1972, pp. 122-43; J. A. Kuypers and V. L. Bengtson. "Social Breakdown and Competence: A

Model of Normal Aging." *Human Development*, 1973, 16, 181-201; Frances M. Carp and Abraham Carp. "Age, Deprivation, and Personal Competence: Effects on Satisfaction." *Research on Aging*, 1981, 3, pp. 279-98.)

personal history. *See* life history.

personal time dependency (PTD). A measurement of the amount of time required to assist an elderly person so that he or she may remain independent in the community. (G. Gurland et al. "Personal Time Dependency in the Elderly of New York City." In *Dependency in the Elderly in New York City*. New York: Community Council of Greater New York, 1978, pp. 9-45.)

Peter Pan syndrome. An extreme form of the denial* of old age in which the older person refuses to face the realities of aging and pretends to be young. (Robert N. Butler and Myrna I. Lewis. *Aging and Mental Health: Positive Psychosocial and Biomedical Approaches*. St. Louis: C. V. Mosby, 1982.)

pet therapy. The use of pet companionship to reduce the elderly's feelings of loneliness and isolation in the home as well as in institutions. Some studies report that pets not only provide older persons with companionship, physical contact, and a sense of responsibility for the pet's care, but that pets may improve their morale and even lower their blood pressure. (C. M. Brickel. "The Therapeutic Roles of Cat Mascots with a Hospital-Based Geriatric Population: A Staff Survey." *The Gerontologist*, 1979, 19, 368-72; Dan Lago, Cathleen M. Connell, and Barbara Knight. "A Companion Animal Program." In Michael A. Smyer and Margaret Gatz, eds., *Mental Health and Aging: Programs and Evaluations*. Beverly Hills, Calif.: Sage, 1983, pp. 165-84.)

phased retirement. *See* gradual retirement.

Philadelphia Geriatric Center (PGC) Morale Scale. This scale focuses on the attitudes that older persons have regarding the quality of their lives. (M. Powell Lawton. "The Dimensions of Morale." In Donald P. Kent, Robert Kastenbaum, and Sylvia Sherwood, eds., *Research Planning and Action for the Elderly*. New York: Behavioral Publications, 1972, pp. 144-65; M. Powell Lawton. "The Philadelphia Geriatric Center Morale Scale: A Revision." *Journal of Gerontology*, 1975, 30, pp. 85-89.)

pigeon drop. A popular scheme for victimizing older persons in which two young women work together to con an older person (usually a woman) out of a large sum of money. There are several variations, but essentially, it works like this. One woman approaches the "pigeon" and begins a conversation and she is then joined by the second woman, who claims that she has just found a large sum of money with no identification and asks for advice. One of the women pretends to go to a lawyer, banker, or elsewhere to find out what to do with the money. After a short time, she returns and says that her lawyer will keep the money for six months and if no one claims it by then, they will divide the money three ways. However, in the meantime to show good faith, each must match her share of the find with her own money. The elderly victim turns over her share to the women and never sees her money again. (Donna St. John. "Beware the Flimflam Man." *Dynamic Maturity*, May 1977, p. 8; Amram Ducovny. *The Billion Dollar Swindle: Frauds Against the Elderly*. New York: Fleet Press, 1969; Letitia T. Alston. *Crime and Older Americans*. Springfield, Ill.: Charles C. Thomas, 1986.)

placebo. A preparation that has no pharmacological effect. (H. W. Smith. *Strategies of Social Research*. Englewood Cliffs, N.J.: Prentice-Hall, 1981.) *See also* double-blind.

planned housing (for the elderly). Housing designated for and designed with specific features for older people (M. Powell Lawton). Examples include public housing, congregate housing,* and retirement communities. (Frances M. Carp. *A Future for the Aged*. Austin: University of Texas Press, 1966; M. P. Lawton. *Environments and Aging*. Monterey, Calif.: Brooks/Cole, 1980, pp. 450-78; M. Powell Lawton. "Housing and Living Environments of Older People." In Robert H. Binstock and Ethel Shanas, eds., *Handbook of Aging and the Social Sciences*. New York: Van Nostrand Reinhold, 1985, pp. 450-78.) *See also* retirement community.

political gerontology. The scientific study of power* as it relates to older persons. Neal E. Cutler defines political gerontology as the "demographic, social, psychological, and political factors in the politics of aging." (N. E. Cutler. "A Foundation for Research in Political Gerontology." *American Political Science Review*, 1977, 71, pp. 1011-26; John B. Williamson, Linda Evans, and Lawrence A. Powell. *The Politics of Aging: Power and Policy*. Springfield, Ill.: Charles C. Thomas, 1982.)

political science. (1) The study of the institutions and ideologies that shape political activity in which some people acquire and exercise power over others. Political scientists study the workings of the government at every level of society as well as the legislative, executive, and judicial branches of government. (2) The "authoritative allocation of resources." (D. Easton). (Harold D. Laswell. *Politics: Who Gets What, When, How?* New York: McGraw-Hill, 1936; D. Easton. *The Political System*. New York: Knopf,

1953; Anthony M. Orum. *Introduction to Political Sociology: The Social Anatomy of the Body Politic*. Englewood Cliffs, N.J.: Prentice-Hall, 1978; Robert B. Hudson and John Strate. "Aging and the Political Systems." In Robert H. Binstock and Ethel Shanas, eds., *Handbook of Aging and the Social Sciences*. New York: Van Nostrand Reinhold, 1985, pp. 554-85.)

polyandry. A rare form of polygamy* in which the wife has two or more husbands at the same time. (George P. Murdock. *Social Structure*. New York: Macmillan, 1949; Meyer F. Nimkoff. *Comparative Family Systems*. Boston: Houghton Mifflin, 1965.) *See also* polygamy, polygyny.

polygamy. Plural mates. This term covers both polygyny* and polyandry.* (George P. Murdock. *Social Structure*. New York: Macmillan, 1949; Meyer F. Nimkoff. *Comparative Family Systems*. Boston: Houghton Mifflin, 1965.)

polygyny. A form of polygamy* in which the husband has two or more wives at the same time. Polygyny provides older men with wealth, a source of prestige, and valuable work hands. As a solution to the shortage of older men in the United States, some writers have suggested polygynous marriages among the elderly. (George P. Murdock. *Social Structure*. New York: Macmillan, 1949; Meyer F. Nimkoff. *Comparative Family Systems*. Boston: Houghton Mifflin, 1965; Victor Kessel. "Polygyny after Sixty." In Herbert A. Otto, ed., *The Family in Search of a Future*. New York: Appleton-Century-Crofts, 1970.) *See also* gerontogamy.

polypharmacy. The unnecessary and excessive use of medication. This pattern of medication consumption is often seen in elderly persons. (William Simonson. *Medications and the Elderly*. Rockville, Md.: Aspen Systems, 1984.)

population. (1) The number of people living in a geographic area and governed by a political unit. Examples include nations, states, and cities. (2) The total collection of individuals and units that the researcher wants to study and draw conclusions about. Also referred to as a universe. (Earl R. Babbie. *The Practice of Social Research*. Belmont, Calif.: Wadsworth, 1983.)

population aging. *See* aging of the population.

population census. *See* census of population.

population pyramid. A diagram that shows the age-sex structure* of a population.* The pyramid is composed of a bar graph that represents age groups* in ascending order (the youngest age group at the bottom and the oldest at the top). A vertical line in the center of the bars divides the pyramid so that the bars on the right represent females and on the left males. Synonymous with age-sex pyramid. Sometimes called the "tree of ages." (Henry S. Shryock and Jacob S. Siegel, and Associates. *The Methods and Materials of Demography*. New York: Academic Press, 1976.)

portability. A type of vesting* that refers to the transfer of pension* rights from one plan to another when a worker changes jobs. (James H. Schulz. *The Economics of Aging*. Belmont, Calif.: Wadsworth, 1985.)

positive correlation. *See* correlation.

postoccupancy evaluation (POE). The assessment of how buildings work for their occupants. Their evaluation is based on questions regarding the occupants' perception of the building, expressions of satisfaction, and observed activities. Housing for the elderly is becoming increasingly studied by the use of this method. (Sandra C. Howell. "Environments and Aging." In Carl Eisdorfer, ed., *Annual Review of Gerontology and Geriatrics*. Vol. 1. New York: Springer, 1980, pp. 237-60.)

postparental period. The period in the life of a married couple after which the last child has left the parental home and before the death* of one of the spouses. (N. Glenn. "Psychological Well-Being in the Post-Parental Stage." *Journal of Marriage and Family*, 1975, 37, 105-10.) *See also* empty nest, family of later life.

poverty. (1) A condition in which persons' incomes are insufficient to meet subsistence needs (absolute poverty). (2) A condition in which persons are unable to maintain the standard of living enjoyed by most members of their society (relative poverty). About one-fifth of the older population are poor or near-poor. (Gabriel Kolko. *Wealth and Power in America: An Analysis of Social Class and Income Distribution*. New York: Praeger, 1962; David A. Peterson. "Financial Adequacy in Retirement: Perceptions of Older Americans." *The Gerontologist*, 1972, 12, pp. 379-83; Thomas Tissue. "Old Age and the Perception of Poverty." *Sociology and Social Research*, 1972, 56, pp. 331-44; Jersey Liang, Eva Kahana, and Edmund Doherty. "Financial Well-Being among the Aged: A Further Elaboration." *Journal of Gerontology*, 1980, 35, pp. 409-20.)

poverty index level. This level is determined by the federal government's poverty index, which was developed in the 1960s by the Social Security Administration in order to administer social welfare programs. The poverty line is based on the amount of income needed to purchase enough food for a

Figure 6
Population Pyramid—the Age Distribution of the U.S. Population

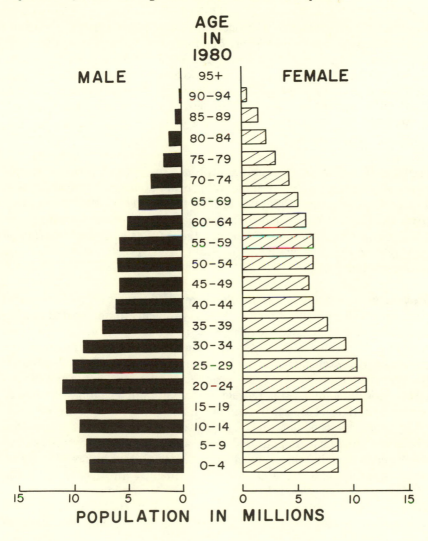

Source: The Social Security Administration.

subsistence diet. The budget is then multiplied by three to determine the poverty level (food expenses are estimated to represent one-third of a poor family's budget). (James H. Schulz. *The Economics of Aging*. Belmont, Calif.: Wadsworth, 1985.)

power. The ability to exercise control over others even against their will. At retirement* individuals lose their occupational status, which often results in a decrease in power. (Max Weber. *Economy and Society*. Guenther Roth and Claus Wittich, eds. New York: Bedminster Press, 1968; George L. Maddox. "Will Senior Power Become a Reality?" In Lissy F. Jarvik, ed., *Aging into the 21st Century: Middle-Agers Today*. New York: Gardner Press, 1978, pp. 185-96; John B. Williamson, Linda Evans, and Lawrence A. Powell. *The Politics of Aging: Power and Policy*. Springfield, Ill.: Charles C. Thomas, 1982.)

prejudice. (1) A negative prejudged attitude* toward a category or group* of people. (2) A favorable or unfavorable belief about the characteristics of a category or a group. Prejudice against the elderly is called "ageism."* (Alex Comfort. "Age Prejudice in America." *Social Policy*, 1976, 7, pp. 3-8; Jack Levin and William C. Levin. *Ageism: Prejudice and Discrimination against the Elderly*. Belmont, Calif.: Wadsworth, 1980.) *See also* discrimination, racism, sexism.

preretirement planning programs. Programs that provide the preretiree with some knowledge about retirement,* what problems to anticipate in retirement, and how to prepare for them. One approach to accomplishing these objectives is through group sessions. These sessions give employees the opportunity to exchange ideas and information freely and to discuss their problems with one another. Each session lasts about two hours and focuses on a major topic involved in retirement preparation. The topics include finances, health, legal aspects of retirement, and the use of leisure time. Most group programs schedule weekly meetings ranging from 6 to 12 weeks. Preretirement programs are sponsored by business and industry as well as community centers, universities, and churches. (Neil G. McCluskey. "Preretirement Education and Preparation for Retirement." In Richard H. Davis, ed., *Aging*. Los Angeles: Ethel Percy Andrus Gerontology Center, University of Southern California Press, 1981, pp. 362-82; Abraham Monk. "Preretirement Planning Programs." In Abraham Monk, ed., *Handbook of Gerontological Services*. New York: Van Nostrand Reinhold, 1985, pp. 322-40.)

presbycusis. The progressive decrease in the ability to hear well that occurs with aging. First high pitches, then other sounds become difficult to differtiate. (Lynne W. Olsho, Stephen W. Harkins, and Martin L. Lenhardt.

"Aging and the Auditory System." In James E. Birren and K. Warner Schaie, eds., *Handbook of the Psychology of Aging.* New York: Van Nostrand Reinhold, 1985, pp. 332-77.)

presbyopia. The inability to focus on close objects. This condition, which results from a gradual loss in the accommodative ability of the lens, is common in old age and usually becomes noticeable about the middle forties. It is commonly referred to as "farsightedness." Also called "hyperopia." (A. P. Weiss. "Sensory Functions." In J. E. Birren, ed., *Handbook of Aging and the Individual.* Chicago: University of Chicago Press, 1959; Donald W. Kline and Frank Schieber. "Vision and Aging." In James E. Birren and K. Warner Schaie, eds., *Handbook of the Psychology of Aging.* New York: Van Nostrand Reinhold, 1985, pp. 296-331.) *See also* myopia.

presbystatis. The loss of equilibrium in old age. This loss plays a major role in the high incidence of falls in older persons. (J. Krmpotic-Nemanic. "Presbycutis, Presbystatis and Presbyosmia as Consequences of the Analogous Biological Process." *Acta Otolaryngology,* 1969, 67, pp. 217-23.)

presenile dementia. An organic mental disorder that is similar to senile dementia* and can appear as early as age 40 or 45. Presenile dementia, as with senile dementia, is characterized by personality disintegration and intellectual deterioration. Three types of presenile dementia are Alzheimer's disease,* Pick's disease, and Creutzfeldt-Jacob's disease. (A. E. Slaby and R. J. Wyatt. *Dementia in the Presenium.* Springfield, Ill.: Charles C. Thomas, 1976.)

pressure groups. *See* aging-based interest groups.

prestige. (1) The social recognition and respect that one receives from others; esteem. In general, the prestige of the elderly is lower than that of younger age groups.* (2) The value* attached to an office or occupation by society.* (Kingsley Davis. *Human Society.* New York: Macmillan, 1948; I. Press and M. McKool, Jr. "Social Structure and Status of the Aged: Toward Some Valid Cross Cultural Generalizations." *Aging and Human Development,* 1972, 3, pp. 297-306; Stephen J. Cutler. "An Approach to the Measurement of Prestige Loss Among the Aged." *Aging and Human Development,* 1972, 3, pp. 285-92; Donald J. Treiman. *Occupational Prestige in Comparative Perspective.* New York: Academic Press, 1977.)

primary aging. The inherited and inevitable declines that occur with aging that are not caused by disease,* trauma, or stress. This term was proposed by Ewald W. Busse in 1959. (E. W. Busse. "Psychopathology." In James E. Birren, ed., *Handbook of Aging and the Individual*. Chicago: University of Chicago Press, 1959, pp. 364-99; Ewald W. Busse and Dan Blazer. "The Theories and Processes of Aging." In E. Busse and D. Blazer, eds., *Handbook of Geriatric Psychiatry*. New York: Van Nostrand Reinhold, 1980, pp. 3-27.) *See also* secondary aging.

primary group. A small, informal group* in which members have an intimate, personal relationship; for example, the family.* This term was introduced by Charles Horton Cooley in 1909. (C. H. Cooley. *Social Organization*. New York: Scribner, 1909; John E. Dono et al. "Primary Groups in Old Age: Structure and Function." *Research on Aging*, 1979, 1, pp. 403-33.) *See also* secondary group, secondary relationship, primary relationship.

primary memory. *See* short-term memory.

primary relationship. A relationship that is personal, spontaneous, inclusive, and an end in itself; for example, the relationship between two friends or between a husband and a wife. Older persons' lifelong patterns of activities often become disrupted when they experience crises in primary relationships. (Kingsley Davis. *Human Society*. New York: Macmillan, 1949; N. Babchuk. "Aging and Primary Relations." *International Journal of Aging and Human Development*, 1978-1979, 9, pp. 137-51.) *See also* secondary relationship, primary group, secondary group.

private pensions. Pensions from employment in the nongovernmental sector. Private pensions may be classified as contributory plans that require employees to pay part of the cost of the pension,* or as noncontributory plans, where the employer pays the entire cost. (Sheila R. Zedlewski. "The Private Pension System to the Year 2000." In Henry J. Aaron and Gary Burtless, eds., *Retirement and Economic Behavior*. Washington, D.C.: Brookings Institution, 1984, pp. 315-44; James H. Schulz. *The Economics of Aging*. Belmont, Calif.: Wadsworth, 1985.) *See also* public pensions.

progeria. A rare premature aging disorder that is characterized by accelerated bodily changes in which the individuals look like little, old wizened persons. This type of progeria is referred to as Hutchinson-Gilford syndrome. Victims usually die during their mid-teens of heart disease. Werner's syndrome or adult progeria is another type of progeria that has a later onset and death* usually occurs by 40 to 50 years of age. (Ewald W. Busse and Dan Blazer. "The Theories and Processes of Aging." In E. Busse and D. Blazer, eds., *Handbook of Geriatric Psychiatry*. New York: Van Nostrand Reinhold, 1980, pp. 3-27.)

progress. Social or cultural change defined as desirable according to some set of values. Most social scientists prefer to use the term "change" instead of progress because it is free from value judgments. The belief in progress is one of the dominant values in American society. In our progress-oriented society, which equates the latest and the newest, with the finest and the best, old people are often made to feel like anachronisms and superannuated members. (William F. Ogburn. *Social Change.* New York: The Viking Press, 1922; Sara Kiesler, James N. Morgan, and Valerie K. Oppenheimer, eds., *Aging: Social Change.* New York: Academic Press, 1981.)

projection. A defense mechanism in which the individual attributes to others his undesirable attitudes. For example, an older man becomes angry at his daughter for not visiting him everyday in the nursing home. He then begins to believe that his daughter is angry at him when in actuality it is he who is angry at her. (Anna Freud. *The Ego and Mechanisms of Defense.* New York: International Universities Press, 1946; Laurance F. Shaffer and Edward J. Shoben. *The Psychology of Adjustment.* Boston: Houghton Mifflin, 1956; George E. Vaillant. *Adaptation to Life.* Boston: Little, Brown, 1977.) *See also* defense mechanisms.

prolongevity. According to Gerald J. Gruman, who coined the term, prolongevity is "the belief that it is possible and desirable to extend significantly the length of life by human action." (G. J. Gruman. "A History of Ideas about the Prolongation of Life: The Evolution of Prolongevity Hypotheses to 1800." *Transactions of the American Philosophical Society*, 1966, vol. 56, pt. 9.)

proposition. A confirmed hypothesis.* (Bernard S. Phillips. *Social Research: Strategy and Tactics.* New York: Macmillan, 1976.)

prospective payment system (PPS). A reimbursement method used by Medicare in which a fixed, predetermined amount for a specific diagnosis is paid to the hospital regardless of the type of services given or the length of the stay. This system, which is also referred to as payment-by-diagnosis, was approved by congress in 1983. (Robert S. Mudge, ed. *Social Security and Retirement: Private Goals, Public Policy.* Washington, D.C.: Congressional Quarterly, 1983; U.S. Senate. *Developments in Aging: 1986.* Vol. 1. A Report of the Special Committee on Aging. Washington, D.C.: U.S. Government Printing Office, 1987.) *See also* diagnosis related groups, Medicare.

prosthetic devices. Substitutes for a body organ or part. Examples of such devices include heart pacemakers,* lenses needed after a cataract* operation, and artificial limbs. (*Your Medicare Handbook.* Washington, D.C.: U.S. Government Printing Office, 1987.)

prosthetic environments. Housing that is designed and modified for the elderly to compensate for or reduce behavioral debilitation. Features included, for example, are guardrails, glare-free lighting, ramps, and nonskid floors. (Ogden R. Lindsley. "Geriatric Behavioral Prosthetics." In Robert Kastenbaum, ed., *New Thoughts on Old Age*. New York: Springer, 1964, pp. 41-60.)

protective services adult. (1) A system of preventive and supportive services for older persons that are too mentally or physically incapacitated to manage their own affairs and to act on their own behalf. (2) An array of legal devices for functionally impaired adults who need protection of person and/or property. (Edna Wasser. "Protective Practice in Serving the Mentally Impaired Aged." *Social Casework*, 1971, 52, pp. 510-22; Martin Bloom and Margaret Neilsen. "The Older Persons in Need of Protective Services. *Social Casework*, 1971, 52, pp. 500-509; Elias S. Cohen. "Protective Services." In Abraham Monk, ed., *Handbook of Gerontological Services*. New York: Van Nostrand Reinhold, 1985, pp. 483-513.) *See also* guardianship.

pseudodementia. Although there is no brain disease present, older patients (especially those suffering from depression*) will sometimes have symptoms that mimic organic mental disorders,* or dementias.* Also written as "pseudo dementia." (Robert N. Butler. "Psychiatry and the Elderly: An Overview." *The American Journal of Psychiatry*, 1975, 132, pp. 893-900; F. Post. "Dementia, Depression and Pseudomentia." In D. F. Benson and D. Blumer, eds., *Psychiatric Aspects of Neurological Disease*. New York: Grune and Stratton, 1975.)

psychiatric ghettos. *See* deinstitutionalization movement.

psychogeriatrics. *See* geriatric psychiatry.

psychological age. The adaptative capacities of individuals to their physical and social environments as well as to their own physical condition. The determination of psychological age would include assessing such areas as learning ability, memory, intelligence, and personality traits. (James E. Birren and Walter R. Cunningham. "Research on the Psychology of Aging: Principles, Concepts, and Theory." In J. E. Birren and K. W. Schaie, eds., *Handbook of the Psychology of Aging*. New York: Van Nostrand Reinhold, 1985, pp. 8-9.) *See also* biological age, chronological age, social age.

psychological aging. The self-regulation that one exercises by making decisions and choices in adapting to biological and social aging. Also referred to as the process of "geronting" by J. J. F. Schroots and James E. Birren. (J.

Schroots and J. Birren. "A Psychological Point of View toward Human Aging and Adaptability." In *Adaptability and Aging*. Proceedings of the 9th International Conference of Social Gerontology, Quebec, Canada, 1980, pp. 43-54; James E. Birren and Walter R. Cunningham. "Research on the Psychology of Aging: Principles, Concepts, and Theory." James E. Birren and K. Warner Schaie, eds., *Handbook of the Psychology of Aging*. New York: Van Nostrand Reinhold, 1985, pp. 8-9.)

psychological death. When the individual defines himself or herself as dead or as good as dead. (Richard A. Kalish. "A Continuum of Subjectively Perceived Death." *The Gerontologist*, 1966, 6, pp. 73-76.)

psychology of aging. The scientific study of age-related changes and differences in behavior. (James E. Birren. *The Psychology of Aging*. Englewood Cliffs, N.J.: Prentice-Hall, 1964; James E. Birren and Walter R. Cunningham. "Research on the Psychology of Aging: Principles, Concepts, and Theory." In James E. Birren and K. Warner Schaie, eds., *Handbook of the Psychology of Aging*. New York: Van Nostrand Reinhold, 1985, pp. 3-34.)

psychosis. A severe mental disorder that impairs an individual's ability to interpret reality and to meet the ordinary demands of daily living. It is characterized by delusions and hallucinations, inappropriate behavior, the inability to think and communicate, and a diminished control of impulses. (James E. Birren and R. Bruce Sloane, eds. *Handbook of Aging and Mental Health*. Englewood Cliffs, N.J.: Prentice-Hall, 1980.)

psychosomatic disorders. Physical symptoms that are influenced by psychological factors. (S. J. Lachman. *Psychosomatic Disorders: A Behavioristic Interpretation*. New York: Wiley, 1972.) *See also* Social Readjustment Rating Scale.

psychotherapy. The treatment of mental and emotional disorders through the use of psychological methods based primarily on verbal or nonverbal communications. Lillien J. Martin was the first person to offer a comprehensive psychotherapy program for the elderly and she coauthored the first publication on psychotherapy for the aged. (L. J. Martin and C. deGrunchy. *Salvaging Old Age*. New York: Macmillan, 1930; K. Gunnar Gotestam. "Behavioral and Dynamic Psychotherapy with the Elderly." James E. Birren and R. Bruce Sloane, eds., *Handbook of Mental Health and Aging*. Englewood Cliffs, N.J.: Prentice-Hall, 1980; June E. Blum and Susan Tross. "Psychodynamic Treatment of the Elderly: A Review of Issues in Theory and Practice." In Carl Eisdorfer, ed., *Annual Review of Gerontology and Geriatrics*. Vol. 1. New York: Springer, 1980, pp. 204-34.)

public pensions. Pensions obtained through employment in the government sector or from social security benefits. (John Myles. *Old Age in the Welfare State: The Political Economy of Public Pensions.* Boston: Little, Brown, 1984.) *See also* private pensions.

pure science. *See* basic research.

Q

questionnaire. A written list of predetermined questions to be filled out by the respondent;* a self-administered interview.* (Charles F. Cannell and Robert L. Kahn. "Interviewing." In Gardner Lindzey and Elliot Aronson, eds., *Handbook of Social Psychology*. Vol. 2. Reading, Mass.: Addison-Wesley, 1968, pp. 526-95.) *See also* interview schedule, survey.

R

racial crossover. *See* crossover phenomenon.

racism. A type of ethnocentrism* in which one is prejudiced toward persons of another race or races because they are believed to be inferior. The problem of racism that is faced by some minority groups is compounded in later life by ageism.* (James W. Vander Zanden. *American Minority Relations: The Sociology of Racial and Ethnic Groups*. New York: Ronald, 1972; Robert Blauner. *Racial Oppression in America*. New York: Harper and Row, 1972; Erdman B. Palmore and Kenneth Manton. "Ageism Compared to Racism and Sexism." *Journal of Gerontology*, 1973, 28, pp. 363-69.) *See also* sexism.

random sample. *See* simple random sample.

range. A measure of variability in a set of scores; the difference between the highest and lowest scores. (Ann E. MacEachron. *Basic Statistics for the Human Services*. Baltimore, Md.: University Park Press, 1982.)

rationalization. (1) A defense mechanism* in which one justifies his or her behavior or thoughts by offering socially acceptable reasons instead of the real reasons. An elderly woman, for example, who dislikes her daughter-in-law turns down an invitation to visit her home by convincing herself the trip would be too tiring. (2) The process in which social life is increasingly ordered by abstract, calculated rules and procedures; the application of scientific methods to production. Rationalization used in this sense is associated with the work of Max Weber. (Anna Freud. *The Ego and Mechanisms of Defense*. New York: International Universities Press, 1946; Laurance F. Shaffer and Edward J. Shoben, Jr. *The Psychology of Adjustment*. Boston: Houghton Mifflin, 1956; Max Weber. *The Theory of Social and Economic Organization*. New York: Oxford University Press, 1947.)

reality orientation. A program for helping persons with dementia to learn by means of repetition of verbal and nonverbal information. For example, subjects are reminded and reviewed on their own names, date, weather, and other information. James C. Folsom started the first reality orientation program in Topeka, Kansas, in 1958 for patients at a Veterans Administration Hospital. (L. Taulbee and J. C. Folsom. "Reality Orientation for Geriatric Patients." *Hospital and Community Psychiatry*, 1966, 17, pp. 133-35; R. S. Citrin and D. N. Dixon. "Reality Orientation: A Milieu Therapy Used in an Institution for the Aged." *The Gerontologist*, 1977, 17, pp. 39-43.)

rectangular survival curve. *See* survival curve.

reference group. Any group* that sets and enforces norms* or standards for an individual or is used by an individual for comparing himself or herself. Herbert H. Hyman coined the term in 1942. The religious community, a retirement community* as well as friends may serve as a reference group for an older person. (H. H. Hyman. "The Psychology of Status." *Archives of Psychology*, 1942, Vol. 38, no. 269, pp. 5-94; Robert K. Merton. *Social Theory and Social Structure*. New York: Free Press, 1968; J. Romeis, R. Albert, and F. D. Acuff. "Reference Group Theory: A Synthesizing Concept for the Disengagement and Interactionist Theories." *International Review of Sociology*, 1971, pp. 66-70.) *See also* relative deprivation.

regression. (1) A defense mechanism* in which one returns to an earlier stage of less mature behavior in the developmental process. An older woman, for example, recovering from an operation insists that her husband feed and dress her even though she is capable of doing it herself. Originally a neurological concept that was introduced by Hughlings Jackson, a British neurologist. (2) In statistics a method of data analysis for predicting a given variable from one or more other variables. (Anna Freud. *The Ego and Mechanisms of Defense*. New York: International Universities Press, 1946; Laurance F. Shaffer and Edward J. Shoben, Jr. *The Psychology of Adjustment*. Boston: Houghton Mifflin, 1956; D. Bienerfeld. "The Two-Way Street: Aspects of Regression in Psychotherapy with Aging Patients. *American Journal of Psychotherapy*, 1985, 39, pp. 86-94; Hubert M. Blalock. *Social Statistics*. New York: McGraw-Hill, 1972.)

regressive intervention. The process of gradually withdrawing the care resources from a person who is severely and irreversibly mentally and/or physically impaired. (W. H. Watson and R. J. Maxwell. *Human Aging and Dying*. New York: St. Martin's Press, 1977.)

rehearsal for retirement. *See* gradual retirement.

rehearsal for widowhood. Preparing oneself in advance for the death of a spouse. (Bernice L. Neugarten. *Middle Age and Aging*. Chicago: University of Chicago Press, 1968.) *See also* anticipatory grief.

relative deprivation. To perceive oneself as being disadvantaged by comparing one's own situation with that of others who have more. A resident of a retirement community,* for example, may believe that his income is inadequate in comparison with other residents. The concept was first introduced by Samuel A. Stouffer and later elaborated on by Robert K. Merton. (S. A. Stouffer et al. *The American Soldier.* Princeton, N.J.: Princeton University Press, 1949; R. K. Merton. *Social Theory and Social Structure.* New York: Free Press, 1968; Gordon L. Bultena and Edward Powers. "Effects of Age-Grade Comparisons on Adjustment in Later Life." In Jaber F. Gubrium, ed., *Time, Roles, and Self in Old Age.* New York: Human Sciences Press, 1976; Jersey Laing and Thomas J. Fairchild. "Relative Deprivation and Perception of Financial Adequacy among the Aged." *Journal of Gerontology,* 1979, 34, pp. 746-59.)

reliability. The extent to which a given measurement or test can be repeated under similar conditions and it yields a consistent result. (Earl R. Babbie. *The Practice of Social Research.* Belmont, Calif.: Wadsworth, 1983.) *See also* validity.

relocation effect. The impact on elderly persons of choosing to move or being forced to move within the community or between or out of institutional settings. The outcome of relocation can either be positive or negative, depending on the situation. (C. K. Aldrich and E. Mendkoff. "Relocation of the Aged and Disabled: A Mortality Study." *Journal of the American Geriatrics Society,* 1963, 11, pp. 185-94; Kenneth F. Ferraro. "The Health Consequences of Relocation among the Aged in the Community." *Journal of Gerontology,* 1983, 38, pp. 90-96.)

reminiscence. The recalling of the past, which is part of a normal life review* process in the elderly. (Robert N. Butler. "The Life Review: An Interpretation of Reminiscence in the Aged." *Psychiatry,* 1963, 26, pp. 65-76; Sharon Merriam. "The Concept and Function of Reminiscence: A Review of the Research." *The Gerontologist,* 1980, 20, pp. 604-8.)

renewal activity. When a person attempts to regress in social age* and to become a peer of persons who are in a younger age grade.* (D. L. Guemple. "Human Resource Management: The Dilemma of the Aging Eskimo." *Sociological Symposium,* 2, 1974, pp. 59-74.) *See also* peer group, regression.

repression. A defense mechanism* in which an individual blocks out unacceptable thoughts, painful memories, or experiences from the conscious part of the mind; for example, an elderly woman may block out the painful memory of a mugging. (Anna Freud. *The Ego and Mechanisms* *of Defense*. New York: International Universities Press, 1946; Laurance F. Shaffer and Edward J. Shoben. *The Psychology of Adjustment*. Boston: Houghton Mifflin, 1956. Sigmund Freud. "Repression." In J. Strachey, ed., *The Standard Edition of the Complete Psychological Works of Sigmund Freud*. Vol. 14. New York: Norton, 1961, pp. 143-58.)

residential segregation. *See* age-segregated community.

respite care. The providing of short-term care to older persons in the community* so that caregivers* can be temporarily relieved of their responsibilities. This relief care may be provided in the home (e.g., homemaker services,* home health services*) or outside the home (e.g., a day-care center/geriatric day hospital,* and overnight respite programs). (Louis Lowy. *Social Policies and Programs on Aging*. Lexington, Mass.: Lexington Books, 1980; Eloise Rathbone-McCuan and Raymond T. Coward. "Respite and Adult Day-Care Services." In Abraham Monk, ed., *Handbook of Gerontological Services*. New York: Van Nostrand Reinhold, 1985, pp. 457-82.)

respondent. One who replies to a questionnaire* or answers the interviewer's questions. Used interchangeably with interviewee, informant, and subject. (Susan G. Philliber, Mary R. Schwab, and G. Sam Sloss. *Social Research*. Itasca, Ill.: Peacock, 1980.) *See also* interview, interview schedule.

rest homes. *See* domiciliary-care facilities.

retired couple's budgets. Three budgets prepared by the Bureau of Labor Statistics that are designed for retired couples in urban areas with the husband aged 65 or over. The budgets list the costs of major items required to meet the normal needs of retired couples at the lower, intermediate, and higher standards of living. (Robert L. Clark. *Inflation and the Economic Well-being of the Elderly*. Baltimore: Johns Hopkins University Press, 1984; James H. Schulz. *The Economics of Aging*. Belmont, Calif.: Wadsworth, 1985.)

Retired Senior Volunteer Program (RSVP). This program is designed to provide community volunteer service for persons aged 60 and over. Volunteers serve through a variety of agencies, organizations, and institutions that include libraries, museums, day-care centers, nursing homes, and adult basic education. Persons in this program receive no hourly stipends as do those in the Foster Grandparent Program* and Senior Companion Program.* RSVP, launched in 1971, is ACTION's* largest program. RSVP was developed from a demonstration project in Staten Island, New York, in the late 1960s known as Serve and Enrich Retirement through Volunteer Experience (SERVE). (M. M. Seguin and B. O'Brien, eds. *Releasing the Potential of the Older Volunteer*. Los Angeles: University of Southern California, Andrus Gerontology Center, 1976; U.S. Senate. *Developments in Aging, 1984*. Vol. 1. A Report of the Special Committee on Aging. Washington, D.C.: U.S. Government Printing Office, 1985, pp. 290-91; RSVP/ACTION, 806 Connecticut Ave. N.W., Washington, D.C. 20525.)

retirement. (1) The acquisition of an economically nonproductive role, which traditionally occurs around age 65, when one leaves his or her primary occupation. (2) A period of time characterized by the absence of occupationally oriented behavior. (3) An event or rite of passage that marks the end of one's primary occcupational life. (4) The process of adjusting to being a retired person. (Gordon F. Streib and S. J. Schneider. *Retirement in American Society: Impact and Process*. Ithaca, N.Y.: Cornell University Press, 1971; Harold L. Sheppard. "Work and Retirement." In Robert H. Binstock and Ethel Shanas, eds., *Handbook of Aging and the Social Sciences*. New York: Van Nostrand Reinhold, 1976, pp. 286-309; Robert Atchley. *The Sociology of Retirement*. Cambridge, Mass.: Schenkman, 1976.)

retirement community. (1) A planned, relatively self-sufficient entity containing shopping, medical, and recreational services that is spatially separated from the larger community* and whose residents are mainly retired or semiretired. The largest retirement community of this type is Sun City, Arizona, developed by Del Webb in 1960. Planned retirement communities in the U.S. date back to the 1920s. (2) A natural, unplanned community that has attracted large numbers of retired persons (e.g., Florida and California). (Gordon L. Bultena and Vivian Wood. "The American Retirement Community: Bane or Blessing?" *Journal of Gerontology*, 1969, 24, pp. 209-17; Jerry Jacobs. *Older Persons and Retirement Communities: Case Studies in Social Gerontology*. Springfield, Ill.: Charles C. Thomas, 1975; Charles F. Longino. "Retirement Communities." In F. J. Berghorn, D. E. Schafer, and Associates, eds., *The Dynamics of Aging*. Boulder, Colo.: Westview Press, 1981, pp. 309-418; Gordon F. Streib, Anthony J. LaGreca, and William E. Folts. "Retirement Communities: People, Planning, Prospects." In R. Newcomer, M. Lawton, and T. Byerts, eds., *Housing an Aging Society*. New York: Van Nostrand Reinhold, 1986, pp. 94-103.)

retirement guilt. Guilt from no longer being employed. (Robert N. Butler and Myrna I. Lewis. *Aging and Mental Health*. St. Louis: C. V. Mosby, 1982.)

retirement planning. *See* preretirement planning programs.

retirement principle. "The labor practice of superannuating elderly workers at a fixed age without regard to physical or mental capacity" (John Myles). (J. Myles. *Old Age in the Welfare State*. Boston: Little, Brown, 1984.)

retirement test. Persons from 65 to 70 years of age are allowed to earn only a certain amount of money and still be eligible to receive their full social security benefits. When this limitation is reached, benefits are reduced one dollar for every two dollars earned. This earnings ceiling increases yearly. After age 70 workers may receive full benefits, regardless of how much they earn. Also referred to as earnings limitation or earnings test. (James H. Schulz. "Liberalizing the Social Security Retirement Test: Who Would Receive the Increased Pension Benefits?" *Journal of Gerontology*, 1978, 33, pp. 262-68.)

retrospective study. *See* ex post facto study.

right to die. *See* living will, death with dignity.

rites of passage. Transitional ceremonies or occasions when an individual or group moves from one status to the next. Examples include confirmation, graduation from college, getting married, and the retirement dinner. Used interchangeably with status passage. The term was introduced by Arnold van Gennep in 1909. (A. van Gennep. *Rites of Passage*. Chicago: University of Chicago Press, 1960; Barney Glazer and Anselm Strauss. *Status Passage*. Chicago: Aldine-Atherton, 1971.)

rocking-chair personality. This term is derived from a study done by Suzanne Reichard, Florine Livson, and Paul G. Petersen in which they identified personality types who adjusted well and poorly to retirement. The rocking-chair types adjusted well to aging and were characterized by their passivity and wish to take life easy. They welcomed retirement and the chance to be free of responsibility. (S. Reichard, F. Livson, and P. G. Petersen. *Aging and Personality*. New York: John Wiley, 1962.)

role. The expected behavior of one who holds a certain status* or social position; the dynamic aspect of status; for example, the role of grandparenthood. (Ralph Linton. *The Study of Man*. New York: Appleton-Century, 1936; Bernard S. Phillips. "A Role Theory Approach to Adjustment in Old Age." *American Sociological Review*, 1957, 22, pp. 212-17; Leslie A. Morgan. "Social Roles in Later Life: Some Recent Research Trends." In Carl Eisdorfer, ed., *Annual Review of Gerontology and Geriatrics*. Vol. 3. New York: Springer, 1982, pp. 55-79.) *See also* role set, sick role, status.

role ambiguity. A condition resulting when there are no clearly defined guidelines or expectations concerning the requirements of a role; for example, the aged role or the retirement role. (Kurt W. Back. "The Ambiguity of Retirement." In Ewald W. Busse and Eric Pfeiffer, eds., *Behavior and Adaptation in Late Life*. Boston: Little, Brown, 1969.)

role discontinuity. The lack of preparation for a role* that one will take on at the next consecutive stage; for example, with the exception of preretirement planning programs* there is little to prepare an individual for the transition from the occupational role to the retirement* role. (Ruth Benedict. "Continuities and Discontinuities in Cultural Conditioning." *Psychiatry*, 1938, 1, pp. 161-67; Matilda W. Riley and Joan Waring. "Age and Aging." In Robert K. Merton and Robert Nisbet, eds., *Contemporary Social Problems*. New York: Harcourt Brace Jovanovich, 1976.)

role exits. *See* role loss.

roleless role. A term that refers to the ambiguous position of older people in our society who, when retired, have no vital function to perform. The term was first introduced by Ernest Burgess. (Ernest W. Burgess. *Aging in Western Societies*. Chicago: University of Chicago Press, 1960.)

role loss. The giving up of an old role* upon concluding a stage of the life course.* Up until old age,* when the individual relinquishes one role he or she is given a new role in return. In old age roles continue to be discarded but new roles usually do not take their place; for example, the death of a spouse ends one's role in the nuclear family,* or retirement* ends one's role in the occupational structure. Zena S. Blau refers to these types of role losses in old age as role exits. (Z. S. Blau. *Aging in a Changing Society*. New York: Franklin Watts, 1981; Irving Rosow. "Status and Role Change through the Life Cycle." In Robert H. Binstock and Ethel Shanas, eds., *Handbook of Aging and the Social Sciences*. New York: Van Nostrand Reinhold, 1985, pp. 62-93.)

role model. An individual whose behavior in a certain role provides a pattern for another individual to follow in performing the same role. One problem faced by the elderly is that they lack appropriate role models. (Irving Rosow. *Socialization to Old Age*. Berkeley: University of California Press, 1974.)

role rehearsal. *See* anticipatory socialization, rehearsal for widowhood.

role reversal. A situation in which an adult child assumes the role of father or mother to his or her elderly parent. Margaret Blenkner and others argue that this is not a normal but a pathological condition of neurotic or disturbed elderly persons. Some writers point out that the older person can never become a child again, making role reversal impossible. (M. Blenkner. "Social Work and Family Relations in Later Life." In Ethel Shanas and Gordon F. Streib, eds., *Social Structure and the Family*. Englewood Cliffs, N.J.: Prentice-Hall, 1965.)

role set. The entire array of related roles associated with a particular status* that an individual occupies. The status of wife, for example, might include the following roles: being a cook, a housekeeper, a mother, a grandmother, and a caregiver to one's elderly mother-in-law. The term was introduced by Robert K. Merton. (R. K. Merton. *Social Theory and Social Structure*. New York: Free Press, 1968.)

S

SAGE. *See* Senior Actualization and Growth Explorations.

sample. A sample consists of the selection of a certain number of units from the entire population* being studied with the aim of drawing inferences about the population as a whole. (Leslie Kish. *Survey Sampling.* New York: Wiley, 1965; Hubert M. Blalock and Ann B. Blalock, eds. *Methodology in Social Research.* New York: McGraw-Hill, 1968; Susan G. Philliber, Mary R. Schwab, and G. Sam Sloss. *Social Research.* Itasca, Ill.: F. E. Peacock, 1980.) *See also* cluster sample, simple random sample, stratified sample.

sandwich generation. Middle-aged persons who have responsibilities toward their dependent children and their aging parents. (A. N. Schwartz. "Psychological Dependency: An Emphasis on the Later Years." In P. K. Ragan, ed., *Aging Parents.* Los Angeles: University of Southern California, Andrus Gerontology Center, 1979; Richard H. Davis. "Middle Years." In R. H. Davis ed., *Aging: Prospects and Issues.* Los Angeles: Andrus Gerontology Center, 1981; Dorothy A. Miller. "The Sandwich Generation: Adult Children of the Aged." *Social Work*, 1981, 26, pp. 419-23.) *See also* middle age, women in the middle.

SCORE. *See* Service Corps of Retired Executives.

secondary aging. Disabilities that result from disease,* trauma, and other hostile factors in the environment.* This term was proposed by Ewald W. Busse in 1959. (E. W. Busse. "Psychopathology." In James E. Birren, ed., *Handbook of Aging and the Individual.* Chicago: University of Chicago Press, 1959, pp. 364-99; Ewald W. Busse and Dan Blazer. "The Theories and Processes of Aging." In E. W. Busse and D. Blazer, eds., *Handbook of Geriatric Psychiatry.* New York: Van Nostrand Reinhold, 1980, pp. 3-27.) *See also* primary aging.

secondary group. A group in which members have an impersonal, superficial, segmental relationship and are joined mostly by secondary relationships, for example, the American Association of Retired Persons.* Although the social psychologist Charles Horton Cooley did not use the term "secondary," it has become widely used for what he was describing.

(Richard H. Hall. *Organizations: Structure and Process*. Englewood Cliffs, N.J.: Prentice-Hall, 1982; Ethel Shanas and Marvin B. Sussman, eds. *Family, Bureaucracy, and the Elderly*. Durham, N.C.: Duke University Press, 1977.) *See also* formal organization, primary group, primary relationship, secondary relationship.

secondary memory. *See* long-term memory.

secondary relationship. A relationship that is characterized by impersonality, external constraints, disparity of ends, and is not inclusive; for example, the relationship between a clerk and a customer. (Kingsley Davis. *Human Society*. New York: Macmillan, 1949.) *See also* primary group, primary relationship, secondary group.

Section 8 program. The largest of the federal housing assistance programs, which provides rent supplements to persons with low incomes. HUD contracts with private owners for the leasing of units to individuals and families who meet the eligibility requirements. HUD pays the difference between the fair market rent and the amount the tenant is required to pay. (M. Powell Lawton. *Environment and Aging*. Monterey, Calif.: Brooks/Cole, 1980; U.S. Senate. *Developments in Aging: 1985*. A Report of the Special Committee on Aging. Washington, D.C.: U.S. Government Printing Office, 1986.)

Section 202 program. First authorized in 1959, it is the primary federal financing method for the building of subsidized rental housing for low-income elderly persons. Through this program the government makes loans to nonprofit sponsors for developing and designing housing to meet the needs of the elderly. This program was suspended in 1959 and later resumed in 1974 after it was strengthened and revitalized. (M. Powell Lawton. *Environment and Aging*. Monterey, Calif.: Brooks/Cole, 1980; U.S. Senate. *Developments in Aging: 1985*. A Report of the Special Committee on Aging. Washington, D.C.: U.S. Government Printing Office, 1986.)

selective dropout. A problem inherent in longitudinal research* in which some subjects are not available for retesting because of death, illness, relocation, or for other reasons. (Jack Botwinick. "Intellectual Abilities." In James E. Birren and K. Warner Schaie, eds., *Handbook of the Psychology of Aging*. New York: Van Nostrand Reinhold, 1977, pp. 580-605.)

selective memory. A defense mechanism, according to Robert N. Butler, in which older persons turn away from an unhappy present and dwell on the pleasant moments of their past. (R. N. Butler and Myrna I. Lewis. *Aging and Mental Health*. St. Louis: C. V. Mosby, 1982.)

self-concept. The view that we have of ourselves; the organization of qualities that the individual attributes to himself or herself. According to Irving Rosow, the loss of roles that the elderly experience deprives them of their social identity and erodes their self-concept. (J. W. Kinch. "A Formalized Theory of Self-Concept." *American Journal of Sociology*, 1963, 63, pp. 481-86; I. Rosow. "The Social Context of the Aging Self." *The Gerontologist*, 1973, 13, pp. 82-87.) *See also* looking-glass self.

self-euthanasia. A euphemism for what some persons would call an appropriate suicide.* (Richard A. Kalish. "The Social Context of Death and Dying." In Robert H. Binstock and Ethel Shanas, eds., *Handbook of Aging and the Social Sciences*. New York: Van Nostrand Reinhold, 1985, pp. 149-70.)

self-fulfilling prophecy. A prediction that starts a chain of events which in turn makes the prediction come true. (Robert K. Merton. *Social Theory and Social Structure*. New York: Free Press, 1968.) *See also* labeling theory, social breakdown syndrome.

self-haters personality type. A personality type identified by Suzanne Reichard and her associates in a study of a group of older men. This type openly rejected themselves and blamed others for their failures. (Suzanne Reichard, Florine Livson, and Paul G. Petersen. *Aging and Personality*. New York: John Wiley, 1962.)

Senate Special Committee on Aging. *See* Special Committee on Aging, U.S. Senate.

senescence. (1) The process of growing old. (2) Old age.* (3) The period of years during which one becomes old. (4) Generalized functional decline, especially in the second half of life. The term was coined by G. Stanley Hall in 1922. His book on senescence was intended to be a companion volume to his earlier work in 1904 on adolescence (another term that he coined). (G. Stanley Hall. *Senescence: The Last Half of Life*. New York: D. Appleton, 1922; Bernard Strehler. *Time, Cells, and Aging*. New York: Academic Press, 1962; Alex Comfort. *Ageing: The Biology of Senescence*. New York: Holt, Rinehart and Winston, 1964.)

senescing. *See* biological aging.

senicide. *See* gerontocide.

senile. (1) Manifesting senility.* (2) Pertaining to old age.* (National Institute on Aging Task Force Report. "Senility Reconsidered: Treatment Possibilities for Mental Impairment in the Elderly." *Journal of the American Medical Association*, 1980, 244, pp. 259-63.)

senile dementia. An organic mental disorder whose onset is usually after age 70. It is characterized by a progressive deterioration of the intellect and personality and an impairment of memory. It is similar, if not indistinguishable, from Alzheimer's disease and may be a late form of it. (E. Miller. *Abnormal Aging: The Psychology of Senile and Presenile Dementia*. London: Wiley, 1977.) *See also* Alzheimer's disease, organic mental disorder, presenile dementia.

senile psychosis. *See* dementia.

senility. (1) A layperson's term to refer to the impairment of mental functions and unusual patterns of behavior that occur in some older persons. (2) The state of being senile.* (3) Old age.* (National Institute on Aging Task Force Report. "Senility Reconsidered: Treatment Possibilities for Mental Impairment in the Elderly." *Journal of the American Medical Association*, 1980, 244, pp. 259-263.)

Senior Actualization and Growth Explorations (SAGE). Started in 1974 by Gay G. Luce, SAGE is designed to encourage self-improvement and growth in people over 60, and to help them to realize their potentialities to the fullest. Techniques and methods utilized to achieve this end include Hatha-yoga classes, biofeedback, meditation, discussion groups, and counseling. (Karen Preuss. *Life Time*. Santa Cruz, Calif.: Unity Press, 1978; Morton A. Lieberman and Nancy Gourash. "Effects of Change Groups on the Elderly." In M. A. Lieberman and Leonard D. Borman, eds., *Self-Help Groups for Coping with Crisis*. San Francisco: Jossey-Bass, 1979, pp. 387-405.)

senior center. A designated community facility that offers programs and services for older persons on a regular basis. Most senior centers provide legal, health, and information and referral services along with cultural, recreational, and educational programs. The first senior center in the United States began in New York City in 1943. Centers offering a wide range of programs and services are called "multipurpose senior centers." (Donald E. Gelfand. *The Aging Network: Programs and Services*. New York: Springer, 1984; Louis Lowy. "Multipurpose Senior Centers." In Abraham Monk, ed., *Handbook of Gerontological Services*. New York: Van Nostrand Reinhold, 1985, pp. 274-301.)

Senior Citizens Home Aide Service. *See* home health services, homemaker services.

Senior Companion Program (SCP). Developed in 1974, this program employs low-income persons 60 years of age and over on a part-time basis. They provide individualized assistance to other adults with emotional, physical, and mental impairments who wish to live independently in their own homes. Like the Foster Grandparent Program,* senior companions are considered volunteers. They work 20 hours per week and receive a small hourly stipend. (U.S. Senate. *Developments in Aging: 1984.* Vol. 1. A Report of the Special Committee on Aging. Washington, D.C.: U.S. Government Printing Office, 1985; Senior Companion Program/ACTION, 806 Connecticut Ave. N.W., Washington, D.C. 20525.) *See also* ACTION.

senior olympics. Started in 1970, this program gives older persons a chance to compete for medals in such sports as softball, tennis, bowling, swimming, and horseshoes. (A. Kamm. "A Senior Olympics." *Journal of Physical Education and Recreation*, 1979, 50, pp. 32-33.)

senior power. The political influence of older persons. (George L. Maddox. "Will Senior Power Become a Reality?" In Lissy F. Jarvik, ed., *Aging into the 21st Century: Middle-Agers Today*. New York: Gardner Press, 1978, pp. 185-96; John B. Williamson, Linda Evans, and Lawrence A. Powell. *The Politics of Aging: Power and Policy*. Springfield, Ill.: Charles C. Thomas, 1982.)

Serve and Enrich Retirement through Volunteer Experience (SERVE). *See* Retired Senior Volunteer Program.

Service Corps of Retired Executives (SCORE). Administered by the Small Business Administration, SCORE is composed of retired business executives who volunteer to do counseling and offer their services in every aspect of business management. SCORE, which began in 1964, now has chapters in every state. (Frances Tenenbaum. *Over 55 Is Not Illegal: A Resource Book for Active Older People*. Boston: Houghton Mifflin, 1979; SCORE, Small Business Administration, 1441 L Street N.W., Washington, D.C. 20416.)

sex composition. The distribution of the population* between the two sexes. Used synonymously with sex structure. (T. Lynn Smith and Paul E. Zopf. *Demography: Principles and Methods*. Port Washington, N.Y.: Alfred Publishing, 1976.) *See also* age composition.

sex differential mortality. Differences in the death* rates between males and females. Currently, in the United States life expectancy* at birth is about seven years longer for women than for men. (R. D. Retherford. *The Changing Sex Differential in Mortality*. Westport, Conn.: Greenwood, 1975.) *See also* differential mortality.

sex distribution. *See* sex ratio.

sexism. The belief that one sex is superior to another; a belief system that legitimizes male dominance and supports unequal treatment. Sexism regarding older women is reflected in our language by such terms as "old maid," "old hag," and "old witch." (Simone de Beauvoir. *The Second Sex.* New York: Alfred Knopf, 1974; Laurel W. Ricardson. *The Dynamics of Sex and Gender: A Sociological Perspective.* Boston: Houghton Mifflin, 1981; Kenneth Manton and Erdman Palmore. "Ageism Compared to Racism and Sexism." *Journal of Gerontology*, 1973, 28, pp. 363-69; Neena L. Chappell and Betty J. Havens. "Old and Female: Testing the Double-Jeopardy Hypothesis." *Sociological Quarterly*, 1980, 21, pp. 157-71.) *See also* ageism, racism.

sex ratio. The proportion of males to females within a population.* It is stated as the number of males per 100 females. This ratio varies dramatically with age. In 1985 there were 82 men between the ages of 65 and 69 years for every 100 women in the same age group. (T. Lynn Smith and Paul E. Zopf. *Demography: Principles and Methods.* Port Washington, N.Y.: Alfred Publishing, 1976.)

sexuality. This term includes the full range of sexual behaviors (e.g., flirting to sexual relations) as well as sexual fantasies. The requirement for sexual activity and the capacity to enjoy it is lifelong. (Robert L. Solnick, ed. *Sexuality and Aging.* Los Angeles: University of Southern California, 1978; Bernard D. Starr. "Sexuality and Aging." In Carl Eisdorfer, ed., *Annual Review of Gerontology and Geriatrics.* New York: Springer, 1985, pp. 97-126; O. H. Oliveira. *Living with Old Age.* Knoxville, Tenn.: Psychological Services, 1987.)

Share-A-Home. A modified form of communal living that consists of non-related older persons who share a household* and divide the expenses. Each person contributes a certain amount of money each month to cover mortgage payments, maintenance on the house, food, and the house manager's salary. The Share-A-Home concept was started by James Gillies in Winter Park, Florida, in 1969. (Rochelle Jones. *The Other Generation: The New Power of Older People.* Englewood Cliffs, N.J.: Prentice-Hall, 1977; Gordon F. Streib, W. Edward Folts, Mary A. Hilker. *Old Homes-New Families: Shared Living for the Elderly.* New York: Columbia University Press, 1984.)

shared housing. A living arrangement in which a homeowner rents out a room or rooms in exchange for either rent or a combination of companionship, housework, yardwork, and/or grocery shopping and rent. Each person has a private bedroom and shares common areas such as the kitchen

and living room. Shared housing is also used to refer to group residences.*
(Dennis Day-Lower. *Shared Housing for Older People: A Planning Manual
for Group Residences*. Shared Housing Resource Center, Inc., 6344 Greene
Street, Philadelphia, Pa. 19144; Stephen R. McConnell and Carolyn E.
Usher. *Intergenerational House-Sharing: A Research Report and Resource
Manual*. Lexington, Mass.: D. C. Heath, 1980.)

shopping-bag women. *See* bag ladies.

short-term disability. *See* disability.

short-term memory (STM). A temporary memory system that stores information from a few seconds to a minute or so and has a limited capacity of
about seven or eight items. Information from short-term memory can either
be forgotten or coded, organized, and transferred to long-term memory.*
There is little or no difference between older and younger persons in short-
term memory. Also called "primary memory" or "working memory."
(Leonard W. Poon. "Differences in Human Memory with Aging: Nature,
Causes, and Clinical Implications." In James E. Birren and K. Warner
Schaie, eds., *Handbook of the Psychology of Aging*. New York: Van
Nostrand Reinhold, 1985, pp. 427-62; Terence M. Hines and James L.
Fozard. "Memory and Aging: Relevance of Recent Developments for
Research and Application." In Carl Eisdorfer, ed., *Annual Review of
Gerontology and Geriatrics*. Vol. 1. New York: Springer, 1980, pp. 97-117.)

sibling bond. An exchange of goods and services based on a shared age
status.* (Arlie Hochschild. *The Unexpected Community*. Berkeley:
University of California Press, 1973.)

sick role. A pattern of behavior expected of someone who is viewed as being
ill and is characterized by a shift from independence to dependence. Illness
may be considered a form of deviance* because the sick person can no
longer perform his or her role obligations. This concept was formulated by
Talcott Parsons. (T. Parsons. "The Sick Role and the Role of the Physician
Reconsidered." *Millbank Medical Fund Quarterly*, Health and Society, 53
[Summer], pp. 257-78; Aaron Lipman and Richard S. Sterne. "Aging in the
United States: Ascription of a Terminal Sick Role." *Sociology and Social
Research*, 1969, 53, pp. 194-203.) *See also* medical sociology.

significant others. Certain persons with whom individuals interact that rank
high in importance for them. Some researchers have found that a person's
significant others are vital to his or her attitudes and adjustments to retirement.* (Cox and Bhak). This concept was introduced by Harry S. Sullivan.
George H. Mead's term "the others" has the same meaning. (G. H. Mead.

Mind, Self, and Society. Chicago: University of Chicago Press, 1934; Harry S. Sullivan. *The Interpersonal Theory of Psychiatry*. New York: Norton, 1953; S. Strykker. "Symbolic Interaction as an Approach to Family Research." *Marriage and Family Living*, 1959, 21, pp. 111-19; Harold Cox and Albert Bhak. "Symbolic Interaction and Retirement Adjustment: An Empirical Assessment." *International Journal of Aging and Human Development*, 1978-1979, 9, pp. 279-86.)

simple random sample. A sample in which each unit of the population* has an equal chance of being chosen. It requires statistical independence so that the drawing of any unit must not depend on any other unit. Simple random samples are often chosen with the aid of a table of random numbers. (Susan G. Philliber, Mary R. Schwab, and G. Sam Sloss. *Social Research*. Itasca, Ill.: F. E. Peacock, 1980; H. W. Smith. *Strategies of Social Research*. Englewood, Cliffs, N.J.: Prentice-Hall, 1975.) *See also* cluster sample, stratified sample.

single organ theories. Physiological theories of aging that attempt to explain aging in terms of a breakdown in the functioning of a single organ. The most popular of the single organ theories attributes aging to the deterioration of the cardiovascular system caused by a reduction in the blood supply. (Nathan W. Shock. "Biological Theories of Aging." In James E. Birren and K. Warner Schaie, eds., *Handbook of the Psychology of Aging*. New York: Van Nostrand Reinhold, 1977, pp. 103-27.)

single-room occupancy hotels (SROs). A living arrangement in which older persons reside in low-rent, inner-city hotel rooms usually without a kitchen and often with a shared or community bath. Older persons with this life-style* have been referred to as the "unseen," "hidden," or "invisible" elderly. (Joyce Stephens. *Loners, Losers, and Lovers: Elderly Tenants in a Slum Hotel*. Seattle: University of Washington Press, 1976; Carl I. Cohen and Jay Sokolovsky. "Social Engagement versus Isolation: The Case of the Aged in SRO Hotels." *The Gerontologist*, 1980, 20, pp. 36-44; J. Kevin Eckert. *The Unseen Elderly*. San Diego, Calif.: The Campanile Press, San Diego State University, 1980.)

skilled nursing facility (SNF). Specially qualified facility that has the staff and equipment to provide round-the-clock, skilled nursing care or rehabilitation services as well as other related health services. (M. Powell Lawton. *Environment and Aging*. Monterey, Calif.: Brooks/Cole, 1980; Linda K. George. "The Institutionalized." In Erdman B. Palmore, ed., *Handbook on the Aged in the United States*. Westport, Conn.: Greenwood, 1984, pp. 339-54; *Your Medicare Handbook*. Washington, D.C.: U.S. Government

Printing Office, 1987.) *See also* extended care facility, intermediate care facility.

social adjustment. An individual's adjustment as evaluated against criteria and standards set by others. (Otto Pollack. *Social Adjustment in Old Age: A Research Planning Report.* New York: Social Science Research Council, 1948; Raymond G. Kuhlen. "Aging and Life Adjustment." In James E. Birren, ed., *Handbook of Aging and the Individual.* Chicago: University of Chicago Press, 1959, pp. 852-97.) *See also* personal adjustment.

social age. (1) "A changing composite of social life styles, attributes, and attitudes at various points of the life cycle" (Charles L. Rose). (2) The position that one holds in an age-grade system* (Bernice L. Neugarten and Gunhild O. Hagestad). (3) The roles,* habits, and behavior of an individual in relation to other members of the society* to which he or she belongs. A determination of social age would include assessing one's dress, lifestyle,* and speech patterns (James E. Birren and Walter R. Cunningham). (C. L. Rose. "Measurement of Social Age." *Aging and Human Development,* 1972, 3, pp. 153-68. Leonard D. Cain. "Aging and the Law." In Robert H. Binstock and Ethel Shanas, eds., *Handbook of Aging and the Social Sciences.* New York: Van Nostrand Reinhold, 1976, pp. 342-68; B. L. Neugarten and G. O. Hagestad. "Age and the Life Course." In Robert H. Binstock and Ethel Shanas, eds., *Handbook of Aging and the Social Sciences.* New York: Van Nostrand Reinhold, 1976, pp. 35-55. J. E. Birren and K. Warner Schaie, eds., *Handbook of the Psychology of Aging.* New York: Van Nostrand Reinhold, 1985, pp. 3-34.) *See also* biological age, chronological age, functional age, psychological age.

social aging. The predictable sequence of changes that takes place in one's roles* and statuses* over the life course.* Also referred to as the process of "eldering" by J.J.F. Schroots and James E. Birren. (J. Schroots and J. Birren. "A Psychological Point of View toward Human Aging and Adaptability." In *Adaptability and Aging.* Proceedings of the 9th International Conference of Social Gerontology, Quebec, Canada, 1980, pp. 43-54.)

social breakdown syndrome (SBS). The concept that older persons are often labeled as incompetent by society and that eventually they label themselves as incompetent. According to Joseph A. Kuypers and Vern L. Bengtson, older persons are susceptible to this type of labeling* because of role loss,* ambiguous norms,* and lack of reference groups* that they experience as they age. The term "social breakdown syndrome" was used earlier by E. M. Gruenberg and J. Zusman to explain the beginning of mental disorder in a population.* (J. Zusman. "Some Explanations of the Changing Appearance of Psychotic Patients: Antecedents of the Social Breakdown Syndrome Concept." *Millbank Memorial Fund Quarterly,* 1964 [Jan.], pp. 363-94; J.

A. Kuypers and V. L. Bengtson. "Social Breakdown and Competence: A Model of Normal Aging." *Human Development*, 1973, 16, pp. 181-201.)

social change. Any significant alteration in the patterns of social structure and social behavior of a society* over time; often used interchangeably with cultural change. Old age,* for example, has undergone a number of social changes in the past 50 years or so. More people are surviving to older ages than ever before, retirement* has become an institutionalized pattern, and the age of 65 (with a slight variation on either side) has become the time when people retire. (William F. Ogburn. *Social Change*. New York: Viking, 1950; Sara B. Kiesler, James N. Morgan, and Valerie K. Oppenheimer, eds. *Aging: Social Change*. New York: Academic Press, 1981; Fred C. Pampel. *Social Change and the Aged*. Lexington, Mass.: Lexington Books, 1981.)

social class. *See* class.

social clock. A term introduced by Bernice L. Neugarten and associates to refer to the norms* widely shared by persons of a society* about the appropriate timing for various life events;* for example, marriage, parenthood, and retirement.* Age norms* act as prods and brakes upon behavior such as speeding up an event or slowing it down. (Bernice L. Neugarten, Joan W. Moore, and John C. Lowe. "Age Norms, Age Constraints, and Adult

Figure 7
Social Breakdown Syndrome as Applied to Old Age

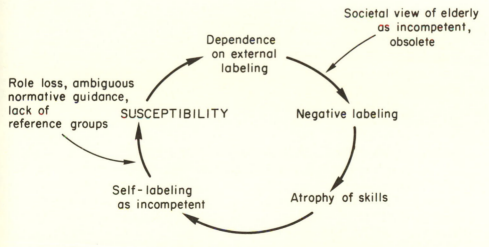

Source: J. A. Kuypers and V. L. Bengtson. "Social Breakdown and Competence: A Model of Normal Aging." *Human Development*, 1973, 16, p. 190. Courtesy of S. Karger AG, Basel.

Socialization." *American Journal of Sociology*, 1965, 70, pp. 710-17; Bernice L. Neugarten and Nancy Datan. "Sociological Perspectives on the Life Cycle." In Paul B. Bates and K. Warner Schaie, eds., *Life Span Development Psychology: Personality and Socialization.* New York: Academic Press, 1973, pp. 53-69.) *See also* off-time/on-time.

social control. The means and processes that a group* or society* uses to get its members to conform to their expectations; a process that counteracts deviate tendencies. Age norms,* for example, are informally enforced through such phrases as "robbing the cradle," "old maid," "act your age," and "early retirement." (E. A. Ross. *Social Control: A Survey of the Foundations of Order.* New York: Macmillan, 1901; Talcott Parsons. *Social System.* New York: Free Press, 1951; Bernice L. Neugarten, Joan W. Moore, and John C. Lowe. "Age Norms, Age Constraints, and Adult Socialization." *American Journal of Sociology*, 1965, 70, pp. 710-17.)

social death. When a person is defined and treated by others as dead even though he or she may be medically alive. (Richard A. Kalish. "A Continuum of Subjectively Perceived Death." *The Gerontologist*, 1966, 6, pp. 73-76.) *See also* psychological death.

social exchange theory. *See* exchange theory (of aging).

social gerontology. A subfield of gerontology that includes the disciplines of sociology,* social psychology,* cultural anthropology,* political science,* and economics.* Social gerontology focuses mainly on the social aspects of aging while deemphasizing the biological and psychological aspects. The term "social gerontology" was coined by E. J. Stieglitz in 1954. (E. J. Stieglitz, ed. *Geriatric Medicine: Medical Care of Later Maturity.* Philadelphia: J. B. Lippincott, 1954; Ernest W. Burgess. "Preface." *Journal of Social Issues*, 1958, 14, pp. 1-2; Clark Tibbitts, ed. *Handbook of Social Gerontology.* Chicago: University of Chicago Press, 1960.)

social institutions. *See* institution.

social integration. (1) The process that ties people into their society. This mainly occurs through their shared values, social roles, and group memberships (Irving Rosow). A basic theme in social gerontology over the past three decades has been the integration of older persons into society. (2) The uniting of different groups with one another. (Emile Durkheim. *Suicide.* Translated by J. A. Spaulding and G. Simpson. Glencoe, Ill.: Free Press, 1951; I. Rosow. *Social Integration of the Aged.* New York: Free Press, 1967; David R. Unruth. *Invisible Lives: Social Worlds of the Aged.* Beverly

Hills: Sage Publications, 1983.) *See also* age integration, altruistic suicide, egoistic suicide, social isolation.

social interaction. *See* interaction.

social isolation. The absence, reduction, or restriction of interpersonal relationships; the deprivation of face-to-face contact. Social isolation has been found to be associated with psychiatric impairment in the elderly. (Marjorie F. Lowenthal. "Social Isolation and Mental Illness In Old Age." *American Sociological Review*, 1964, 29, pp. 54-70; Ruth Bennett, ed. *Aging, Isolation, and Resocialization*. New York: Van Nostrand Reinhold, 1980.) *See also* social integration.

socialization. A lifelong process through which individuals learn and internalize the culture* and social roles of their society. Although socialization is most obvious during childhood, it continues to occur whenever one moves into a different social position, and there are new roles to learn and new expectations to adapt to, such as the role of a grandparent, retiree, and widow. Irving Rosow maintains that one of the problems of growing old in our society is that the elderly are not socialized to an aged role.* Often used interchangeably with "enculturation," which is the term preferred by anthropologists. (O. G. Brim and S. Wheeler. *Socialization after Childhood: Two Essays*. New York: John Wiley, 1966; David A. Goslin. *Handbook of Socialization Theory and Research*. Chicago: Rand McNally, 1969; I. Rosow. *Socialization to Old Age*. Berkeley, Calif.: University of California Press, 1974.) *See also* adult socialization.

social mobility. The movement of individuals or groups between different levels of the social hierarchy; changes in the social position of individuals or groups in the stratification system from one social class* or strata* to another. Certain groups experience downward social mobility in their later years. This would include widows whose husbands' pensions are reduced or terminated at their death or persons who have had adequate incomes during their working years but depend solely on social security* at retirement.* According to Irving Rosow, older persons in the middle class find downward mobility harder to accept than those in the working class. (Seymour M. Lipset and Reinhard Bendix. *Social Mobility in Industrial Societies*. Berkeley: University of California Press, 1959; Judah Matras. *Social Inequality, Stratification, and Mobility*. Englewood Cliffs, N.J.: Prentice-Hall, 1984; I. Rosow. *Social Integration of the Aged*. New York: Free Press, 1967; Thomas Tissue. "Downward Mobility in Old Age." *Social Problems*, 1970, 18, pp. 67-77.) *See also* group, intergenerational mobility, social stratification.

social movement. An organized group effort to promote or resist change in a society;* for example, the Gray Panthers,* or the Townsend Movement.* (Neil J. Smelser. *Theory of Collective Behavior.* New York: Free Press, 1962; Ralph H. Turner and Lewis M. Killian. *Collective Behavior.* Englewood Cliffs, N.J.: Prentice-Hall, 1986; Abraham Holtzman. *The Townsend Movement.* New York: Bookman, 1963; Michael K. Carlie. "The Politics of Age: Interest Group or Social Movement?" *The Gerontologist*, 1969, 9, pp. 259-63; Pauline K. Ragan and James J. Dowd. "The Emerging Political Consciousness of the Aged: A Generational Interpretation." *Journal of Social Issues*, 1974, 30, pp. 137-58.) *See also* End Poverty in California, Ham and Eggs Movement, McClain Movement.

social network. The system of relationships in which a person is involved and maintains contact; for example, one's social network may include family, friends, neighbors, and acquaintances. In later life one's social networks may become helping networks, especially if the elderly person is physically or mentally disabled. The term was introduced by Arthur R. Radcliffe-Brown in 1940. (A. R. Radcliffe-Brown. "On Social Structure." *Journal of the Royal Anthropological Institute*, 1940, 70, pp. 1-12; Marjorie F. Lowenthal and Betsy Robinson. "Social Networks and Social Isolation." In Robert H. Binstock and Ethel Shanas, eds., *Handbook of Aging and the Social Sciences.* New York: Van Nostrand Reinhold, 1977, pp. 432-56; David L. Shaw and Judith B. Gordon. "Social Network Analysis and Intervention with the Elderly." *The Gerontologist*, 1980, 20, pp. 463-67; Toni C. Antonucci. "Personal Characteristics, Social Support, and Social Behavior." In Robert H. Binstock and Ethel Shanas, eds., *Handbook of Aging and the Social Sciences.* New York: Van Nostrand Reinhold, 1985, pp. 94-128.)

social norms. *See* norms.

Social Participation Scale. This scale was designed to measure the number and intensity of involvements in groups and organizations. It was developed by F. S. Chapin in 1939. (F. S. Chapin. "Social Participation and Social Intelligence." *American Sociological Review*, 1939, 4, pp. 157-66.) *See also* group.

social policy. An action or procedure designed by local, state, or federal government officials as well as members of large organizations to remedy a social problem.* Social policies toward the elderly have shifted from reliance on one's family or on charity toward the assumption of societal responsibility through entitlement benefits. (Howard E. Freeman and Clarence C. Sherwood. *Social Research and Social Policy.* Englewood Cliffs, N.J.: Prentice-Hall, 1970; Louis Lowy. *Social Policies and Programs on Aging.* Lexington, Mass.: Lexington Books, 1980.)

social power. *See* power.

social problem. A condition that a significant number of people believe to be undesirable and feel should be corrected; for example, ageism.* Many conditions that have existed among the elderly in the past and were accepted as inevitable are now being redefined as social problems that can be changed through social action. (Joseph Julian and William Kornblum. *Social Problems*. Englewood Cliffs, N.J.: Prentice-Hall, 1986; Elizabeth S. Johnson and John B. Williamson. *Growing Old: The Social Problems of Aging*. New York: Holt, Rinehart and Winston, 1980.)

social psychology. The scientific study of the influence of the social context on human personality and individual behavior. (Gordon W. Allport. "The Historical Background of Modern Social Psychology." In Gardner Lindzey and Elliot Aronson, eds., *Handbook of Social Psychology*. Vol. 1. New York: Random House, 1985, pp. 1-46.)

Social Readjustment Rating Scale. This scale provides a way to evaluate empirically how stress from changes in one's daily life may affect susceptibility to an illness or precede the onset of disease. This scale contains 43 commonly occurring events that cause stress with weights ranging from 100 (death of a spouse) down to 11 (a minor traffic violation). (Thomas H. Holmes and Richard H. Rahe. "The Social Readjustment Rating Scale." *Journal of Psychosomatic Research*, 1967, 11, pp. 213-18.) *See also* general adaptation syndrome, life events.

social sciences. Disciplines that apply scientific methods to the study of various aspects of human behavior and society.* These disciplines are sociology,* cultural anthropology,* political science,* economics,* and social psychology.* Sometimes history is included as well as some aspects of geography. (Robert H. Binstock and Ethel Shanas, eds., *Handbook of Aging and the Social Sciences*. New York: Van Nostrand Reinhold, 1985.) *See also* social gerontology.

social security. The popular term for the Old-Age, Survivors, and Disability Insurance (OASDI) program. Social security is the single most important income to the elderly. Basic benefits are paid at age 65 based upon the worker's career earnings of covered employment. Early retirement benefits may be paid at age 62, but the amount is permanently reduced by 20 percent. Funding for social security comes from payroll taxes paid by nearly all employers and employees. The Social Security Act was signed into law in 1935 by Franklin D. Roosevelt to cover workers in industry and commerce when they retired. Originally it was known as old age insurance (OAI). In 1939 it was amended to provide benefits to workers' dependents at retirement as well as the workers' survivors at the death of the worker (OASI). It was further amended in 1950 to provide coverage to self-employed persons, household and farm workers, state and local employees, clergymen, and members of the armed forces. In 1956 coverage was extended to protect disabled workers (OASDI). The term "social security" was coined by Abraham Epstein in 1933. (M. Derthick. *The Politics of Social Security*. Washington, D.C.: Brookings Institute, 1979; Louis Lowy. *Social Policies and Programs on Aging*. Lexington, Mass.: Lexington Books, 1980; James H. Schulz. *The Economics of Aging*. Belmont, Calif.: Wadsworth, 1985; U.S. Senate. *Developments in Aging: 1985*. Vol. 1. Special Committee on Aging. Washington, D.C.: U.S. Government Printing Office, 1986, pp. 1-40; Social Security Administration. *Social Security Handbook*. Washington, D.C.: U.S. Government Printing Office, 1986.)

social services. "Organized societal approaches to the amelioration or eradication of those conditions which are viewed at any historical point of time as unacceptable and for which knowledge and skills can be applied to make them more acceptable" (Walter M. Beattie). Examples of social services specifically directed toward the older population include Friendly Visitors, senior centers, information and referral services,* and day care centers/geriatric day hospitals.* (W. M. Beattie. "Aging and the Social Services." In Robert H. Binstock and Ethel Shanas, eds., *Handbook of Aging and the Social Sciences*. New York: Van Nostrand Reinhold, 1977, pp. 619-42.) Louis Lowy. *Social Policies and Programs on Aging*. Lexington, Mass.: Lexington Books, 1980.)

social status. *See* status.

social strata. (1) Persons in a society who are ranked at a relatively similar level on the basis of such dimensions as prestige,* power,* or wealth. In this sense, social strata is equivalent to social classes. (2) The categorizing of persons in a society on the basis of certain shared characteristics; for example, persons aged 65 and over. The singular is social stratum. (Gordon F. Streib. "Social Stratification and Aging." In Robert H. Binstock and Ethel Shanas, eds., *Handbook of Aging and the Social Sciences*. New York: Van Nostrand Reinhold, 1985, pp. 339-68.) *See also* class.

social stratification. Structured social inequality; the ranking of individuals into higher and lower social positions according to their share of social rewards. These rewards generally consist of power,* prestige* and wealth. Talcott Parsons defines social stratification as "the differential ranking of the human individuals who compose a given social system and their treatment as superior and inferior relative to one another in certain socially important respects." One of the most important determinants of social stratification, if not the most important, is occupation. Therefore, the study of social stratification among older persons who are retired requires a different orientation. Also in retirement* some older persons experience a lowering of their social stratification ranking (downward social mobility*). (Talcott Parsons. "An Analytic Approach to the Theory of Social Stratification." In *Essays in Social Theory: Pure and Applied*. Glencoe, Ill.: Free Press, 1949; Reinhard Bendix and Seymour Lipset, eds. *Class, Status, and Power*. New York: Free Press, 1966; James J. Dowd. *Stratification among the Aged*. Monterey, Calif.: Brooks/Cole, 1980; Gordon F. Streib. "Social Stratification and Aging." In Robert H. Binstock and Ethel Shanas, eds., *Handbook of Aging and the Social Sciences*. New York: Van Nostrand Reinhold, 1985, pp. 339-68.) *See also* age stratification, social mobility.

social support system. *See* support system.

social survey. *See* survey.

society. An autonomous human group* that shares the same territory and culture,* has a sense of unity and a feeling of belonging, and engages in activities that satisfy its needs and interests. The status and treatment of the aged varies from one society to another. Often used synonymously with "culture" but the two terms have different meanings. (Gerhard Lenski and Jean Lenski. *Human Societies*. New York: McGraw-Hill, 1982.)

society of widows. A group composed largely of older widows who provide a social network* for each other. (Zena S. Blau. "Structural Constraints on Friendships in Old Age." *American Sociological Review*, 1961, 26, pp. 429-39; Helena Z. Lopata. *Widowhood in an American City*. Cambridge, Mass.: Schenkman, 1973; Richard A. Kalish. "The Social Context of Death and Dying." In Robert H. Binstock and Ethel Shanas, eds., *Handbook of Aging and the Social Sciences*. New York: Van Nostrand Reinhold, 1985, pp. 149-70.)

socioeconomic status (SES). A ranked position in a social stratification system. It is measured by taking into account a number of factors. The most commonly used ones are education, occupation, and income. It allows social scientists to deal with stratification without assuming there are distinct classes. In general, higher socioeconomic status is related to greater longevity, life satisfaction, and better health. (Reinhard Bendix and Seymour Lipset, eds. *Class, Status, and Power*. New York: Free Press, 1966; Judah Matras. *Social Inequality, Stratification, and Mobility*. Englewood Cliffs, N.J.: Prentice-Hall, 1984; Gordon F. Streib. "Socioeconomic Strata." In Erdman B. Palmore, ed., *Handbook on the Aged in the United States*. Westport, Conn.: Greenwood Press, 1984, pp. 77-92.) *See also* class, social stratification.

socioenvironmental theory of aging. This theory assumes that the environment* of action for the elderly is built on the interrelationship of two dimensions, the social context and the individual context. The social context refers to the normative outcomes of social homogeneity, residential proximity, and local protectiveness. The individual context includes those resources such as health, solvency, and social support that have an impact on behavior flexibility. (Jaber F. Gubrium. "Toward a Socio-Environmental Theory of Aging." *The Gerontologist*, 1972, 12, pp. 281-84; Jaber F. Gubrium. *The Myth of the Golden Years: A Socio-Environmental Theory of Aging*. Springfield, Ill.: Charles C. Thomas, 1973.)

Figure 8
Diagram of the Socioenvironmental Approach

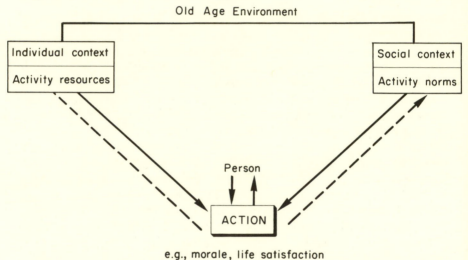

Source: Jaber F. Gubrium. "Toward a Socioenvironmental Theory of Aging." *The Gerontologist*, 1972, 12, pp. 281-84. Reprinted with permission.

sociogenic aging. The effect that societal attitudes, prejudices, and misconceptions about age have on the elderly. (Alex Comfort. "Age Prejudice in America." *Social Policy*, 1976, 7, pp. 3-8.) *See also* ageism, prejudice.

sociology. The scientific study of human interaction* and group life; an empirical science that studies society* and the social behavior of human beings. Auguste Comte coined the term "sociology" in 1824 from the Latin root "socio" meaning society and the Greek ending "logy" meaning the "study of." The term did not gain wide usage until Comte's publication of *Course of Positive Philosophy* in 1838. (Peter Berger. *An Invitation to*

Sociology: A Humanistic Approach. Garden City, N.Y.: Anchor Books, 1963; Harry E. Barnes. *An Introduction to the History of Sociology.* Chicago: University of Chicago Press, 1966; Lewis A. Coser. *Masters of Sociological Thought: Ideas in Historical and Social Context.* New York: Harcourt, Brace, 1971.)

sociology of aging. The scientific study of the interaction* of older people in society.* The sociology of aging emphasizes the roles and statuses that change with age in relation to the major social institutions and examines the adjustments that individuals make to these changes and the consequences of these actions. The sociologist is interested in the impact that the rapidly increasing number of older people have on society, as well as the effect of society on older people. The sociology of aging is a specialized field within the discipline of sociology. Also referred to as "gero-sociology." (Diana K. Harris and William E. Cole. *The Sociology of Aging.* Boston: Houghton Mifflin, 1980.)

somatic mutation theory. According to this theory, which is based on the work of A. J. Curtis, aging* results from an increase in the number of somatic cell mutations. When cells become injured from radiation or from other causes, they undergo mutations or changes in their inherited characteristics. These mutations are often harmful and once developed tend to persist. (A. J. Curtis. *Biological Mechanisms of Aging.* Springfield, Ill.: Charles C. Thomas, 1966; F. M. Burnet. *Intrinsic Mutagenesis: A Genetic Approach to Aging.* New York: Wiley, 1974.)

Special Committee on Aging, U.S. Senate. Formed in 1961 to focus on the concerns of the elderly through hearings, committee prints, and newsletters. The committee's report, *Developments in Aging*, is published yearly. (U.S. Senate. Dirksen Office Building, Room G-33, Washington, D.C. 20510.)

spurious correlation. A correlation between two variables that is purely coincidental, and there is no direct causal link. (Bernard S. Phillips. *Social Research: Strategies and Tactics.* New York: Macmillan, 1976.)

SRO. *See* single-room occupancy hotels.

stage theory of dying. Proposed by Elisabeth Kübler-Ross, this theory identifies five stages of psychological adjustment to impending death: (1) denial; (2) anger; (3) bargaining; (4) depression; and (5) acceptance. (Elisabeth Kübler-Ross. *On Death and Dying.* New York: Macmillan, 1969.)

standard deviation. The square root of the variance; a measure of the dispersion or spread of scores clustered about the mean.* (Ann E. MacEachron.

Basic Statistics in the Human Services: An Applied Approach. Baltimore: University Park Press, 1982.)

State Units on Aging (SUAs). These units are the focal point for statewide aging services. They administer, monitor, and assess area agencies' programs and activities. SUAs vary in organizational structure from separate commissions within the governor's office to subunits within health and human service agencies. (Carroll L. Estes. *The Aging Enterprise*. San Francisco: Jossey-Bass, 1979; Louis Lowy. *Social Policies and Programs on Aging*. Lexington, Mass.: Lexington Books, 1980.) *See also* National Association of State Units on Aging.

status. (1) The place or position that an individual occupies in a group* or society;* for example, a retiree. Status changes are inevitable accompaniments of old age. The static aspect of role.* (2) Rank or prestige.* (Ralph Linton. *The Study of Man*. New York: Appleton-Century-Crofts, 1936; Irving Rosow. "Status and Role Change through the Life Cycle." Robert H. Binstock and Ethel Shanas, eds., *Handbook of Aging and the Social Sciences*. New York: Van Nostrand Reinhold, 1985, pp. 62-93.) *See also* master status, role.

status crystallization. The consistency between one's various statuses; for example, being an elderly black female and living below the poverty level. Used interchangeably with status congruence. The term was derived from the work of Max Weber by Gerhard Lenski. (G. Lenski. "Status Crystallization: A Non-Vertical Dimension of Social Status." *American Sociological Review*, 1954, 19, 405-14; G. Lenski. *Power and Privilege: A Theory of Social Stratification*. New York: McGraw-Hill, 1966.) *See also* status.

status inconsistency. The incompatibility between one's various statuses. Examples of this concept would include a retired university professor who has experienced a decline in status but his educational level still remains high; or an elderly multimillionaire who becomes mentally incapacitated. Used interchangeably with status discrepancy and status incongruity. The term was derived from the work of Max Weber by Gerhard Lenski. (G. Lenski. "Status Crystallization: A Non-Vertical Dimension of Social Status." *American Sociological Review*, 1954, 19, 405-14; G. Lenski. *Power and Privilege: A Theory of Social Stratification*. New York: McGraw-Hill, 1966; L. Beeghley. *Social Stratification in America*. Santa Monica, Calif.: Goodyear, 1978; James E. Trela. "Status Inconsistency and Political Action in Old Age." In Jaber F. Gubrium, ed., *Time, Roles, and Self in Old Age*. New York: Human Sciences Press, 1976, pp. 126-47.) *See also* status.

status passage. *See* rites of passage.

stem family. A nuclear family* plus one or more other relatives that do not comprise a second nuclear family. One child, usually the oldest son, remains in the household after marriage with his wife and children. He inherits the family property after his father's death and assumes some responsibility for his younger sisters and brothers; a type of extended family.* The concept of stem family is associated with the work of Frederick Le Play (R. D. Lee, ed. *Population Patterns in the Past*. New York: Academic Press, 1977; William J. Goode. *The Family*. Englewood Cliffs, N.J.: Prentice-Hall, 1982.) *See also* modified extended family, nuclear family.

stereotypes. Oversimplified, exaggerated beliefs about a group* or category; the aged are often negatively stereotyped as being sick, senile, and sexually inactive. Walter Lippmann first introduced the term into the social sciences in 1922. (Walter Lippmann. *Public Opinion*. New York: Harcourt, Brace, 1922; Jacob Tuckman and Irving Lorge. " 'When Aging Begins' and Stereotypes about Aging." *Journal of Gerontology*, 1953, 8, pp. 489-92; Nathan Kogan. "Beliefs, Attitudes and Stereotypes about Old People: A New Look at Some Old Issues." *Research on Aging*, 1979, 1, pp. 11-36.)

strata. *See* social strata.

stratification. *See* age stratification, social stratification.

stratified sample. A sample* that is obtained by dividing the population* into subsets and then selecting a simple random sample* from each. (Leslie Kish. *Survey Sampling*. New York: Wiley, 1965; Bernard S. Phillips. *Social Research: Strategy and Tactics*. New York: Macmillan, 1976; Earl R. Babbie. *Survey Research Methods*. Belmont, Calif.: Wadsworth, 1983.) *See also* cluster sample.

stress theory. This theory asserts that aging* comes from a gradual build-up of stresses caused from living. These stresses leave residuals that persist, accumulate, and eventually exhaust the reserve capacities of the organism. (H. Selye. "The Future for Aging Research." In Nathan W. Shock, ed., *Perspectives in Experimental Gerontology*. Springfield, Ill.: Charles C. Thomas, 1966, pp. 375-87.)

stroke. *See* cerebrovascular accident.

structured interview. An interview* in which the wording and order of questions is controlled by the interviewer, so that the respondent* is limited to answering on the basis of certain alternatives or categories. (Herman A. Hyman et al. *Interviewing in Social Research*. Chicago: University of Chicago Press, 1954.) *See also* closed-ended question, depth interview.

subculture. A group* that is part of the larger culture* of a society,* but at the same time contains its own distinctive values,* norms* and lifestyle.* According to Arnold M. Rose, the aged in the United States are developing a subculture. (A. M. Rose. "The Subculture of the Aging: A Topic for Sociological Research." *The Gerontologist*, 1962, 2, pp. 123-27; Arlie R. Hochschild. *The Unexpected Community: Portrait of an Old Age Subculture.* Berkeley: University of California Press, 1973.) *See also* aging subculture.

subjective age. *See* age identification.

successful aging. *See* life satisfaction.

suicide. Any intentional act of self-destruction in which a person committing the act could not be expected to survive. The suicide rate for the white elderly male is highest of any age group in the United States. (Emile Durkheim. *Suicide.* Translated by J. A. Spaulding and G. Simpson. Glencoe, Ill.: Free Press, 1951; Asser Stenback. "Depression and Suicidal Behavior in Old Age." In James E. Birren and R. Bruce Sloane, eds., *Handbook of Mental Health and Aging.* Englewood Cliffs, N.J.: Prentice-Hall, 1980, pp. 616-52; Friedrich V. Wenz. "Aging and Suicide: Maturation or Cohort Effect?" *International Journal of Aging and Human Development*, 1980, 11, pp. 297-305; Nancy J. Osgood. *Suicide in the Elderly.* Rockville, Md.: Aspen Systems Corp., 1984; Kenneth G. Manton, Dan G. Blazer, and Max A. Woodbury. "Suicide in Middle Age and Later Life: Sex and Race Specific Life Table and Cohort Analyses." *Journal of Gerontology*, 1987, 42, pp. 219-27.) *See also* altruistic suicide, anomic suicide, egoistic suicide.

sunbelt. The southern and southwestern states; Jeanne C. Biggar defines the sunbelt "as all states on the boundary from Virginia south and west through California plus Oklahoma, Arkansas and Missouri." From 1950 to the present the number of persons age 60 and over moving to the sunbelt has nearly doubled. (J. C. Biggar. "Reassessing Elderly Sunbelt Migration." *Research on Aging*, 1980, 2, p. 177.) *See also* countermigration.

sundown syndrome. *See* disorientation.

superego. In psychoanalytic theory one of the three basic personality structures. The superego is roughly equivalent to the conscience and is associated with morals, ethics, and self-criticism. In the course of aging,* changes in the superego may take place; for example, the supergo may become more relaxed and one may enjoy a sense of freedom or experience retirement* as a time for well-earned leisure after being on good behavior for most of one's life. (Laurance F. Shaffer and Edward J. Shoben. *The Psychology of Adjustment.* Boston: Houghton Mifflin, 1956; Sigmund Freud. "The Id and the Ego.'' In J. Strachey, ed., *The Standard Edition of the Complete Psychological Works of Sigmund Freud*. Vol. 19. New York: Norton, 1961.)

Supplemental Security Income (SSI). A federal program that pays monthly checks to persons in financial need who are age 65 or older, or who are blind or disabled. It is the first federal program to provide a guaranteed minimum income for any segment of the population. Implemented in 1974, it replaced Old Age Assistance,* Aid to the Blind, and Aid to the Disabled, the federal-state assistance programs for the deserving poor that were established under the Social Security Act of 1935. SSI is administered by the Social Security Administration under Title XVI of the Social Security Act. (Paul L. Grimaldi. *Supplemental Security Income*. Washington, D.C.: American Enterprise Institute, 1980; Louis Lowy. *Social Policies and Programs on Aging*. Lexington, Mass.: Lexington Books, 1980.)

support ratio. *See* age dependency ratio.

support system. Any action, behavior, or object that assists persons to maintain their lifestyles, provide for their well-being, and meet their goals. Writers have distinguished various types of support, which include social, emotional, material, economic, self-esteem, and approval. Most older people generally maintain some sources for support systems. (Helena Z. Lopata. *Women as Widows: Support System*. Cambridge, Mass.: Schenkman, 1979; Ethel Shanas. "The Family as a Social Support System in Old Age." *The Gerontologist*, 1979, 19, pp. 169-74.)

survey. A systematic way to gather data about individuals and groups by using interviews or mailed questionnaires. Surveys are often conducted for the purpose of discovering the distribution of certain traits or attributes in a population; for example, a survey could be conducted to reveal the distribution of attitudes toward cohabitation among those aged 65 and over. (Earl Babbie. *The Practice of Social Research*. Belmont, Calif.: Wadsworth, 1983.)

survival curve. A curve that shows the number of survivors at each age. The percentage of the population remaining alive is usually plotted on the vertical axis and the year of age at death is plotted on the horizontal axis. After age 75 the curve dips dramatically. The survival curve is becoming increasingly rectangular in the United States as more persons live to older ages. Also called rectangular survival curve. (James F. Fries and Lawrence M. Crapo. *Vitality and Aging: Implications of the Rectangular Curve*. San Francisco: W. H. Freeman, 1981.)

Figure 9
The Rectangular Survival Curve

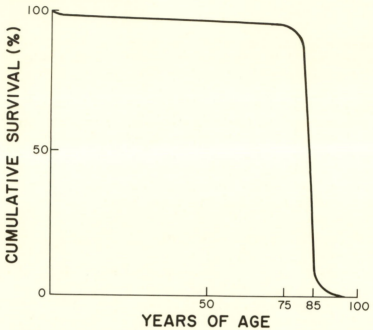

Source: James F. Fries and Lawrence M. Crapo. *Vitality and Aging: Implications of the Rectangular Curve*. San Francisco: W. H. Freeman, 1981, p. x. Copyright © 1981 W. H. Freeman and Company. Reprinted with permission.

survivor's benefits. Benefits paid to an employee's survivor through a private pension plan and/or social security. (James H. Schulz. *The Economics of Aging*. Belmont, Calif.: Wadsworth, 1985.)

symbiotic relationship. A mutually dependent relationship between two people. Often in later life mutual interdependence becomes a more salient feature of a marriage, especially when one or both partners are in poor health. (Margaret Clark and Barbara G. Anderson. *Culture and Aging*. Springfield, Ill.: Charles C. Thomas, 1967; Lillian E. Troll. "The Family of Later Life: A Decade of Review." *Journal of Marriage and the Family*, 1971, 33, pp. 263-90.)

synchronic method. *See* cross-sectional design.

synchronized retirement. A situation in which both husband and wife retire at the same time. Also called "dual retirement." (Timothy H. Brubaker. *Later Life Families*. Beverly Hills, Calif.: Sage, 1985.) *See also* dissynchronized retirement.

T

telephone reassurance. A service usually performed by volunteers who call older persons who live alone on a daily or semiweekly basis to find if any emergency has occurred or if they need assistance. It also provides the client with psychological and social support. (V. R. Van Coevering. *Guidelines for a Telephone Reassurance Service.* Ann Arbor: Institute of Gerontology, University of Michigan, 1973; Louis Lowy. *Social Policies and Programs on Aging.* Lexington, Mass.: D. C. Heath, 1980.) *See also* Friendly Visitors, Lifeline services.

terminal decline. The assertion that there is a drop in intellectual functioning during five or less years prior to natural death.* This hypothesis was first noted by Robert W. Kleemeier in 1962. Also referred to as terminal drop. (R. W. Kleemeier. "Intellectual Change in the Senium." *Proceedings of the Social Statistics Section of the American Statistical Association,* 1962, pp. 290-95; Morton A. Lieberman. "Psychological Correlates of Impending Death." *Journal of Gerontology,"* 1965, 20, pp. 181-90; Klaus F. Riegel and Ruth M. Riegel. "Development, Drop, and Death." *Developmental Psychology,* 1972, 6, pp. 306-19.)

thanatology. The study of death* and dying.* This term is derived from the Greek word "thanatos" meaning death. (Robert Fulton. *Death and Identity.* Bowie, Md.: Charles Press, 1976; John W. Riley. "Dying and the Meanings of Death." In Ralph H. Turner, ed., *Annual Review of Sociology.* Vol. 9. Palo Alto, Calif.: Annual Reviews, 1983.)

three-generation family. *See* multigeneration family.

time-lag design. The comparison of individuals of the same age at different times to investigate changes in attitudes and behavior. For example, such a study might involve the comparison of the attitudes of 65-year-old persons toward cohabitation in 1960 with persons aged 65 in 1980. (Paul B. Baltes, Hayne W. Reese, and John R. Nesselroade. *Life-span Developmental Psychology: Introduction to Research Methods.* Monterey, Calif.: Brooks/Cole, 1977.)

time-of-measurement effect. *See* period effect.

timetable norms. *See* career timetable.

total institution. Erving Goffman defines total institution as "a place of residence and work where a large number of like-situated individuals, cut off from the wider society for an appreciable period of time, together lead an enclosed, formally administered round of life." Their housing, feeding, and sometimes even personal care is supervised by custodians. Examples of total institutions include nursing homes, hospitals, prisons, and boarding schools. The term was introduced by Erving Goffman in 1960. (Erving Goffman. "Characteristics of Total Institutions." In M. R. Stein, A. J. Vidich, and D. M. White, eds., *Identity and Anxiety: Survival of the Person in Mass Society*. Glencoe, Ill.: Free Press, 1960; Erving Goffman. *Asylums: Essays on the Social Situation of Mental Patients and Other Inmates*. Chicago: Aldine, 1961.) *See also* institutional inmates, institution, nursing home.

Townsend Movement. The first major organization to try to improve the economic conditions of the elderly. In 1934, Dr. Francis Townsend, a retired California physician, advocated an old-age pension of $200 per month for everyone over the age of 60 on the condition that they would not work and that they would spend all the money by the last day of every month. He argued that by making the elderly the "circulators of money," it would stimulate the economy, end the Depression, and help eliminate poverty among the elderly. The official name of this movement was "Old Age Revolving Pensions, Ltd.," and their motto was "Youth for Work, Age for Leisure." With the passage of social security legislation, the main thrust of the Townsend Movement was blunted. (Abraham Holtzman. *The Townsend Movement*. New York: Bookman Associates, 1963, pp. 199-207.)

triple-blind. *See* double-blind.

two worlds of aging. This phrase refers to one segment of the older population who are in good shape both financially and physically, and the other segment of the older population that is poor and chronically ill. Some researchers contend that the gap is widening between them and that public policies subsidize the financially well-off elderly at the expense of those that are destitute. (S. Crystal. *America's Old Age Crisis*. New York: Basic Books, 1982.)

U

U.S. Administration on Aging. *See* Administration on Aging.

U.S. Senate. *See* Special Committee on Aging, U.S. Senate.

unseen elderly. *See* single-room occupancy hotels.

unstructured interview. *See* depth interview.

V

validity. The extent to which a given instrument measures what it is supposed to measure. (J. C. Nunnally. *Psychometric Theory*. New York: McGraw-Hill, 1967; Earl R. Babbie. *The Practice of Social Research*. Belmont, Calif.: Wadsworth, 1983.) *See also* reliability.

value. (1) A socially learned and shared conception of desirability; usually expressed in such phrases as good or bad, right or wrong, beautiful or ugly, and so on. One approach to studying the aged and aging is through analyzing some of the dominant cultural values of a society; for example, in American society some major value themes include the work ethic, youth orientation, and independence. (2) Any object of desire or need. (3) In economics, the price of a good or service as determined by its exchange value. (4) A number representing a quantity or magnitude. (J. R. Hicks. *Value and Capital*. New York: Oxford University Press, 1946; Talcott Parsons. *The Social System*. Glencoe, Ill.: Free Press, 1951; Robin M. Williams. *American Society*. Alfred A. Knopf, 1970; Harold L. Orbach. "Social Values and the Institutionalization of Retirement." In Richard H. Williams, Clark Tibbitts, and Wilma Donahue, eds., *Processes of Aging: Social and Psychological Perspectives*. Vol. 2. New York: Atherton Press, 1963, pp. 389-402; Margaret Clark. "Cultural Values and Dependency in Later Life." In Donald O. Cowgill and Lowell D. Holmes, eds., *Aging and Modernization*. New York: Appleton-Century-Crofts, 1972, pp. 263-74.)

variable. A concept that takes on different values, states, or categories. (Susan G. Philliber, Mary R. Schwab, and G. Sam Sloss. *Social Research*. Itasca, Ill.: Peacock, 1980.) *See also* dependent variable, independent variable, value.

vesting. This term refers to the right of employees to receive the pension benefits they have accumulated in a retirement plan even if they leave the plan before retirement.* (Louis Lowy. *Social Policies and Programs on Aging*. Lexington, Mass.: Lexington Books, 1980; James H. Schulz. *The Economics of Aging*. Belmont, Calif.: Wadsworth, 1985.)

vital capacity. The breathing capacity of the lungs; the maximum amount of air that an individual can exhale after a maximum inhalation. Vital capacity is one of the most useful indices of health* and vigor. It is often used to study functional age.* (Morris Rockstein and Marvin Sussman. *Biology of Aging*. Belmont, Calif.: Wadsworth, 1979; David Sparrow and Scott T. Weiss. "Respiratory Physiology." In Carl Eisdorfer, ed., *Annual Review of Gerontology and Geriatrics*. Vol. 6. New York: Springer, 1986, pp. 197-214.)

vital event. A change in one's status* that results in a change in the composition of the population;* for example, marriage, divorce, and death.* Also called a vital statistic. (Henry S. Shryock, Jacob S. Siegel, and Associates. *Methods and Materials of Demography*. New York: Academic Press, 1976.)

voluntary association. A type of formal organization* that individuals join by choice, is nonprofit, and has a specific purpose; for example, the American Association of Retired Persons,* the National Council on the Aging,* and the Gerontological Society of America.* Used interchangeably with formal voluntary organization and voluntary group. (N. Babchuk and A. Booth. "Voluntary Association Memberships: A Longitudinal Analysis. *American Sociological Review*, 1969, 34, pp. 31-45; Stephen J. Cutler. "Aging and Voluntary Association Participation." *Journal of Gerontology*, 1977, 32, pp. 470-79; Nicholas Babchuk et al. "The Voluntary Associations of the Aged." *Journal of Gerontology*, 1979, 34, pp. 579-87.)

voluntary euthanasia. In cases of terminal illness, when the suffering becomes intolerable, the patient may choose to die before death* occurs naturally. (Joseph Fletcher. *Morals and Medicine*. Boston: Beacon Press, 1960; David Meyers. "The Legal Aspects of Voluntary Euthanasia." In John Behnke and Sisela Bok, eds., *The Dilemmas of Euthanasia*. Garden City, N.Y.: Anchor Books, 1975; Derek Humphry and Ann Wickett. *The Right to Die: Understanding Euthanasia*. New York: Harper and Row, 1986.) *See also* involuntary euthanasia.

W

WAIS. *See* Wechsler Adult Intelligence Scale.

waste-accumulation theory. This nongenetic cellular theory of aging assumes that harmful substances and waste products that cannot be eliminated build up within various cells. Over time, these wastes interfere with the normal functioning of the cells. (Bernard L. Strehler. "On the Histochemistry and Ultrastructure of Age Pigment." In B. L. Strehler, ed., *Advances in Gerontological Research*. Vol. 1. New York: Academic Press, 1964, pp. 343-84.)

wear-and-tear theory. A theory of aging that assumes that the living organism is like a machine and from extended usage its parts wear out and the machine breaks down. Similarly, aging is seen as a product of the gradual deterioration of the organs of the body. This is one of the older theories of aging and dates back to Aristotle. (G. A. Sacher. "Abnutzungstheorie." In Nathan W. Shock, ed., *Perspectives in Experimental Gerontology*. Springfield, Ill.: Charles C. Thomas, 1966.)

Wechsler Adult Intelligence Scale (WAIS). The most widely used adult intelligence test today. It consists of 11 subtests with each measuring a different but related ability. (D. Wechsler. *Manual for the Wechsler Adult Intelligence Scale*. New York: Psychological Corporation, 1955.)

Werner's syndrome. *See* progeria.

White House Conferences on Aging. Conferences, which have occurred every ten years since 1961, that bring people together from across the nation to make recommendations that can be used in developing a proposed national policy on aging for the coming decade. This policy, together with recommendations for its implementation, are then presented to the president and to Congress. The idea to sponsor such conferences originated in a bill introduced by Congressman John E. Fogarty in the second session of the 85th Congress in January 1958. Initially, the bill called for the convening of the first White House conference by December 1958. This date was later changed to December 1961 to allow time for preliminary state conferences and to stimulate grass-roots interest in the national conference. (Henry J. Pratt. *The Gray Lobby*. Chicago: University of Chicago Press, 1976.)

wholistic health. *See* holistic health care.

Widow-to-Widow program. A mutual support group in which widows are trained as volunteers to help other widows. The program's goal is to identify new widows and to assist them in coping with practical and psychological problems resulting from the loss of their spouses. This program was developed by Phyllis Silverman in Boston in the mid-1960s. (Phyllis R. Silverman. "The Widow-to-Widow Program." *Archives of the Foundation of Thanatology*, 1970, 2, pp. 133-35; Phyllis Silverman and A. Cooperband. "On Widowhood: Mutual Help and the Elderly Widow." *Journal of Geriatric Psychiatry*, 1975, 8, pp. 9-27.)

wisdom. A composite of attributes that includes a mastery over emotional responses, increased experience, the ability to overcome personal and environmental limitations, and a concern to review relevant information before acting. (James E. Birren. "Age, Competence, Creativity, and Wisdom." In Robert N. Butler and Herbert P. Gleason, eds., *Productive Aging: Enhancing Vitality in Later Life*. New York: Springer, 1985, pp. 29-36.)

women in the middle. Females who have responsibilities both toward their dependent children and parents. (Elaine M. Brody. " 'Women in the Middle' and Family Help to Older People." *The Gerontologist*, 1981, 21, pp. 471-80.) *See also* sandwich generation.

work ethic. The view that hard work and advancement in one's career are morally good regardless of any practical consequences. The work ethic stresses the central role of work in an individual's life and its importance in determining one's status and identity. At retirement this ethic presents a problem for some older persons. The work ethic is a secularization of the Protestant ethic that fostered the notion that to work was to pray and that success through hard work constituted proof that one had been chosen by God for salvation in the next life. (Max Weber. *The Protestant Ethic and the Spirit of Capitalism*. New York: Scribner, 1958.)

working age population. The age range of persons in the work force. For cross-national comparisons, the ages of 15-64 are often used for males and 15-59 for females. (Henry Shryock, Jacob Siegel, and Associates. *The Methods and Materials of Demography*. New York: Academic Press, 1976.) *See also* age dependency ratio.

working retired. Those who work after officially retiring. (Gerda G. Fillenbaum. "The Working Retired." *Journal of Gerontology*, 1971, 26, pp. 82-89.)

work-life extension. A movement to increase older workers' participation in the labor force by either delaying retirement* or having retirees reenter the labor force. (Deborah D. Newquist. "Toward Assessing Health and Functional Capacity for Policy Development on Work-Life Extension." In James E. Birren, Pauline K. Robinson, and Judy E. Livingston, eds., *Age, Health, and Employment*. Englewood Cliffs, N.J.: Prentice-Hall, 1986, pp. 27-44.)

"world we have lost" myth. The false belief that family ties have declined and that older persons were better off in earlier times than they are today. (Peter Laslett. *"The World We Have Lost" Myth*. New York: Scribner, 1983.)

wrinkles. The lines and creases in the skin that occur as one ages are due to a decrease in the moisture and lubrication provided by the sweat and oil glands of the dermis (the layer of skin under the epidermis). The skin then becomes drier and the lines and creases become more accentuated. Also with time, the bones, fat, and muscle gradually shrink while the skin stretches. As a result, the skin begins to sag and wrinkle. (Albert M. Kligman, Gary L. Grove, and Arthur K. Balin. "Aging of the Human Skin." In Caleb E. Finch and Edward L. Schneider, eds., *Handbook of the Biology of Aging*. New York: Van Nostrand Reinhold, 1985, pp. 820-41.)

Y

YAVIS. Introduced by W. Schofield in 1964 as an acronym for the young, attractive, verbal, intelligent, and successful patient. Psychologists and psychiatrists prefer this type of patient to an elderly patient for psychotherapy* and, as a result, the elderly are often discriminated against in treatment. (W. Schofield. *Psychotherapy: Purchase of Friendship*. Englewood Cliffs, N.J.: Prentice-Hall, 1964.)

young-old. Generally used for persons who are 65 to 74 years of age; sometimes used for persons 60 to 74 years of age. Bernice L. Neugarten introduced the term in 1974 in referring to persons 65 to 74 years of age. (B. L. Neugarten. "Age Groups in American Society and the Rise of the Young-Old." *Annals of the American Academy of Political and Social Science*. Vol. 415. 1974, pp. 187-98; B. L. Neugarten. "The Future of the Young-Old." *The Gerontologist*, 1975, 15, pt. 2, pp. 4-9.) *See also* old-old, oldest-old.

youth-centered society. This phrase is often used to describe American society,* which in general extols the virtues and qualities of youth. This emphasis on youth tends to devalue old age and often leads to prejudice* and discrimination* against the elderly. (R. L. Rapson. *The Cult of Youth in Middle Class America*. Lexington, Mass.: Lexington Books, 1971.)

Z

zero population growth (ZPG). A stationary population* in which birth and death* rates are equal and the number of immigrants to a society* and the number of emigrants from a society are in balance. (Ethel Shanas and Philip M. Hauser. "Zero Population Growth and the Family Life of Old People." *Journal of Social Issues*, 1974, 30, pp. 79-92; R. L. Clark and J. J. Spengler. *The Economics of Individual and Population Aging*. New York: Cambridge University Press, 1980; F. Denton and B. Spencer. "Macroeconomic Aspects of the Transition to Zero Population Growth." In C. Garbacz, ed., *Economic Resources for the Elderly: Prospects for the Future*. Boulder, Colo.: Westview Press, 1983.)

Name Index

About the Author

DIANA K. HARRIS teaches in the Department of Sociology at the University of Tennessee at Knoxville. She is the author of *The Elderly in America, Sociology of Aging, Sociology of Aging: An Annotated Bibliography and Sourcebook,* and articles dealing with aging.